'Rome is most attractive place, all the charming accidents of light and shadow touch up some ruin or some column or some church, lovely or historical or both.' (Journal entry: 24 December 1844)

TWO VICTORIAN LADIES

ON THE

CONTINENT

1844-45

AN ANONYMOUS JOURNAL

edited with notes by

Michael Heafford.

POSTILLION BOOKS, CAMBRIDGE

2008

First published in 2008 by Postillion Books,
PO Box 261, Cambridge CB22 5WT.

ISBN 978-0-9558712-0-7

Printed and bound in Great Britain by Joshua Horgan, 246 Marston Road,
Oxford OX3 0EL

Contents.

Illustrations.

Cover illustration: Two ladies painting the view from the churchyard at Thun, Switzerland (see Journal entry for 25 June 1844). Watercolour by R.G. Wale, dated June 1867.

Frontispiece: View of the Arch of Septimus Severus in the Roman Forum taken from the passage leading to the Capitol, the Capitol and Apennines in the distance. From an engraving by W.B. Cooke in H. Noel Humphreys, *Rome and its surrounding scenery*, London, 1840.

Line drawings in the text are copied from the original manuscript.

Introduction.

The purchase of an anonymous 500-page manuscript journal from a bookdealer and published here for the first time provided two leads to follow: the one to the manuscript itself and the tour described in it, the other to archives and record offices to seek out the identity of the two ladies and more about the circumstances under which the tour was undertaken. Both leads proved fascinating. A consideration of the first will serve as an introduction to the journal, while an outline of the pursuit of identities and backgrounds will be added as a postscript. Readers may, of course, choose to read both or neither, before engaging with the journal itself.

The tour, its itinerary and its participants.
On 8 April 1844, the writer sat down in a hotel in Boulogne and wrote home with the news of a safe Channel crossing. We may deduce that the writer is a Miss W. - though to make even this deduction it is necessary to read some 350 pages into the manuscript. Miss W., a woman probably in her 30s or 40s, had in her charge a teenager by the name of Minnie. There is no indication that they were related, rather that Miss W. was acting as a sort of tutor to the young girl. On 9 April, they left Boulogne by *diligence,* the large, officially regulated stage-coach, and arrived in Paris the following day. They took up lodgings, clearly pre-arranged, with the family of a doctor, Monsieur Laguerre. That for Minnie the tour was to have a strong educational component becomes immediately apparent: a French teacher was engaged to come twice a week, a piano was hired, and a music teacher found. The three or four weekly lessons still left plenty of time for seeing the sights and for visiting people. Contacts were taken up and visits made. These included a visit to the Chateau de Vincennes where the Commandant was a friend of Monsieur Laguerre, and another to Marly where they stayed with the family of Monsieur Saintine, a popular writer of the time. On Sundays in Paris, as elsewhere on the tour, the two ladies made every effort to attend a church service at least once.

At the end of May, the moment had come to move on. Passing through Strasburg and Basel, they reached Bern on 3 June. They found lodgings with Madame Henzi, the widow of a professor. Here a German teacher was engaged to come twice a week. There was no need to hire a piano as there already was one in the apartment. They quickly began to receive invitations from members of the Bernese aristocracy, particularly from the Freudenreich family, residents of Chateau Bremgarten, and from Mlle. Wurstemberger, a young woman actively engaged in social causes. After three weeks in town, they set off on two mountain tours, both to the Bernese Oberland, but the second extended to the Lucern area as well. On 22 July, they made the ascension of the Rigi, considered an essential component of a Swiss tour.

After these excursions, they moved into French Switzerland. Not having finalised lodgings in Geneva, they first stayed a fortnight in Vevey on the north-eastern shore of the Lake of Geneva. Having settled arrangements for lodgings at the pension of Madame Wolff in Geneva, they moved there on 12 August. They quickly met up not only with the Anglican community and its clergyman, but also with well-known Genevan evangelicals of the time. Geneva was the usual starting point for an excursion to Chamonix, and this the two ladies were able to undertake in a four-day tour in the second half of August. They also made other standard visits such as to Ferney and to Coppet, the former residences of Voltaire and of Madame de Staël respectively.

With summer ending, the intention was to move south into Italy. It had been arranged that, at this point, a third person would join the two ladies, and they now waited for the arrival of a young man named William. He does not appear to have been related to either of the two ladies, but it must be assumed that he had been extremely carefully vetted. When, after some delay, he finally joined them, they set off from Geneva on 25 September, crossed the Simplon pass, spent a few days in Milan, and finally arrived at Florence on 22 October. Their stay here proved much more eventful than they could possibly have imagined, for it was on 3 November 1844 that Florence suffered its most serious flooding before that in November 1966. Ignoring warnings that they were going to their deaths, the party managed to escape from the city on 6 November and arrived in Rome on the 12th.

Here they settled for the winter, with Miss W. making arrangements similar to those adopted at Paris and Bern. Lodgings were found just off the Corso and near the Piazza di Spagna, that central and fashionable quarter long popular with British visitors. A piano was hired, and music and language lessons arranged. These regular and formal activities fell into the background as Miss W. and her two charges undertook visits to see the sights of Rome. At the same time, they were quickly caught up in a round of social activities. These were clearly facilitated both by letters of introduction which they brought with them and by previous acquaintances from Britain. The latter seem to have included Miss Douglasse and her cousin Dr Pollock who feature regularly in the journal entries. By the beginning of December, Miss W. recorded that they had 'so many irons in the fire that it is hard to keep all going.' While regularly attending English church services on a Sunday, they also paid many visits to Catholic churches to listen to particular preachers and to witness some of the special ceremonies. Those involving the Pope understandably had particular appeal.

On 25 January, Carnival began, and they threw themselves into the street processions and lively social activities. When these ended abruptly with the onset of Lent, they returned to a calmer way of life: the language and music lessons, the visits to churches and Roman sites, meetings with British and Italian friends. At the beginning of March, the two ladies received an audience with the Pope, a formal affair in which they were just two of many ladies presented. They also made a couple of shorter excursions outside the town, to Tivoli and to Albano, before finally leaving for Naples on 10 April.

They spent a month in Naples exploring the city and visiting the many nearby sights: Pompeii, Vesuvius, Amalfi, and Capri. On 12 May, they headed north again, stopping a few days in Rome, where they were joined by Miss Douglasse and Dr Pollock who were to accompany them to Venice. They passed through Spoleto to Loreto where they visited the shrine. A steamer then took them on to Trieste - they all, with the exception of Miss W., succumbed to sea-sickness - and another conveyed them on to Venice which they reached on 29 May. Here, on 3 June 1845, over a year since the two ladies had left England, in the middle of a description of a trip on a gondola, the journal was brought to a sudden and unexplained end with the words 'the stillness....'

The interest of the journal.
After being excluded from the Continent for a twenty-year period, except during a few months after the Treaty of Amiens in 1802, the British poured across the Channel after the defeat of Napoleon. The profusion of visitors led, in turn, to an explosion in travel literature. 'The public has banquetted,' wrote Francis Hall in 1819, 'on Travels, Agricultural, Philosophical, and Political; on Visits, and Visitations, from Six Months to Six Weeks; on Letters and Observations; on "Reflections during a Residence," and "Notes during an Abode;" on "walks in, round, and about Paris;" on "Sketches of Scenery," and "Scenic Delineations;" on Journeys, voluntary and forced; on Excursions on Horseback, and on Foot; by Old Routes, and New Routes, and Unusual Routes.' All these works, as well as recording for the travellers themselves the details of their tours, served a twofold purpose: on the one hand, they satisfied the demands of those

who, without budging from their own firesides, wished to experience the excitement of confronting the foreign world as described by their compatriots, i.e. the armchair traveller audience. On the other, they provided much practical and historical information of value to prospective travellers. The combination within a single volume of, on the one hand, a personal adventure narrative with, on the other, a presentation of objective information about the history of buildings, the cost of inns, and the range of available modes of transport, was often not a comfortable one. As the years passed, however, more purposeful and structured guide-books began to emerge as a clearly distinguishable genre, a trend which culminated in 1836 with the publication of the first of the famous *Murray's Handbooks*. Thus Miss W.'s journal, written in the 1840s, belongs to the new era inasmuch as the writer consciously seeks to exclude guide-book information from her narrative. She regularly enjoins her mother to 'see Murray' for historical descriptions and, at one point (2 August 1844), formally states: 'I do not pretend to give you guide book information; it would take too much time; you must read "your Murray"; it will contribute greatly to your information and pleasure as it does to ours.' By this exclusion, we get a much fresher and more personal response to the experiences of travel.

Miss W. maintains a lively style, and describes the major incidents of the tour in memorable detail: the christening the two ladies attend in a Swiss village, their shock and amazement at encountering a woman dressed in male attire, Minnie's carelessness in leaving her watch behind in an awful Italian inn, the floods in Florence which delay their departure, the Carnival in Rome, and their presentation to the Pope. The narrative is enhanced by the way the characters of the two ladies emerge: Miss W., much concerned with her health, touchy on issues of morality, nevertheless possessing a sense of humour which regularly breaks into the journal; Minnie, energetic and playful one moment, lethargic or sleepy the next, resentful towards those who underestimate her age, not allowing her homesickness to detract too much from her fun at encountering new people and situations.

By the very nature of the genre, journal writing presents material in a fragmented and anecdotal way rather than discursively. However, by picking out comments thematically, insights into the experiences and modes of travel can be derived from passing remarks and often inexplicit allusions. For this reason, I decided not to follow some editors of similar material by editing out sections of the original text on the grounds they contain no more than routine descriptions of travel or of personal daily life. This approach can easily lead to the excision of detail which may seem trivial, but which, in fact, has some significance. For instance, by piecing together the references to how they travelled, we can gain an overall impression of the varying modes of transport available at the time: the centrally organised network of stage-coaches (*diligences*) in France, the privately hired voituriers in Switzerland and Italy, an array of smaller hired gigs and chaises for transport within town, horses and mules for covering rough terrain, especially in the mountains. Railways were just beginning to make an appearance - the ladies travelled by train over the short distances between Paris and Versailles, between Strasburg and Basel, and between Naples and Pompeii. In spite of the discomfort of sea travel, a steamer was preferred to road travel up the east Italian coast from Loreto to Trieste and on to Venice.

The journal also provides evidence of how contacts were built up both before and during the journey in order to ease the passage of and provide some measure of security to the two women. Miss W. has obtained from acquaintances at home a number of letters of introduction which enable her and Minnie to receive hospitality and guidance at the places where they stay. These contacts in turn provided further letters of introduction to individuals living at subsequent destinations. It is apparent that Miss W. had in London become acquainted with Frances Bunsen, the British-born wife of the Prussian envoy, Christian Bunsen. The latter had met his wife in Rome where they had lived for some fifteen years. They had then moved to Bern before he had been appointed to London. It follows that Frau Bunsen was ideally placed to propose contacts both in Bern and in Rome. She undoubtedly provided letters of introduction to influential members of Bernese society: to the Freudenreichs, to Frau von Zerleder and to Sophie von Wurstemberger, all of whom she knew well. After arrival in Rome, Miss W. explicitly mentions that she has delivered letters of introduction provided by Frau Bunsen (24 December 1844).

Fascinating too is the way in which the journal reveals the religious attitudes and practices of the ladies, many shared with their travelling compatriots. In Britain, Sunday was considered a day for churchgoing and for quiet reflection and reading within the family circle. When travelling on the Continent, there was, therefore, immediate disapproval of all the forms of commercial activity and of public entertainment on a Sunday which were regularly encountered. Unless completely unavoidable, even travelling on the Lord's Day was considered unacceptable. Thus when occasionally the two ladies found themselves on a Sunday in a small village with a modest inn, they nevertheless made a point of staying two nights there. While their perception of a properly spent Sunday would have included attendance at at least one church service, it was not always easy for them to find an appropriate one to attend. Only a few large cities had a designated Anglican church or one which Anglicans were able to share with other Protestant denominations. Otherwise they had either to attend the local Protestant church or to worship in a private room. Thus they attended Anglican services with resident ministers in Paris, Geneva and Rome, Protestant churches in Bern and the Oberland, Evangelical meetings in Geneva, and, where no suitable church service was available, they held their own private prayers. In addition to the range of Protestant forms of worship, Continental travel also involved visits to many Catholic churches, an activity which, especially in Rome, included experiencing a range of religious ceremonies held on particular days. This very direct confrontation with Catholicism and its practitioners could, depending on circumstance, feed anti-Catholic prejudice or mitigate it. Certainly participating in a church service as a 'sightseer' could lead to difficult situations as Miss W. discovered when attending High Mass at the Church of St. Eustache in Paris (16 May 1844). However, her Protestantism did not prevent her mixing socially with Vatican clergy during her stay in Rome, nor indeed her seeking an audience with the Pope.

These experiences are all the more interesting from being written by a woman who was travelling as mentor to a teenage girl for whom the tour was intended to have an educational and 'finishing' purpose. As a result, Miss W.'s account of her tour differs sharply from most contemporary travel accounts written by women travellers on the Continent, for these recorded journeys 'protected' by male companions, e.g. fathers, husbands or brothers. Here, however, we are made conscious of the particular challenges faced by Miss W.: 'I shall never forget the desolation which came over me on feeling myself absolutely launched among strangers. Nothing but the recollection that the journey had been decided to be a right step after much thought and much prayer for guidance could have prevented this feeling from degenerating into a pain.' (10 April 1844). While cut off from her family, she had to protect her charge and herself from unwelcome advances and from possible subversive influences. Although Miss W. does not discuss this concern at any length, during the course of the journal she makes a number of comments which manifest it: for instance, her caution at travelling in the *coupé* of a coach (that part of the coach in the front which contained three seats), her decision in Rome not to call on the Polish couple they had met at Florence, her reluctance to take a cab which involved sitting next to the driver, her decision never to go to the theatre in Rome, and her general recognition of the added protection which William gave them on the Italian section of their tour. At the same time, her own confidence seems to grow. She draws attention to those occasions when any one tries to take advantage of her, and she is critical when she and Minnie are excluded from doing things because they are female.

The very explicit educational purpose of the tour points clearly to foreign travel being perceived as a means of developing the artistic, intellectual and social skills of women, at least by the promoter of this tour. It becomes clear that Miss W. also seizes the opportunity to participate in the educational activities she has arranged for Minnie. In this respect, therefore, the tour resembles a Grand Tour of the eighteenth century - except that here tutor and pupil are both women and seem to belong to the upper-middle class and not to the aristocracy. The journal provides an example of how travel could give opportunities to women to acquire not merely knowledge, but also a real measure of self-confidence and self-esteem.

The Manuscript and its Editing.
The manuscript is written on some 500 single sheets of lined quarto paper and bound in an untitled cloth binding. The text presented in the volume is not made up of the letters actually sent by Miss W. to her mother, but seems to be a careful copy of these made by the writer at some point after her return to England. Perhaps she wished to give a copy to Minnie or to create a copy for herself. On only one or two occasions does Miss W. suggest she has amended the original, for instance on 13 June 1844 where she indicates that she has left out some comments relating to the death of one of her aunts. The status of the manuscript as a subsequent copy of the original letters does suggest that the abrupt mid-sentence ending of the final letter was deliberately maintained and therefore might have some significance.

Like many journal writers of the time, Miss W. made extensive use of initials when referring to people. Where these could be identified with certainty or near certainty, I have added the full name in square brackets, but otherwise left them as written in the original. I have provided notes when I felt these would be useful. Inevitably, as a result of mistaken assumptions about a reader's knowledge, this provision may come across as somewhat random. Some names and allusions remained obscure even after investigation and on these I have not made any individual references to my inability to elucidate. As far as punctuation was concerned, Miss W., like most other journal writers of the time, was very casual - after all, the journal was intended for home consumption only. In my insertions and adjustments, I have tried to highlight the sense of the text, but possibly not always avoiding the danger of making it come across in a more staccato manner than it should. A few misspellings have been corrected in square brackets, as have some obvious omissions and errors, but only where these might have led to confusion and where the intended text seemed apparent. Otherwise, syntactical and spelling errors have been left uncorrected. For instance, the writer appears inconsistent in her use of capitals on words denoting nationality, often promoting it on *English*, but neglecting it on *french*! It is hoped that my fairly minimal editorial interventions will have made the text easier to read without distorting the style or effacing the idiosyncrasies of the writer.

Acknowledgements.
I should like to thank all those of my friends who have offered advice, help and encouragement. I am particularly grateful to Sue Robin, a direct descent of Minnie, who provided me with much useful background information about her ancestor.

Introductory letter

Hotel des Bains,
Boulogne.
April 8 1844.

My dear Mother,[1]

If you could see how very comfortable we are, it would do you good. I say like the boy who was going to be drowned 'How I wish my Mother was here'. Josiah[2] would tell you he introduced us to Mr L. who, with his bride and her maid, are here for a few days. He reminds me of Dr Martin and is most excessively kind. After amusing us and doing everything agreeable on board, he proposed we should join in the same Hotel. His wife is a good-natured sprightly girl. Our voyage was most pleasant (I do not mean to deny having a heavy heart when I thought of home and of the arduous undertaking in which I had engaged), but all the circumstances of weather, civility, etc. were entirely favourable. For descriptions of the humours of a steamer, see Charles Dickens, Hood and others. I had too anxious a mind to be in a comical mood. The captain called to our aid the Commissionaire of [the hotel] 'Des Bains' who has taken charge of luggage and passports. Mr and Mrs L. are pleased with the hotel to which we have introduced them. We have charming rooms: Minnie and I two adjoining and communicating. The Diligence leaves this place at 11 tomorrow morning and arrives in Paris at ten next morning. Minnie takes the pen 'There are a good many of the peasantry about which makes the place rather entertaining. I do wish you could know how extra comfortable we have been coming and are still and shall be more for a good dinner which I hope will arrive directly. The luggage is here so I must see after it.' This idle girl! While I was talking about the Diligence, we cannot get the whole *coupé*[3] so I have engaged two places in the *intérieur*. What a delightful day. I hope you are now arriving from your drive with a good appetite and thinking cheerfully of the travellers.

******

---

[1] This letter was probably actually sent to Miss W's mother after their arrival in Boulogne. With the next entry, she appears to begin an epistolary journal which served the dual purpose of a personal diary of each day and a means of conveying detailed news to her mother and other members of the family circle.

[2] The writer's brother.

[3] The *coupé* was the most expensive part of the diligence as it was usually enclosed and faced forward. It seated three and, presumably, Miss W. could not risk taking two places in case the third was occupied by an unsuitable travelling companion. The *intérieur*, behind the *coupé*, seated six or more, and numbers suggested safety.

1

The Journal

Here begins my journal of all sorts of little matters only fit to be seen by loving eyes. Last night we set out after dinner for a walk through the town and on the ramparts. The place looked better than usual between the three lights of a beautiful glow from the setting sun, the brilliant stars, and the lamps. Minnie was excessively entertained and has taken up the most vehement nationality, or, in fact, a still narrower partiality, for nothing is so good as what we have in our own home. We peeped into a church where burned one lamp. No service was going on but about 20 holiday folks were kneeling at their private devotions. All the world here is making holiday and there is a capital view of clean caps and spruce uniforms. I have learned from Mrs L.s maid that all our things were thoroughly overhauled [1] so as to excite her very great indignation. I fear we must have the trouble of repacking tomorrow.

9th [April]. We had a very merry breakfast. The amphibious shrimp women delighted Minnie. In fact, we were like great boys and girls on a frolic, in spite of my weight of care. I declined a walk that I might not be put into a bustle on setting off on a fatiguing expedition, and it was well, for the people very carelessly sent me a passport for myself only which might have been very inconvenient if not immediately rectified.[2] Mr L. accompanied us to the Diligence. Our fellow passengers were two frenchmen, one of whom spoke English, and both were very civil to us, and an Englishman who spoke scarcely at all. The annoyance of a Diligence (this being my first experience) is simply the excessive fatigue of so long a journey with only 20 minutes interval for dining and two 5 minutes just to stand upright. Also to me (what was entertainment to Minnie), the outrageous noisiness of men and horses. We had 9 [at] once all neighing and jingling away together helter skelter up hill and down dale, and the whip snapping over their heads like a pistol. The night was lovely. I did not even put on my cloak though we had one window down. There was starlight enough to drive by at midnight before the moon rose. You may guess I had both time and inclination to think of those left behind in the intervals of a sort of stupefaction which did not amount to a doze.

10 April. We arrived in Paris unusually early about half past 7. On alighting the officers of the *octroi* attempted to examine my luggage to see

---

[1] In the Customs House.

[2] Both ladies were travelling on a British Foreign Office passport - several people, not necessarily related, could travel thus on a single passport. This passport would have been exchanged at Boulogne for a temporary French passport, and it was into this that Minnie's name had not been transcribed.

if 'I had brandy!'[1] They let me off upon my assurance that I had none. Mme Laguerre's servant procured me a coach.

2 rue des trois Frères, Paris.[2] Found a woodfire lighted for us and, when we had vainly attempted to lie still for a while (my head was in too much of a whirl), we washed and then enjoyed our breakfast. We had been for a time tormented by heat and dust and arrived most dirty creatures. Our apartments are quite french, small, and, at first, we both felt them gloomy. I shall never forget the feeling of desolation which came over me on feeling myself absolutely launched among strangers. Nothing but the recollection that the journey had been decided to be a right step after much thought and much prayer for guidance could have prevented this feeling from degenerating into a pain. We soon became reconciled to our little snuggery and think the only thing essential to comfort is one we can obtain: more water and a tub to wash in. Finding we could not keep quiet, we unpacked and arranged our room, then dressed and read till Mme L[aguerre] made her appearance. She is in person something like Mrs E.M., but on a larger scale that does not prejudice me *against* her, quite a french woman, and appears obliging. Her husband is a large ruddy handsome man looking like an Englishman. Mr J. H[ey] said he liked his manner. There is a daughter who speaks a very little English and a Mrs and Miss S. who are not offensive. That is all we know at present. Just before the 2nd breakfast came Mr. J. H[ey] to look after us and was very polite. I was too tired to encounter the bustle of walking. Therefore, we proposed taking a little carriage (a sort of Fly) and delivering letters and cards. Mr J. H[ey] ordered one for us, and we drove first to Rue Faubourg St Martin, then to Chaillot. Very pleasant it was: the fountains playing, every thing looked glittering and many-coloured. Poor Minnie was so thoroughly beaten that she fell fast asleep. Mrs J. H[ey] paid us a visit. She is very prepossessing in manner and appearance, speaks English with a foreign accent, is not at all intrusive, but very willing to help us. As Mme de C.'s card was here for me, I called on her. She is a gentle ladylike woman, has been very pretty, and is still delicately fair, most friendly to us, and glad we like our situation so well. I ought to tell you Mrs J. H[ey] says our apartments are excellent for Paris and surprisingly clean. By way of reversing the medal, I found two huge Bugs!!! this morning (11th) and am going to have my bedstead changed forthwith for an iron one. I do not think we shall be much annoyed when that is done. There is so much polished wood and marble which will not shelter them. At 6.30 we dined. There was a nephew instead of M. L[aguerre], an odd-looking youth but quiet and polite. We had a very

---

1 The *octroi* was the body authorised to levy duty when specified articles were brought into a town. These internal customs controls could involve multiple inspections, even on a short journey.

2 The Rue des Trois Frères lay to the north of the Boulevard de Rochechouart and to the south of where the Sacré-Coeur now stands. The street still exists.

3

tolerable dinner, not like Meurice's[1] but good enough. Mme is absolutely *en desespoir* that I do not drink wine or eat made dishes. We talked nothing but french and were prodigiously complimented about it - the fact being that I made many blunders but still got on fluently and was determined not to be afraid. After dinner, we declined remaining in the drawing room, and also drinking tea with our countrywomen, whom I mean to avoid, though there is nothing unpleasant in them, but the mother speaks only English.

11th April. We both slept uninterruptedly till 7 this morning, and, having by the help of a large screen contrived to make a dressing closet and astonished the maid by demands of water, we were pretty comfortable. Our rooms are terribly noisy all day. We are next door to a piano manufactury and a large concert room, and an adjoining house is under repair, but, as our windows look upon a succession of small courts and gardens, we are quiet at night. Minnie is invited to practise on the drawing room piano as Miss S. does, who plays very well, but this is inconvenient. We had a good breakfast, the very essence of Coffee with milk and bread and butter. You would smile at our breakfast equipage, no plates, not even for the 18 inches of roll, two big kitchen knives, and the butter in a teacup. However, this only serves for a joke. We eat none the less. How should we not be content, since we have wax candles, mirrors, and yellow velvet sofa and chairs. Today after lunch (at which by the bye we have hot meat), we call for Mr and Mrs J. H[ey] to take us to choose a piano and make various purchases. The weather is delightful, our window is wide open, and we enjoy the air. Our waiting maid is a nice cheerful rosy-cheeked girl who speaks parisian french very fairly. Minnie begs I will give her love to you. She continues to prefer every thing English and wishes she was at home again sometimes. I have not had very terrible fits of the nervous yet, only a little, and feel much better in health than I expected to be so soon after the journey and the anxiety about it which was the worst part. Before you receive this, I hope to hear you are better; nothing will do me so much good. Tell Josiah that at first I wished Mr L. further for being so perseveringly entertaining, but could not help acknowledging that it was good for me. It must be quite superfluous to send love to anyone who is to see this letter - nothing but my love to them could make me suppose they would wade through it. Good bye, dear Mother, I wish you could see us as busy at our little table as if we were at home.

---

[1] The leading hotel of Paris lay in the fashionable rue de Rivoli and was much frequented by the British. According to Galignani's Paris Guide of the time, it was almost as well known as the rue de Rivoli itself. Miss W. must have become acquainted with it on a previous visit to Paris.

Rue des trois frères.
I have yesterday's afternoon's journal to give. Mme L[aguerre] and her daughter accompanied us to Mrs J. Hey. She has very pretty apartments. I still like her. She is very obliging. We were out from 2 till 6, seeking in vain a good Piano, changing money, franking letters, and ordering stays of such a grand personage, that she had quite a levée waiting for admission into her elegant little boudoir, all draped with silk and adorned with mirrors and biscuit china. We had no time for anything but to walk in the Tuilleries a few minutes, while Mrs H[ey] made a call, and then hurried home, overtaken by a shower. Notwithstanding my precaution in writing before hand, I find no piano, no master ready, so I must bestir myself if I wish to have any thing done. It is Mlle. L[aguerre] and not Miss S. who plays so well, and she can tell us all about french music. M. L[aguerre] was very agreeable at dinner. He is a medical man and appears well informed. At dinner, I am placed on one side of Mme, and Mrs S. on the other, our young people next to us, and the others beside M[onsieur]. We have quite a french meal: soup, bouillie, rotie, fowls, fish, cheese and fruit. M[onsieur] has his little cup of strong coffee and brandy. Then we adjourn to the drawing room and, at 8, Minnie and I come up to our own room to tea.

12th. Again in search of a piano. We have ordered a pretty good one but very dear, and spoken to a music Master [M. Hallé] who, however, is not sure he has an hour to spare. Every thing we have yet ordered or bought is as dear as in London. We have a pleasing french Master [M. Bertin], evening Mondays and Thursdays at 10 - 'Important' as the puffs say. Minnie is to have a Tuscan bonnet bound with white crape trimmed with white ribbon and pink bows inside, not nearly so fine as we could buy at home for the same price, but I dare say the shape and trimming will be in good taste. Mine is to be white silk drawn in flat slips with a cap of blond and blue gauze ribbons. Mrs H[ey] employs firstrate people but now we have obtained these *very* important articles, I shall look out myself for cheaper things. Think of giving 12frs for a very little collar! - nothing else would do according to the true parisian taste, but now I think I have done my duty in that way. Mme de C. called during our absence.

13th April. Your welcome letter makes Paris bright to me. I am very thankful, yet not half thankful enough to hear a good account of you. In my heart I kiss all the people who show you attention. We often wish for you, yet you would not always be comfortable. Mme L[aguerre] is continually adding some little embellishment to our rooms: flowers, a pretty little table, large tub for washing, etc. My room is quite free from visitors now, and we really have no longer any reasonable wants. Our countrywomen are somewhat insipid, and I am very hardhearted because I am determined to speak only French. More shopping with Mme L[aguerre]. We saw the Exchange and the Church of St. Roche. A parisian pun - they call about in the streets chickweed for birds (*mourons*) and ask 'quelles sont les femmes les plus sensibles (tenderhearted) de Paris?' – answer: 'Celles qui s'écrient mourons pour les petits oiseaux.' [1] Mme L[aguerre] having accompanied our countrywomen to the play, we were left with Mlle. I asked her to play to us and we found her so pleasant that we stayed in the drawing room longer than usual. When we come away, at 8 generally, we are too tired to do any thing but work and read an entertaining french story. At 10, we have prayers and go to bed.

Sunday. Read separately and together till nearly 11.30, then went to the French protestant church, Rue de Provence.[2] The service is very like that of our Independants, but few English there. Mme de C., her daughters and son attend and have promised us a hymn book for next time. We had an excellent sermon 'all things shall work together for good to those who love the Lord'.[3] I followed it and the prayer without distraction, still rather longing for our own Liturgy and, if the weather had not been threatening, we should have gone in the afternoon to the Chaillot[4] to hear it. After lunch, we read, wrote, sang, and talked English. This latter is our Sunday treat - I would have no unnecessary restraint in our communications on the especial subjects of this day - and then we indulge in a particular recollection of all dear to us, and, after all, one's mother tongue is the language of the soul and the heart, however the intellect may delight in variety. After dinner, we went to Church again. I thought we might go alone as it was not dark and so near, but M. L[aguerre] was so polite as to escort us, and the footman attended us home. On arriving, we were requested to go into the drawing room. There we found M. Saintine,[5] a very popular author in Paris and known in England as the author of *Picciola*, his wife and beautiful child, and another young french couple, the wife being the intimate friend of Mlle L[aguerre]. Being Sunday, we soon took our leave.

15th April. French lesson very entertaining. You would laugh to see how zealously Minnie purifies the chair and table from the snuff M. Bertin scatters and what grimaces she makes during the operations. Mlle L[aguerre]. accompanied us shopping, to carry Mme Bunsen's note to a

---

1 *Mourons* means both 'chickweed' and, from the verb *mourir*, 'let us die'.
2 The rue de Provence was within easy walking distance of the rue des Trois Frères.
3 See Romans, Ch.8, v.28.
4 The Church of England's Chapel Marboeuf was in the rue de Chaillot. This lay off the northern end of the Champs Elysées and was therefore some distance from the rue des Trois Frères. The chapel had been established in 1824 and its minister in the 1840s was the Rev. Robert Lovett (1799-1880).
5 Saintine was the pseudonym of Joseph Xavier Boniface (1798-1865), a writer of comedies and vaudevilles, but best known for his novel *Picciola*, published in 1836.

distant place,[1] to call on Mme Martin who was out, and then to the fine old Church of St. Eustache. Mr J. H[ey] met us on our return. A stranger dined with us and we had some lively talk. Mlle L[aguerre] lends us books and music. She has a charming little bedroom with bookcases and all manner of pretty things.

16th April. At our early breakfast came Mr J. H[ey] to learn the result of an enquiry I had made for him about country houses. Then we went all six ladies in a Landau to Vincennes. M. Le Commandant is a friend of M. Laguerre's and allowed us to see the donjon not usually shown. We mounted several hundred steps in the tower, rested in cells where the ministers were imprisoned in the revolution of Charles 10 (of which M. L[aguerre] gave us a lively description at dinner). Mirabeau was also confined there three years. They are extending the fortifications which now contain 1000 men and 1200 horses. The latter dine at the sound of a trumpet like their masters. There is a beautiful armoury, not so large, I think, as that which used to be at our Tower, but more picturesque. From the tower, there is a view of all Paris and the country for many miles round. The Chapel is gothic and very handsome outside. A great stiff monument to the Duke d'Enghien[2] disgraces the altar and its beautiful balustrades. M. le Commandant (a Falstaff in figure) was very polite; I was much amused. We had to go through Paris and saw the place Royale and Colonne Julien.[3] This expedition took the whole afternoon.

17th April. What a dear good creature my dear Mother is to write so soon again, and what a comfort to have a good account of you all, especially that you are out of the doctor's hands. Minnie and I found our way alone to a Ladies Bazaar held for the benefit of free protestant schools. Mme de C.'s two daughters held stalls where, of course, I made a point of purchasing. There were some elegant french women and children. We did nothing more as we had to dine with Mrs Howard. They live in french style elegantly and are certainly very well bred and agreeable on the surface, beyond which I have not yet penetrated. Another lady dined with us. Mrs H[oward] has a fine voice but is so timid that I question if it gives any one pleasure. Her private exercise of it seems to be merely practising difficulties under a master, and she cannot, or does not, exert it when anyone is present. We returned soon after tea and sat up chatting about you later than we ought.

---

[1] Frances Bunsen (1791-1876), née Waddington, had married Christian Bunsen in Rome in 1817. He was appointed Prussian ambassador in Bern in 1839, and ambassador in London between 1841 and 1854. As we shall discover later, Mrs Bunsen had also given Miss W. a number of letters of introduction to acquaintances at Bern and Rome.
[2] The Duc d'Enghien (1772-1814) had been executed on the orders of Napoleon after being falsely implicated in a plot to assassinate the First Consul.
[3] Presumably the Colonne de Juillet in the centre of the Place de la Bastille is meant.

18th April. French lesson. Much praised for our writing - I am translating Bulwer's *Rienzi* and Minnie Miss Edgeworth's *Helen*.[1] Went with Mlle L[aguerre] and her pleasing friend to the Luxembourg to see the choice works of modern painters. There were some good pictures, especially small historical and social subjects; the landscapes inferior to our own. I found I could not gain admission for Minnie to several objects of curiosity there which I had seen in my former visits to Paris. We could only see the exterior of the palace and walk in the gardens where multitudes of all classes and ages were amusing themselves. We were excessively tired and, having found it very difficult to procure a coach, we all 4 got into an omnibus and rode for 3d from one end of Paris to the other. These vehicles are under such strict discipline that it is less disagreeable than in our own. It was hard work to keep our eyes open till ten at night.

19th April. Set out at 9 expecting a private view of the pictures now exhibiting at the Louvre and hung before the works of the old masters so as to hide them. However, to our mortification, we had mistaken the time. We saw instead the old Church St Germain l'Auxerrois with its beautiful carved wood and stained glass, the exterior of the Tuilleries, and walked about in and out of shops in the gayest part of Paris till nearly one. We saw and heard relieving guard at the Tuilleries, which is a pretty martial pomp. In the afternoon came M. Hallé[2] to give Minnie her first music lesson. He is very mild and young, but has an industrious way of setting about his task. Of course, he wanted Minnie to have more exercises. However, Mlle L[aguerre] kindly lent them to her, and he ordered a Sonata of Beethoven's. In the evening, we were left to dine with Mlle L[aguerre] and M. L[aguerre], the nephew, and had a pleasant chat. The young man is only shy; he appears well informed when compelled to talk. We then invited Mlle to English tea in our apartments. I offered to read Shakespeare or Milton with her, but she would not, so we continued all french. She played and sang to us.

20th April. Went early with Mlle L[aguerre] to the Marché aux Fleurs, a pretty sight. The women are so picturesque with their huge straw hats and so diverting in their effrontery in trying to cheat and retreating with the best grace in the world when they find it will not do. Minnie bought a beautiful geranium for Mrs H[ey] and I two flowers for Mlle. Mme. often brings us

1 Bulwer Lytton's novel *Rienzi* was set in fourteenth century Rome and published in 1835. Maria Edgeworth's *Helen* was published in 1834 and was highly popular over the ensuing years.
2 Charles Hallé had arrived in Paris from his native Westphalia in 1836. As well as giving piano recitals, he took on an increasing number of pupils. He was aged 35 when he gave lessons to Minnie. He was in contact with the famous musical personages of the period, Chopin and Liszt for instance, but the two ladies do not seem to have penetrated into this wider musical world through him.

nosegays from the house at Marli. Owing to a mistake in getting a coach, we walked about two hours - so tired I was; yet, in the afternoon, went out again with Mrs H[ey] to purchase a Barège[1] and silk dress, and see the Milliner whom we missed after toiling up 3 pairs of stairs, and walked about till I was ready to sink. Mrs H[ey] and Minnie were so dreadfully particular that I was quite ashamed and weary, though obliged for their care. It is quite lawful in Paris to dress in contrast to the Harlequins, therefore my silk is as modest and quiet as I could wish, but as dear as in London.

21st April. Refreshing quiet of Sunday. The pause, alone, in the whirl of this external life, is most valuable to us both. There we may feel our hold on things real and lasting. Morning at the french service which we continue to like very much. Afternoon at the English at Chaillot. Did not get a coach till we had walked some way. Such a gay scene in the Champs Elysées, crowded with folks in their Sunday's best, on foot and in carriages of all sorts, not to mention men and women riding, whirligigs, mountebank shows, gambling tricks, all in short which makes up an English fair. Minnie is extremely indignant at this open profanation of Sunday. It was very profitable to hear our own Liturgy and a sermon from Mr Lovett. I think we shall often go in the afternoon, when there is no difficulty in getting sittings. I saw Mrs R., but she did not recognise me apparently. She looks very well. At Dinner there was M. L[aguerre] junior, another nephew, who goes by the name of the 'gros Eduard' with a forest of black whisker and beard, and some other gentlemen. We soon came up to our books and Hymns.

22nd April. Quite knocked up by the two last days, not bilious or nervous, but too much weakened, so I have ordered the tonic prescription and hope to give a good account of myself tomorrow. Our Washerwoman is not so dear as I expected and does our linen beautifully. M. Bertin went with Mr J.H[ey] to the Bank where he managed all pleasantly for me, and, since my return, I have made myself mistress of the matter, exchanges, etc. Mr and Mrs H[ey] go to Seau [Sceaux] on the first of May and he invited us to spend a few days with them which we shall like. We are also to go to M. S[aintine]'s country house. It will be amusing to see the french country life. Both parties prepare by purchasing coarse cotton wrapping gowns and huge coarse uncut leghorns.[2] We hear English news sometimes and many little bits of Parisian fun from M. L[aguerre] at dinner. M. le Commandant dined with us; he is not to my taste but still entertaining. I am confused by the conversation when they all talk at once, very fast, very loud, and using all sorts of colloquial phrases, but I have received one new idea, neither

---

1 Barège - a thin gauze-like fabric for ladies' dresses, usually made or silk and worsted.
2 Leghorns - hats made from plaited straw, on these presumably untrimmed.

9

moral, metaphysical nor political, but of roast pigeons! They were almost like woodcocks, only imagine what profound science must have been employed in effecting this transformation. Also, one day, I tasted french salad to find out what sort of thing Father liked, but it was only oil + salt. We were long at table afterwards. Some of the party sat down to whist. Mlle came up with us and read a little Milton.

23rd April. I am better this morning but find it prudent to keep quite quiet. Therefore I have put off Mlle Mouton and the much required new gown. Went to dine at Mr H[ey]'s with the intention of seeing the horsemanship in the Champs Elysees, but as they saw I was not strong, they kindly insisted upon giving it up. Two french gentlemen and a lady came in. We had a specimen of Parisian gossip. It is enough to make one's hair stand on end to hear 'fools make a mock of sin' thus.[1] The conversation was frivolous and mischievous.

24th April. I am much better this morning so as to require nothing but a continuation of the same measures for recovery. Yesterday, after the 2nd breakfast, we sat chatting in the little garden here as if it were July - we have missed Mme Martin 3 times and must write to fix an hour. Your welcome letter just came. I must refer to it in my next. I am glad Mary continues pretty strong. Give my kind regards to her and tell her Miss Malvars does not forget the kind care she took of her and desires to be remembered. I do not think she would much like France. Every one of the little comforts furnished by my friends has proved extremely useful. Minnie and I took a gentle walk for a little shopping. We dined late and stayed late in the drawing room talking of french and English games.

25th April. I am much better today and may as well finish my letter before M. Bertin comes, for I shall have nothing more to say after, till we have been out. I think you will be ruined in postage if I have not the charity to tell you it is not now necessary to frank your letters to Paris.

Rue des trois frères.
I must begin with messages, not to the kind friends who will see this letter, that is superfluous, but to Louisa D. because she is a dear good girl to be so attentive to you. Give her my love and tell her I say so. Minnie absolutely refuses oranges, as my father cannot prepare them for her (by the bye, it is only at Mr H[ey]'s that we get such a luxury). I enjoy notwithstanding - they are 4d a piece. We have no great excitement at present. Minnie passes her mornings quietly in study and is not much charmed with sight seeing. Hitherto she certainly dislikes the national differences more than I do. M. L[aguerre] seems a good family man, very busy, but also very entertaining.

---

[1] See Proverbs Ch.14, v.9.

Yesterday, for a grand treat, he drove his daughters to Marli, and rose at 5 to return this morning at 12.30. He has his first breakfast with us. The young men are kept in strict etiquette - we see no more of them than is desirable. But I have skipped over the 25th. We went to a missionary meeting where, besides the interest of the subject, we had a specimen of french eloquence. But the heat was intense and my head ached too much to bear it more than 2 and a half hours. It was not half over when I came away. After lying down for a while, went shopping with Mlle L[aguerre] principally on her own account. After dinner, as she was alone, we stayed with her till Mr H[ey] came politely to enquire how I was.

26th April. Everyone says it is tremendously hot, so no wonder I am exhausted. We have made two fruitless visits today, the 1st to Mme de C. M. Hallé is now here.

27th April. Went with Mme L[aguerre] first by railway to Versailles.[1] The waiting rooms are much smarter than ours and very well arranged. Everything is extremely orderly, but they go slowly. It was a delicious day and, though not yet strong, I enjoyed it. I declined seeing any thing at Versailles, but a few of the streets and avenues through which we passed. It is a courtly town. There we took an open fly, and had a pleasant drive to Marli, sat some time on a dry sunny bank waiting for Mlle. Then we mounted the aqueduct which conveys water to Versailles (a great wonder in mechanics when steam engines were not used). Thence there was an extensive prospect, and more interesting than a bird's eye view generally is. On our descent, Mlle S[aintine], Mme S[aintine] and her little girl, met us, and we walked through part of the forest up a very steep hill in the village of Marli to M. S[aintine]'s villa which is close by the little church. All this was very entertaining. I peeped in at the village school and wished there was more truth taught to all those bright looking little creatures. Comparing M. S[aintine]'s house to others in the neighbourhood of Paris, it seems to hold about the same rank that Babergh does in England, but is actually greatly inferior. All the houses here look like those to let in England, and all the gardens as if they had been unoccupied three years and there remained only such flowers as persist in growing of themselves. What a figure Aunt Fanny's garden would cut here and Baylham would be a chateau, not to mention the Parsonage. As all the windows here have wooden outside blinds like the storm blinds at Brighton, and they, as well as the rest of the house, are of a chalky whiteness, they are not harmonious in the landscape, in spite of their picturesque roofs. The insides of the two we have seen are equally bare, badly painted white panneling, bad paper, very few bells, bad locks, no carpets, brick for the secondary staircases and

---

[1] The two lines between Paris and Versailles, the 'rive droite' and the 'rive gauche', had been opened in 1839 and 1840 respectively.

bedrooms; on the other side, light, airy, cool. From M. L[aguerre]'s house, a charming view over the forest at the 1st and 2nd floor. As I was very tired, Mme kindly insisted on my lying down in a bedroom after our lunch. There I listened to the larks for an hour and half, at the end of which time I found myself in the condition of the well known starling saying 'I can't get out'. The lock would not open from within, so I shouted to the gardener from the window to be released. Minnie, meanwhile, was being lionized by Mlle. There is an Irish oddity living in the house, a very inferior edition of F.P. She had lived with Mme L[aguerre] but chose to remain the whole winter in Marli alone. We dined with M. and Mme S[aintine] where everything was thoroughly french country life. M. S[aintine] writes a great deal in this retreat and recreates himself with his rosebushes, botany, and his pretty child. He is one of the comical contrasts to the idea one would form of the sentimental author of *Picciola*: instead of a 'sallow sublime sort of Werther-faced man',[1] he is a little round punch, his very features all made up of circles, thick beef and pudding lips, and a profusion of light curly hair, slow and heavy in speech like a Bavarian. Mme S[aintine] seems a domestic intelligent woman who shares in some measure her husband's pursuits and enjoys escaping from Paris. We sat chatting in the garden, but out of consideration for me, did not go into the forest to see some chestnut trees immortalised in one of M. S[aintine]'s romances. Minnie enjoyed playing with the little girl who, on her part, was charmed with the condescension, and it was a capital exercise of french, but unhappily she stayed out too late. It grew suddenly cold and she caught a sore throat. At 8.30 came a vehicle like the things in which cottage bread, dyed shawls, candles, and other sweetmeats are carried in England, but with windows at the sides. On the front bench sat the driver (an old acquaintance of Mme) with a young man. On the back we three contrived to squeeze together. The machine had but two wheels. The little rat who drew us, animated by the incessant chatter and marvellous whistle of his master, trotted down steep and rough descents without bringing his nose nearer than within 4 inches of the ground. It was a lovely moonlight. The Seine with its bridges, and the terminus brilliantly lighted, made a pretty scene. Minnie was sorry to exchange our little cart for the prosaic railroad. However, she made one nap till, at a little past ten, we arrived in Paris. I do not think the excursion did me harm but rather good. I have a change of misery - my digestion is disordered as might have been expected.

28th April. Heard a most striking sermon from M. Punot, formerly an advocate. Mme de C. tells me he was induced to examine Xtianity by the circumstance that, though young and holding a distinguished position in society, he was so dissatisfied and tired of this life that he had meditated suicide, till he enquired of a friend what was the source of his cheerfulness,

---

[1] Thomas Moore, *The Fudge Family in Paris*, London, 1818, lett. 5, l.98.

and found in love to Christ the secret of content. We were detained till late and did not venture to Chaillot. After dinner we were glad to coddle over the fire not without talking of all dear to us.

29th April. M.Bertin. Afternoon went out to purchase a french Cachemire and a veil. Mrs H[ey] kindly went with us and I bought both, quite pretty enough for me, at much less than the extravagant price I had been told was required. At dinner, the huge Colonel of Vincennes and two other men. They made the most outrageous noise and I, not feeling well, was quite annoyed. I stayed while the gentlemen played whist to hear some good singing. My favourite Mme Naqué came in the evening. Minnie having a cold and I being rather dismal, we treated ourselves to tea and a fire. The society in this house is something similar in rank to our own, only as Mme is a great lover of music and formerly superintended the education of the young girls placed under the care of her husband to be cured of deformities, she knows many professors. M. Naqué is a civil engineer. M. Ernest L[aguerre] has been to Algiers as army surgeon and is now, I believe, secretary to one of the great hospitals in Paris.

30th April. Not feeling well, I did not undertake any fatiguing expedition. We saw the beautiful church of the Madeleine and the flower market close by.

May. I dismiss the 1st and 2nd with only the observation that I was not well and very stupid; on the 1st, however, we met the Judges going to pay their compliments to the King.

3rd May. I am forced to confess that, after a night of fever and unrest, being obliged to give up going out and, rather puzzled by the continuance of this influenza, I felt bound by my promise about health to take some advice. Fearing my dear mother would be vexed if I had a french doctor, I was embarrassed - it seemed so strange to introduce another into M. L[aguerre]'s house, who by the bye seems to me a very sensible man. However, the thought hung over me like a duty, so I told M. L[aguerre] the truth which he received most politely, and, as I learned afterwards, had suggested to his wife on seeing me look ill the night before, that I had better send for the Physician to the B.Embassy. He arrived - what one might call an old-fashioned fussy little doctor. He was extremely particular in his examination, and seemed to think it very impertinent to have 'le gripe' [flu] without sore throat. The night was somewhat better, though still very restless, but today I feel better and more able to understand my case. To add to my trouble, though not to my alarm, I have the rheumatism in my head.

4th May. When the Dr. came, he took my slight hint about requiring only rest and care, and did not take any more of my heavy dollars, both which I thought very civil. So now I am left to Mme L[aguerre], always subject to my own exceptions in favour of an English stomach which will not be drenched with broth. Oh, for one glass of the despised filtered water at home. I am so thirsty and have only toast, and water which I detest, and milk and water of which I am half afraid. Your pleasant letter came this morning and did me as much good as a cordial. I picture your exquisite neatness, garden and all, not without great longings, as you may guess. I assure you Minnie does not neglect her office; on the contrary, she is sufficiently savage and arbitrary, but it is very difficult to avoid too much fatigue when one is connected with others. I shall try, however. The first instance is giving up going tonight to a very fine concert for which we have excellent places. I am very sorry to lose it and to send Minnie without me, though I have no hesitation in trusting her to the care of Mme. L[aguerre] with whom she has now gone to buy mittens for the occasion. The concert proved splendid.

5th May. Went to the church close by us and did not venture further.

6th May. Went about Minnie's stays which give endless trouble, partly because the 'grande artiste' will not believe she requires room to breathe, and partly because there is such a press of fashionables waiting to be modelled that she can hardly attend to us small folks. Ventured to dine downstairs. There were a great many noisy french men and I was most glad to get away.

7th May. This morning I am as well as I am likely to be here, keeping to the strictest diet, not even taking coffee, and reserving all my strength for what I am obliged to do, having given up even my french lesson, and quite laid aside music. Minnie does not look well. In fact, we are neither of us qualified for Parisians and long to be off. As I do not mean to kill myself by travelling 2 days and three nights, we shall go by Nancy, Strasbourgh and Bâle, resting at each place. Now do you distinctly understand that if you could see me just now, you would not find reason to be anxious. By nursing myself, I hope to get through the rest of my time here, and as it is only strength that I want, mountain air will be excellent. Oh! this incessant din, not one moment's quiet.

8th May. Ann's letter brings me the distressing news of Mrs P.'s death: poor dear Fanny, I grieve for her. I knew Mrs P. was likely to be summoned suddenly, and doubt not that she was a christian long tried in adversity. I am greatly shocked for poor F. I am going on well, but Minnie has a slight attack of influenza and looks miserable. What would Mr H[egan] say to her longing to get away from Paris. Yesterday we saw

Notre Dame, St Etienne du Mont, the Pantheon, and the outside of innumerable colleges and schools. Of course we did not walk, except home from the Palais Royale; it was rather too much exertion. You cannot think how motherly Mme Laguerre is to me. One of her recipes which does me a great deal of good is chicken Broth with lettuce boiled in it. I have a tea cup full in the afternoon which prevents my being faint if we wait till 7 for dinner, and it refreshes and quiets me extremely. Returned from seeing the Gobelin Tapestry, where it was very hot and crowded, seeing on our way the Pont Austrelitz, and a long extent of Boulevards. Minnie and I no worse, but poor Mlle L[aguerre] who was with us had a bilious attack which made her hysterical. She scared Minnie. I was rather hard-hearted. From what her mother said, I hope she will be quite well tomorrow. Mrs F. called - we were out. For a wonder went to bed without feeling over-tired.

9th May.   Minnie still poorly. M. Bertin is quite an original, full of information, having a perfect appreciation of all that is beautiful in literature, and truly polished manners. There is a simple *bonhomie* about him which makes him believe we are interested in the minutest details of his domestic affairs, and in fact creates the interest, for one cannot help sympathising with his kindliness, so we exchange messages with his wife, who has lately been confined, and willingly accepted his excuse for being late, that he had to send the linen to the wash, his wife not having left her bed. Minnie is indignant at his strewing the chairs and tables with snuff, and his lack of clean shirts, notwithstanding all which we like him extremely - he is so intelligent and painstaking. Busy indoctrinating a french locksmith about a key to our large trunk, the tiresome *Octroi* having broken the old one.[1] Went to the Hotel des Invalides where there are great additions since my last visit to the plans in relief of towns and countries; they are very entertaining.[2] Then to the Champ de Mars to see the military school. Arrived there, we found all the *beau monde* of Paris assembled at a race. We got out of our carriage and were close to the course in time to see one round and the winning, quite a novelty to both of us, and a stupidish affair. Coming through the Champs Elysées, there was a most brilliant scene. Mlle L[aguerre] declared she never saw such equipages, the road well watered and thronged with *elegantes* of all sorts. It is really a beautiful specimen of pomp from the Barrière de l'Etoile to and beyond the place de la Concord: fountains sparkling, trees *greening* (as the Germans have it), graceful outlines of architecture, prancing horses and pretty women with still prettier Parasols - forgive my inserting this last article, they are so striking in colour. We were none of us the worse for our expedition. At dinner, M. L[aguerre] appeared in a military frock garnished with huge

---

1 See entry for 10 April.
2 The collection of relief models, some of which dated back to the seventeenth century, had been moved from the Louvre to the Invalides in the 1770s.

metal buttons and great red worsted epaulettes. He was summoned to mount guard all night as one of the national guard. It seems very burdensome for a man in his profession to be obliged to do this six times a year besides extras, but one could not help thinking at the sight of his good-humoured face and fine person, those are the men who are likely to preserve peace. This regulation promotes cordiality between the upper and middle classes who meet here on an equality. No substitute is allowed, everybody above a certain degree is compelled to serve personally.

May 10. As a further proof that I have recovered from my illness, you must know that I was on foot 3 hours this morning at the Louvre seeing the modern pictures which for the most part are sad rubbish, quite inferior to our R. Academy exhibition. There were a few good things. Very tired but not ill.

11th May. Mrs J. H[ey] appeared early and took Minnie to see an old acquaintance. Meanwhile I settled accounts with Mme for the 1st month, found all straight and perfectly understood. Had to wait for others, were too late to do any good, caught in a shower, paddled through the sloppy streets in thin shoes, all very uncomfortable indeed.

12th May. In the evening at the Eglise Evangelique. Saw Mme de C. who had kindly called on Saturday, having heard I was ill. In the afternoon, sent for a carriage to go to Mr Lovett's church, could not get one, tried three omnibuses, all full, tried for a cab in vain till it was too late; all the world was gadding. We can only secure the English Service by ordering a job coach the day before. The service at the Oratoire is at such an inconvenient time (12.30) that we could only go once if we went there. We had a violent tempest in the afternoon, much lightning and rain, so we had the less reason to regret not going to church as we should probably have taken cold. I am so tired in the evenings that twice I have fallen asleep while reading aloud.

13th May. M. Bertin. In the afternoon to Père la Chaise[1] driven by the most tiresome of coachmen who would not even condescend to answer our entreaties that he would make his horses trot now and then. We pay something for seeing Paris in this brilliant state. Every thing is excessively dear and difficult to procure. The number of passports signed last week in Paris was nearly double that of the population. It is said the inhabitants have consumed all the poultry and vegetables which should have served for next month; the unhappy little chickens come to an untimely end. Two shopkeepers told Mme L[aguerre] they had sold off all their old stock (haberdashery and grocery), so you may guess it is not easy to get any

---

[1] The most famous cemetery in Paris.

thing done at all and impossible to get any thing cheap. Very near losing a day by a gentleman being dilatory and undecided. However, by walking some distance, we procured a coach and went to St Denis to see the tombs of the ancient Kings. Being less tired than usual, we stayed with the family (who were alone) till past nine. M. L[aguerre] was very entertaining; we had a great deal of conversation about French Orators and politics. Mlle played some national and popular airs which I have bought for Minnie.

15th May. Your letter, my dear Mother and Aunt, which was sure to do me good. Indeed, I feel very well this morning and shall send this letter sooner than I intended to remove any lingering anxiety. Minnie is well too, but we shall neither of us be strong here, I am sure. We are too excitable, and there is no bracing air to counterbalance the effects of perpetual excitement. Poor Fanny, how I grieve for her. If there were the least probability of being of any use to her, I would delay my departure from Paris, but if she has not already gone by Marseilles, she will surely be here before the 27th. We are to take the whole *coupé* of the Diligence to Nancy ..... Counting my chickens before etc. - the *coupé* taken from this time till June in the morning coaches, and we do not choose to travel two nights. We must be content with the interior. To the banker's and Galignani's to get a peep at the handbook for France that we might be provided with all convenient information.[1] Mme Naquet dined with us. After dinner we chatted and they all helped Minnie to hem her new handkerchiefs.

16th May. This morning Aunt Kirby's letter. Give her my love and thanks. I was charmed to hear such a good account of dear Uncle and all the circle. Tell her also that we are both well and only require change of air to strengthen us. Paris did not agree with me before; probably I should never be thoroughly well here. This being a festival and not Sunday, we took the opportunity of hearing high mass at St Eustache where the music is said to be particularly well conducted. The chanting was dull, and the voices not sweet in their individual tones though harmoniously mingled, but the Kyrie, Sanctus and Benedictus were beautiful, as was a sort of voluntary where the air, bright and delicate, floated (as it were) upon a mist of harmonies. This is a fine old church though built in all manner of *dis*orders as far as I can judge. The splendid dresses, perfumes, candles, etc. were pretty as a spectacle for a few minutes, melancholy as a senseless worship. There was a procession of marble hewers, who, decorated with ribbands and flowers, brought rings of cake about 2 and a half feet in diameter surrounded by tapers 3 feet high. A smartly dressed woman and girl carried tapers at the head of the procession. Afterwards they brought pieces of the cake in a basket to a few of the congregation. I scandalised my neighbours

---

[1] Galignani's reading rooms contained a subscription library offering readers many English books and newspapers.

by my obstinate heresy, but must say I should not willingly have placed myself in the midst of those who were worshipping, but Mlle L[aguerre] was with us, and we followed her unwittingly till we could not retreat. One old woman gave me a poke and desired me very roughly to stand up when the host passed. I took no notice. Another, more lenient, said 'you are not of the religion?' I shook my head 'but protestants stand up'. I made another gesture of dissent and thought to myself, more shame for them, but I would not move a finger towards the least appearance of joining in the service. Of course, we were very quiet and I would have gone out if our presence had seemed likely to make any disturbance. We were there from before 10 till 1. You may guess we came back tired and hungry. Minnie says she could never have believed that a civilized people had such a ridiculous worship if she had not seen it. My neighbour was very busily reading prayers which were totally unconnected with the service going on.

17th May. Went early to an exhibition of improvements in the arts which takes place every five years. We were 3 hours on foot and saw many curious things but in such a cursory way that it was like looking in at shop windows. After a hasty lunch went to that tiresome Mme Bourgagnet.[1] Returned for M. Hallé to give his last lesson.

18th May. Went early to the Louvre for the chance of permission to see those of the ancient pictures not hidden by the moderns. Passed two hours in the Spanish and Standish galleries.[2] Then, as it was too far to return to lunch, we went to a restaurant (Mlle L[aguerre] and Mme Naquet were with us) and ate a reasonable dinner. Then to the Jardin des Plantes. Let me remark, by the way, this was our first bad day in Paris. It rained heavily all day long, and, as we did not know our way, we saw a great deal more of the gardens than was agreeable under the circumstances. Though I did move one man to let me in by my piteous representations, another was inexorable and we had to trudge ever so far for tickets. We saw but half, the beasts not at all. Returned for one last lesson from M. Bertin who made us all sorts of pretty speeches; he has been pleasant and useful. I feel much more confidence in speaking and writing than before. We chatted till 9 with Mme and Mlle. The former says she is *désolée* that we do not go again to Marli and does not like to part with us at all. I am sure we have reason to be very thankful for the kind-heartedness she has shown upon every occasion.

---

[1] The dressmaker from whom stays for Minnie were ordered - see entries for 11 April and 6 May.

[2] The Standish collection had been bequeathed to Louis Philippe in 1838 by Frank Hall Standish (1799-1840) of Duxbury Hall, Lancashire, but was subsequently sold in 1850 along with the contents of the Galérie Espagnole, in order to cover the liabilities of the dethroned King.

19th May.   Hotel des Reservoirs, Versailles.
In the morning, as usual, at the Eglise Evangelique, where we heard an eloquent stranger, M. Blanc from Metz. In the afternoon, determined not to be disappointed of the English service, we arrived nearly three quarters of an hour too soon. The Rev. Mr Lovett was also waiting for admission, who politely answered my question about next Sunday's sacrament and showed us to seats. We walked home, notwithstanding a slight sprinkling of rain. At dinner, we met for the 2nd time a friend of M. L[aguerre]'s, quite a Lady's old man, who was prodigiously flattering to Minnie whom he took for 13. He affected to regret extremely that he was going to Nancy so soon as the 22nd because he could not have the honour of protecting us and showing us the town, whereupon Mme L[aguerre] suggested that he might bespeak apartments for us at the Hotel. I added, take places for us in the Diligence to Strasbourg. This he readily undertook, and, if he does it, we shall avoid being detained. We escaped soon after dinner to our quiet reading.

20th May. A pouring rain which put a stop to our seeing St Cloud[1] on our way here [Versailles] in company with Mlle L[aguerre] and Mme Naquet. We meant to delay our departure only till 10.30, but, from the difficulty of getting a coach, were too late for that train and were obliged to wait in the terminus nearly an hour, during part of which time I was agreeably occupied in reading a kind letter from Aunts Kedington and Fanny. We arrived (pattering away then and still going on tonight). The douanier was very civil and merely opened our bag. We came here where I had already secured apartments and very good they are. After eating an egg apiece, we set out for the Palace close bye, walked 3 hours in the galleries, and had only just done, though excessively tired, when we were turned out. We repose before a blazing fire and hope, with our books and new handkerchiefs to hem, to get through the evening right cheerily and have a fine day tomorrow.

21st May. A very good night and capital breakfast, but Alas! torrents of rain. However, with cork boots, rough cloaks, and umbrellas, we sallied forth to the Library, found we were an hour too early, so I proposed to Minnie, who seemed nothing daunted, to see at least the great alley, some of the courts and the Chapel. We did so and she was pleased with their magnificence; even the rain could not spoil the grandeur of the effect. The flowers were luxuriant though dripping. These external things do certainly awaken a strong sympathy through our senses - not only is the harmony

---

1 The royal palace and park of St.Cloud lay on the route between Paris and Versailles. The palace was burnt down on 13th October 1870 during the Franco-Prussian war.

and grandeur of the scene pleasant, but one feels conscious of a bearing more dignified and graceful than usual, where every thing around suggests the idea of majesty and refinement. It is certainly very pleasant, though far inferior to the free step and heavenward eye which a lovely country induces. There are charming varieties of mental and physical character arising from the different positions in which mankind are providentially placed. Returning to the Library, we saw the curious coloured drawings representing the tournaments given by Louis 14th in the fantastic dresses pretending to represent the costume for different countries and ages; also a book of female costumes of his time. I forgot to mention how extremely I admired the statue of Joan of Arc done by the Princess Marie of France (there are many casts of it sold about the streets of London).[1] It is life size, she is armed except the helmet; the sculpture is good whoever had done it, recommendable for a woman, marvellous for a princess. It is quite Schiller's Joan: heroic, fanatic, womanly. We then had our wet things dried, took a second breakfast, and resolved that as the rain would *not* go, we would, so we returned to Paris, and were kindly welcomed by Mme and M. L[aguerre] who had expressed more pity on us than we deserved. Mr and Mrs J. H[ey] were to have joined us today at Versailles, but the weather settled that matter. Our cavalier at dinner, a specimen of French persiflage - we heard abundance of droll puns. Came up early and packed the heavy trunk to gain a free day on Friday. Went to the Passport Office. Mr J. H[ey] came to say we could not be accommodated at his country house at Sceaux for the night, because Mrs J. H[ey] had been obliged to receive an intimate friend with her child and servant. The Lady's mother had died suddenly and her husband being absent, it was thought desirable to take her out of the way and keep her ignorant of her loss until his return. Took advantage of our leisure to spend two more hours at the Exposition industrielle. The most remarkable thing I saw was wood into whose vessels different coloured liquids had been injected, capable of being worked up and polished like any other wood, and where the colours were not cutting and unnatural, producing a very pleasing effect. There were crape gowns embroidered with flies' wings (Cantharides). Such a desperate crowd - we were between 5 and 10 minutes following the stream before we could get in - the lowest people amongst them all orderly, but by no means all fragrant.

23 May. A funny expedition to Sceaux about 8 miles from Paris. We had some distance to go to the Omnibus, therefore a stupid young 'tiger' (fresh imported) was sent for a vehicle. To our consternation, he brought a Cab, open, in which the driver sits besides his passengers. We looked aghast; the driver was so sensible of the unsuitableness that he offered to fetch another fly, but he had such a good countenance, looked so clean, and, moreover, I

---

1 Princess Marie was the daughter of Louis-Philippe.

was so afraid of missing the stage that we packed in. Our driver was the quintessence of politeness, and his call to heedless passengers most musical, most melancholy. We saw Paris in its nightcap. Like its inhabitants, it is not at all ashamed of being a dirty figure in a morning. We were constantly stopped by scavenger's carts, for which women did the sweeping, and market people of all sorts. We had to wait 20 minutes in a coffee room for the arrival of the Omnibus delayed by the bad state of a piece of the road, during which the waiter related the overthrow of two Omnibuses the day before, and that, since that, passengers were obliged to get out and walk over the bad part. However, it was just safe for us. On our arrival, Mr J. H[ey] met us. His house is pretty, though small, the garden English in its style, french in its rough state, plenty of fruit, we partook of the berries from it. In the afternoon, we had 2 hours rambles in the wood. Just round Sceaux, there are fruits and vegetables for the Paris markets. Being interspersed with small patches of grain and no hedges, they look very much like our cottage allotments. It seems a strange system, but I am told the labourers are fed here by their employers and have 25 frs a month besides. The country has a pretty undulation of hill and valley, and plenty of wood but no water. We were alone in the omnibus returning with a pair of most vicious horses fighting all the way. The driver left them for a moment and off they went. Minnie caught hold of the reins through the window which checked them again. They tried to do the same at the imminent peril of turning us over on a heap of stones, while the population of *la jeune France* looked on without stirring a finger for our help. At last, we were whisked to Paris in double quick time. There I dared neither go into the coffee house, nor wait in the streets while I sent for a coach, so we went in search of one. We were disappointed at two stands. I did not know my way and began to be frightened (it was nearly 9 o'clock). At last a very civil woman directed us to a stand, and glad was I to find myself safe here. Minnie thought the whole matter high fun, especially driving an Omnibus!

24th May. Again to the Jardin des Plantes. Called on Mme de C.

25th May. Paying and packing.

26th May. Morning service at Chaillot that we might partake of the sacrament; felt united with you in our best and happiest moments through union with Christ our common head. We retired early to prepare for the morrow.

27th May. At 5, we rose. After our luggage was dispatched, we took coffee, the whole family being up to wish us good bye. They were most affectionate and attentive to the last. M. L[aguerre] and M. Leon both accompanied us to the diligence which, notwithstanding we were desired to be so early, did not start till 8. It was cold and showery, but that was better than dust. We arrived 5 hours before we expected which was a treat - only think of the barbarity of caging us up till today, 28th at 11, with only just time to dine yesterday at 1, and take coffee this morning at 7.30. Minnie and I took tea off preserves and rolls which Mme Laguerre would stuff into our baskets besides our biscuits, and very acceptable they were. She would fain have added a bottle of wine. How you would stare to see us sitting down amicably and exchanging civilities with the guard who was a very well behaved man, and of course we were not so foolish as to exhibit any dislike to their accustomed manner of proceeding. The guard's manners would have done credit to a higher station. Every one was very civil to us, the only Ladies, and we were well fed. The country at first is rather pretty but, in the evening, we came into a district surpassing in poorness and dreariness Bodmin down, Salisbury plain, or the Lincolnshire fens. There is a new road over what was a chalky desert and is now little better. There are one or two new villages with half-finished houses, the creation of the road. Otherwise there is scarcely inhabitant or habitation to be seen in 6 hours drive between Vitry and Ligny, neither hedges, trees, or hills. All the way to Nancy, we met but one carriage, only two or three diligences, and many carts. At Ligny, the native place of M. L[aguerre], the country is pretty, and thence to Toul, like Dorking. Near Nancy are beautiful wooded hills.

Nancy, Hotel de France. Found splendid rooms engaged for us which were very expensive and we were not comfortable. After refreshing ourselves, we sallied forth, with a smart stripling as guide, to see this very pretty town which lies in a plain (not a hollow) surrounded by hills. The streets radiate from the centre; they are all wide and most of them terminate in an arch, or some other picturesque object, leading the eye to the hills beyond. The public walks are shaded by fine trees. The town looks clean, bright and handsome every way - the Hotel de Ville (a palace now appropriated to the magistrature), the round chapel containing the tombs of the Dukes of Lorraine, patrons of this place, the statue of Stanislas, King of Poland,[1] author of its splendour, all help to embellish, though the latter is not good in itself, the cathedral like a poor imitation of St Pauls. In the museum is a lock of Buonaparte's hair and there are some middling pictures. Dined at the table d'hôte; all appeared french except two German ladies. After a good dinner, we dozed over a blazing fire, but, with all this comfort, I felt very disconsolate at feeling myself among strangers only, and that our future proceedings must depend upon my own prudence and activity.

29th May. Rose refreshed, engaged a nice open carriage and civil driver to take us to the chapel Bon Secours in the Faubourg. There is the tomb of

---

[1] Stanislas Leczinski, King of Poland, having abdicated in 1735, resided in Nancy as Duke of Lorraine until his death in 1766, when the duchy and its capital passed to France.

Stanislas, well sculptured. The chapel is more Italian than French, small, no columns, only pilasters, almost all marble of different colours, pulpit sculptured marble, painted roof. We then thought we should like a drive in that part of the environs which we do not see coming or going - saw the valley of the Meurthe and abundance of country houses nestled in the trees on the sides of the hills. Then we walked about the town, went into two churches in one of which is a monument to Girardet.[1] Time is endeavouring to cast the veil of oblivion over him, the genius of painting interposes, a good thought badly executed. The other church, St Sebastian, in the style of St Pauls. It is the time of the great annual fair of 20 days. The town is thronged. It is very entertaining to see the peasants from all the surrounding country in their Sunday's best. We walked among the booths, made purchases, and gazed about, nearly two hours, since which we have had an early dinner, being obliged to set off for Strasbourg at 6 this evening. Your letter and Ann's and Clara's came to cheer me. To spare you crossing, I do not comment on their interesting contents. We read them for the 3rd time last night; they drove away a fit of the nervous.

Bale Hotel 3 Rois [deleted]

What a business this letter writing is, my dear Mother. I sent you an almost interminable scribble from Strasbourg yesterday and now begin again.

29th May. In spite of my reluctance, another night's travelling; our two gentlemen fellow travellers very polite. The country was interesting, but at eleven a dense warm fog so dimmed the moon that I could only judge of the hills by a faint outline and by the alternations of creeping up and helter skelter down in our vehicle. It is marvellous these diligences are not often overthrown, but horses and drivers really do their work capitally. Luneville is a wretched tumbledown place. The route was strikingly different from that to Nancy, so much more intersected by roads and so many more villages. Falsburg is so fortified that I think all the inhabitants must feel 'I can't get out'. At day-break, we came into the country of the Vosges. Oh! so pretty, almost mountains, partially covered with forests, and many summits crowned with ruined castles exactly like those represented on the banks of the Rhine. The road winds among them, presenting them in all varieties of position, and the mist wreathed itself around them like an adornment. After a long delay at the customs in which we were not the least molested, we arrived at Strasbourg at 9. Breakfasted, dispatched a messenger to M. Emile L[aguerre], then set out to see the Cathedral and town. The exterior of the former answered my expectations. It is very elegant, though one-eared; the interior is not equally fine. For the wonders of the clock, I refer you to a print which I hope to show you. It is a most curious piece of mechanism in which natural history, grecian mythology,

---

[1] Jean Girardet 1709-1778, painter.

23

and christianity, are brought to illustrate the course of time; cocks, planets, old time, the hours, and the apostles perform curious evolutions. We marched about most independantly. The costume of Alsace is picturesque for women: the hair turned quite back from the face, braided in two long tails behind, with the addition of a thick tress of black worsted from which hang long black ribbons, a small cap of silk embroidered like old curtains, often with gold and silver, a band of broad black ribbon tied in two long bows and ends exactly over the middle of the forehead like a huge crow flapping its black wings there, boddice laced, embroidered and spangled white sleeves, strong contrasts in colours, (ex.gr.) scarlet boddices, green petticoat with yellow border, short, very tidy white stockings and high shoes. Men in long surtouts, sometimes red, but generally dark, with an edging of something light, and a huge three-cornered hat. I never heard such a jargon as at Strasbourg between French and German; both those nations disclaim the dialect. A very civil verger was doing the honours of the cathedral to us, and, as German seemed more natural to him than french, I was manufacturing a german phrase to explain myself when he put the finishing stroke to my mystification by saying in his best English 'twelve our' (12 o'clock). Strasbourg is a dirty stupid place, but such picturesque roofs and gable ends, five stories of garret windows in the roofs. The railway train to Basle professes to leave S[trasbourg] at 4.30 and arrive in 3 and a half [hours].[1] We went at 3, were stopped a mile and half before we reached Bâle; at 9 had to clamber into the open *coupé* of an omnibus, where in a few minutes our view was darkened by two bulky opaque substances which proved to be the conducteur's legs as he descended that way to his seat. M.Emile L[aguerre] came at one, a handsome gentlemanly young man. He escorted us to the train and professed great regret that he had not more time to lionize us[2] at Strasbourg where, however, he confessed there was very little to see. Our journey to Bâle was charming, the hills or rather mountains of Alsace on each side. It was a showery evening, and they looked too aerial for real earth, soft and delicate as the image of a beautiful thing; there is still snow on the highest.

31st May. 3 Kings, Bâle. We are very comfortable in a handsome room on the 2nd floor of this magnificent Inn. We could not get two rooms but our beds are in an alcove. We breakfast (at a separate table) in a noble dining room. The Rhine rushes past washing its very walls. Disdaining a *valet de place*, we set off to see the Cathedral and the paintings of Holbein in the library - it is not now shown, but on special request. My patches of german and french to help me in this enquiry were comical but, however, intelligible. German prevails here, so I mean to take it up in good earnest.

---

[1] The line from Strasburg to St. Louis, on the French side of the border, had opened in 1840. The final couple of kilometres of track into Basel itself opened on 15 June 1844.

[2] i.e. to show us the sights.

The pen drawings by Holbein were capital; the 'dance of death', attributed to him but probably before his time, very curious, and drawn with great spirit. The bridge across that noble Rhine affords a fine view of the mountains on each side. We could have loitered there only, for hours, to gaze on the passers - every thing was so new and entertaining. The Cathedral is of dark red stone and is painted still darker, which looks gloomy. The pinnacles are light in construction, interesting from its antiquity (1009) and as being one of the churches early rescued from Popery. There is a beautiful terrace on one side close to the Rhine but high above it. I forgot to say that, last night, the foreground to the beautiful hills was frequently the spire of a village church, the most comfortable scattered cottages imaginable with each its garden, most fertile fields, and plenty of inhabitants. We dined at the 1 o'clock table d'hote where we met a gentleman with whom we travelled most of the way from Strasbourg, one of those whose face is a letter of recommendation and whose conversation assures you you are not mistaken. He claimed acquaintance without being intrusive. We fancy he is a french artist of talent, travelling with his wife whom we heard him mention to another gentleman, from the indications afforded by a large portfolio and the ribbon of the Legion of honour. At 5.30 we walked out with a very intelligent *Valet de place* to see the best views around the town, of the Rhine and the hills, also the gates, etc. There are preparations making on a grand scale for a fête held every two years in one or other of the Swiss confederate towns which, according to their means, furnish amusement, food, and prizes for rifle shooting. Basle is the richest and does things handsomely. A space as big as St James Park is sprinkled over with wooden tenements to serve for rest and refreshment, or shelter if required. They are to be painted into imitations of grandeur. It must be a pretty sight to see the various costumes. I forgot to mention the monuments in the Cloisters of the Cathedral to Oecolampadius, Grynaeus and Meyer.[1] We went a long pleasant walk to a little church perched on the top of a high hill whence there is quite a panorama view - the dark red spires of the Cathedral rise up against the blue mountain grandly. The town hall is Burgundian gothic, picturesque. More of Holbein's early and faulty pictures, an odd little figure representing a servant of the magistrate as they used to dress in the colours of their respective cantons - that of Bâle being black and white, one side of him was clothed in black, the other in white. We walked three hours and a half, and what a tea we have eaten. We have been most cruelly tired, especially with travelling by night, but it shows that we are much stronger, that we can do it without growing worse, and we *do* grow better. No wonder we could not get a sitting room - the Duchess of Kent arrived two hours before us, and every thing was so quietly conducted that we did not know it till next day. We have engaged a Voiturier to take us to Berne at the recommendation of the respectable

---

[1] Protestant reformers, followers of Zwingli, active in the early sixteenth century.

Landlord. The man looks honest and is most benevolently attentive to us. Our carriage is a sort of slight Britscha[1] with a great deal of glass. We have it half open or shut. We have a pair of tolerable horses. At 7 we set off, having been ready long before, but we could not move our cool coachee.

Bale. The Cathedral has two spires; is of dark red sandstone, was begun by Henry 2 in 1010. There is the tomb of the wife of Rudolph of Hapsburg; on the left of the Altar, the tombstone of Erasmus. The council room unaltered since the memorable council with its moth eaten cushions and tarnished leathers. Beautiful view of the Rhine, the town, and black forest hills. Holbein's sepia drawings of the passion of Christ, portrait of Erasmus, of his own wife and children, of himself. The dance of death attributed to him was in existence during the council of Bâle 50 years before his birth. Until 1795, the clocks of Bâle were an hour before those of other places. There is a tradition that a conspiracy to deliver the town to the enemy at midnight was defeated by the clocks striking one instead of 12. The custom of pious inscriptions over the doors frequent here, (ex)
Auf Gott ist meine Hoffnung bau
Und wohne in der Alten Sau. [2]
The town gates are shut on Sunday during church time.

June 1st. Oh! the first day among the mountains. If you could but be here, if I could but send you some of my pleasure, I have plenty to spare. It is no use to rave about those dignified grey Giants or the busy gamesome river at their feet, look for the prints and description of the valley of the Birs, or Val Moutier. The day was sunny after a misty morning. We took a bit of a sketch while our driver was preparing and horses resting. At Saugron we walked through the most picturesque part of one of the defiles, and I think our coachman rather loitered at the next, being a man of taste, and pleased with our appreciation of his country. By the bye, it would be a treat to Father to hear our german talk, and how we eke out our sentences by 'nods and becks and wreathed smiles'.[3] I did not feel at all terrified on the road as I had expected, though many times, when within a stones throw of the turn, I could not imagine how any thing but a bird could get out, and many times there was barely room for the river and us. The beauty was such as I expected, the grandeur somewhat less, but the pleasure was extreme. As we were emerging from the last gorge, there came rushing suddenly a cold wind. We put on our cloaks, but a complete shutting up was soon necessary. The clouds came down on the mountain tops; lightning of the most lovely colours darted in all directions; a lilac spark played on the lamp of our carriage; the thunder rolled, and every mountain joined in

---

[1] The britzscha was an open carriage with a folding top.
[2] 'On God I build my hopes, And dwell within the Ancient Pig.'
[3] From Milton's *Allegro*, l.28.

chorus; rain and hail fell in torrents so that we could seldom see the mountains along whose base we were travelling for an hour and a half. It was rather a trial of nerves for the first day of mountain journey, but I am very glad to have seen such a storm without being extremely frightened or the least hurt. I omitted to mention that at St Jacob, a quarter of a mile from Bâle, there is a cross in memory of a battle fought there in 1444, when 1600 Swiss withstood for 10 hours 16000 french under Louis 11th (then dauphin). They slew 3 times their own number of the enemy and only 10 escaped alive. A little further is Dornach where also the Swiss gained an honourable victory.[1] There are iron furnaces and forges in the valley of the Birs, but they only add a little life to the scene without detracting from its sublimity. We were much pitied on our arrival at this clean but thorough Swiss Inn (Crown, Tavannes) but we do not feel as if we much required it. Minnie, who enjoyed her day, is fast asleep, but I could not resist writing to you.

June 2nd. I have been fretting at my stupidity in having omitted in my last to wish dear Father many happy returns of his birthday. I thought of it every time but the right; and I thought of Maria too with affectionate wishes for her & hers. Sunday among the mountains. We were up early and went to the little village church at 9 before the mists of last night's storm had rolled away; such a rough little place and simple congregation. The greatest man there was our host who accompanied us. The clergyman had lived 30 years among these mountains and was much beloved. He preached in German on reconcilement to God through Christ. The form of service was the same as the Eglise Evangelique in Paris. There was a baptism, a shorter ceremony than ours but similar. The baby was wrapped up in a very gay sort of embroidered table cloth. Before service began, a man read the Bible from the pulpit. There is catechising for the children and exposition for the young people in the afternoon. We went out for a ramble at 5 and were soon joined by mine hostess, a pleasant obliging woman who knew a few words of French and made out the rest by German. She took us a beautiful walk to the source of the Birs. Then we went to her cowhouse, dairy and garden. The villagers meanwhile were diverting themselves by playing ball and something like throwing the handkerchief, in a ring. Men and women of 30 were among them. The amusement did not seem to me disorderly, but only suited to rude people. We were charmed with our evening walk, including the fun of watching the agile little black lambs jump over one another to follow the shepherd. Our windows commanded the Pierre Pertuis, a natural arch 40 feet high through which the road passes. At first deceived by the magnitudes all around, I wondered how our carriage would be crammed through it till I observed an enormous

---

[1] The Confederates defeated the army of the Emperor Maximilian at Dornach in 1499.

Diligence, looking like a toy drawn by six mice, coming through it. By a Latin inscription it appears to have stood on the boundary of the Sequani.[1]

June 3rd. Set out again at 7 among the mountain defiles, passing through scenery scarcely less wild and beautiful than Val Moutier. We walked up two mountain roads today. Through the carriage being open, we had a good view always. Between Bienne and Aarberg, we had a fine view of the Lakes Bienne, Neufchatel and Morat. We flattered ourselves we saw the snow mountains, and snow indeed it was, but, as we afterwards heard, it was only the secondary range. After a bad dinner at Aarberg, we arrived here (Berne) at six, delighted with our last three days, forswearing Diligences and upholding Voituriers for ever. And here let me tell you, we have not met with a single instance of incivility while travelling, but several times, from people of all ranks, such politeness as deserves rather to be called brotherly kindness. Notwithstanding all our enjoyments, we are rather knocked up and very glad to rest. A letter from M.G. recommending us to go into the Revd. Mr H.'s family at Geneva.[2]

June 5th 1844   Rue de l'Isle, Berne.[3]
Since the gentlemen tell you, you may spend a fortune in postage, I will describe our present abode at length. By the bye mind, and enquire about franking your letters here - I was very near missing several posts yesterday by misinformation; only by good luck I could read the notices. Mme. Henzi is a little modest housewifely woman, very obliging in her manners, the eldest daughter a pretty girl of 18, very shy but well bred. There is a fine spirited looking boy of 16, the other 3 boys and a girl of 15 we have not yet seen. We have a spruce little maid who speaks very good french. She is quite puzzled at our requiring so little attendance. Our sitting room is about 22 feet square and the bedroom adjoining about two thirds that size; the floors wood in a diamond pattern, immense stoves of white porcelain opening from without, no chimney. In the drawing room, there are 3 large windows, in the bedroom, 2, with cushions in the seats, where we may sit and look upon [the river] Aar, from which we are separated only by a narrow road, and small houses whose roofs are below the terrace of our garden. Beyond is a wooded hill, roads, fields, and country houses; on the left, the snowy mountains of which our view is somewhat intercepted by a house, and entirely [by] the mist which has scarcely

---

[1] The inscription was much defaced, but Murray's Guide furnished a transcription of what could still be deciphered along with the information that the arch had separated the Sequani from the Rauraci.
[2] Presumably, Rev. William Hare, the Anglican Chaplain in Geneva, but he had been succeeded earlier in the year by the Rev. William Lawrenson.
[3] The Rue de l'Isle (Inselgasse) lay near the route of the present Kochergasse. The house itself was presumably destroyed when the Federal Parliament building was extended in the 1880s.

allowed us a peep at them since the first evening of our arrival. I pity those who pass hastily through these countries; their pleasure is so much at the mercy of the weather. Every thing is delicately clean here; our breakfast and tea very nice; dinner from a hotel very bad yesterday, better today. We dine at 1.30 i.e. half an hour later than the Bernese. Mlle W[urstemberger][1] called yesterday; her extreme liveliness of manner and rosy cheeks reminded me a little of what J.R. was. She seems between 20 & 30, speaks English fluently, and appears the busiest of mortals. She was very friendly and I am happy to say does not leave the neighbourhood soon. She advised me to present Mme B[unsen]'s note in person to Mme de F[reudenreich][2] about 11 in the morning! Yesterday afternoon, we walked out with Mlle H[enzi]. After having put my letter in the post on the strength of her assurance that I need not frank it, I discovered a notice which said we must. We went then to the general post Office, paid the money, left the address, and the postmaster promised to frank it, notwithstanding which you might never have had it if Col. M. had not happened to look at the addresses of letters in the window, and, seeing your name, had the great kindness to pay and send it. This morning, in a little phaeton, we had the most charming drive to Mme de F[reudenreich]'s chateau. She is an elegant interesting woman, received us very kindly, and invited us for Friday evening. Col. M. has just called. He is gentlemanly and agreeable, how obliging you may guess from what I said above. I am going to have a German master for Minnie here, finding that the pronunciation in Vienna is as bad as it is here. There are occasional exceptions in both places. Mme H[enzi] and her family, having resided many years in Livonia (where her husband was Professor[3]), are among the exceptions, so that, although we have hitherto spoken only French, we might with great advantage speak German, and, besides, the mountains are not within a day's excursion, and subjects for the pencil are within 10 minutes walk - therefore we can arrange our time for study. We have a very good piano.

6th June. At 7.30 a message from Mme H[enzi] to bid us look out at the mountains. There they were, magnificent Ghosts in all their glory (it was only the 2nd range we had seen before). We could not be content with the window, but put on our cloaks and went into the garden to enjoy the view. It was just the outline you saw in Murray's guide.[4] I could scarcely believe

---

[1] Sophie von Wurstemberger (1809-1878) was an active benefactress of the sick and poor in Bern. She was known to and had been visited by British non-conformists such as Elizabeth Fry, the Gurneys and John Yeardley.

[2] Eugenie Martha , née Falconnet, the wife of Beat Friedrich von Freudenreich, the owner of Schloss Bremgarten.

[3] Samuel Rudolf Gottlieb Henzi had taught Persian and Hawaiian in Dorpat, Livonia (today Tartu in Estonia) and had died in 1829.

[4] Murray's Handbook contained a small panoramic sketch of the Alps 'as seen from the neighbourhood of Bern.'

them to be real. It is not in the nature of things that painting would represent them. Even in reality, with all the advantages of atmosphere, the eye requires educating to appreciate their grandeur, but it is an ever growing pleasure. Minnie's knee is very weak which is rather an anxiety to me. I would not suffer her to strain it, and therefore took the phaeton, had a charming drive at the foot of the Gurten,[1] and sketched. After dinner, a German professor, Herr Gelpke,[2] who speaks neither french nor english, but has a very good name for talent; such a shaggy creature, like the prints of comets with the coma foreshortened. We begin in good earnest on Saturday and are already as busy as at Paris or at home, 3 books apiece to read, drawings to finish, letters, and accounts!! the climax of horrors, how shall I ever keep them, paying in all manner of coins which will not multiply into each other. Mlle W[urstemberger] again. She approves our professor and courageous determination to plunge into German at once; she invites us for Wednesday. Col. M. tells us Mr H. is suddenly called to the Ionian Islands. In the evening, we watched the changes on the mountains from the terrace of our garden. They are so great that it is like a Diorama;[3] they stand out and disappear by turns, some parts glitter, others are a delicate salmon colour, other colours we have yet to see; there was a rainbow also. Mme H[enzi] brought her daughter Anna[4] to see us. She is within a day of Minnie's age, in the style of E. du B. but more lively.

7th June. We have been this morning across the ferry over the rapid Aar. The boat is guided by a rope. We sketched but found it very hot and fatiguing for every step is up or down. The ugliest feature I have seen is that the bridges are almost all clumsy wooden structures like a range of cart sheds, roofed at an acute angle to prevent their being broken down by snow. The public walks are most delightful, of great extent, shaded by fine trees, and commanding lovely views. The people live so much out of doors in the summer that family groups enliven the scene everywhere in the villages and public walks. Most respectable people sit and take refreshment at tables under the trees; sometimes it is a picnic. At this season all the rivers are busy sawing wood and all the maids beating mattresses in the sun. We had a most romantic drive to Chateau Bremgarten. Our driver, not knowing the place, took us by a short bad road overhanging the river and excessively steep. It was very pretty but too dangerous for us to return that way in the dusk. With Madame de F[reudenreich], we found her mother, an

---

[1] A hill on the outskirts of Bern from which, weather permitting, there are fine views of the Oberland Alps.
[2] Ernst Friedrich Gelpke (1807-1871) had been born near Leipzig, but moved to Bern where he had become a citizen in 1837.
[3] The Diorama was a popular form of entertainment in London: painted scenes, usually foreign views, were presented to an audience; by manipulating the sources of light, various atmospheric effects could be created.
[4] Mme Henzi's younger daughter was born in 1829.

englishwoman,[1] her sister and sister's husband, a pleasing frenchman. The sister is a dashing woman. M. de F[reudenreich] who does not speak english, is gentlemanly, but not otherwise prepossessing. They are all perfectly well bred, but the loveliest creature I almost ever saw is the eldest girl 12 years old. I could hardly keep my eyes off her - she is so charming in manner and person. There are 2 younger pretty children besides the baby and a boy of 14. The chateau is small, in a sequestered little nook on the steep banks of the Aar, more than 100 ft. above it, where it turns abrupt round a wooded hill and makes M. de F[reudenreich]'s domain a little peninsula. We walked in the garden and heard a most interesting history of a young girl whose tomb we saw. Daughter of Mr Morier,[2] she was a girl of remarkable talent, being at 14 mistress of several languages, besides many other acquirements useful and ornamental. In the prospect of early death, she showed christian hope and patience, but on one point her mind seemed morbidly sensitive: she could not bear to be buried out of England. So, with tender consideration for the parents' sympathy with their lost darling, the Fr[eudenreichs] offered a burying place in their own grounds, that her ashes might at least repose among those who love her, though in a foreign land.

We had a pleasant drive home through the gloom of the forest. I had been cautioned to take care of my throat against the fogs of the river - not without reason, for, although I did so, I had last night an increase of the irritation which has continued ever since the cold wind in the pass of Moutiers. I have almost recovered from the effects of the journey, and expect to be quite strong very soon. Minnie grows fat upon it, and looks very well. We have had our first lesson from Professor Gelpke. The little french he speaks is so bad we can scarcely understand him. He is a thorough german, so we must scramble forward in his own language which will certainly push Minnie on, however difficult it may [be]. He reads both french and english so as to be able to correct our translations. Being professor of german literature at the College, he is likely to be a good guide in his own language; indeed, he seems very intelligent. After this, we spent an hour in the museum. The Steinbock and the Lämmergeier (stuffed specimens) attracted me and some fine large raised charts of Switzerland which always amuse me. Then we took a long stroll in the beautiful public walk, the forest of Bremgarten. The wood scenery alone would please, but in some parts you look beyond to the silver-crowned Alps with their purple robes lying at their feet. Mlle Rosa accompanied us, and drank tea with us, and Anna came in in the evening to play duets with Minnie.

---

[1] Anna Hunter (1760-1859) had married Jean Louis Théodore Falconnet.
[2] David Richard Morier, British Minister Plenipotentiary in Switzerland between 1832 and 1846. He lost two daughters to a measles epidemic in 1839. Their memorial was subsequently incorporated into Bremgarten cemetery where it can still be seen.

9th June. In the morning to the french church with Mme.; heard a very poor sermon from a smart young orator. In the evening walked on the Altenberg about a mile from the town overlooking the river. Mme M. came after tea. Between 9 and 10, the warm dry evening tempted us into the garden.

10th June. Up at 6 to prepare for Herr G[elpke]. We had a spirited lesson; we all worked so hard at understanding one another. If I could but take German alone for a month, I should talk fluently, but three languages at once is rather puzzling for an unlucky wight who has so little verbal memory. We went to recreate ourselves in the Munster court or platform overlooking the Aar, shaded by fine trees and abounding with benches. There we drew for an hour, not having much chance of subject, but just practising in the open air. It is so burning hot that, except in the streets where there are heavy arcades, or under the trees, it would be intolerable. I have made Minnie into a Bernese girl by a large straw hat which is not only a shade for her face and neck but very becoming. I beg all friends who see this letter to observe it has my full address Rue de l'Isle Maison Aebi, Berne, and that I shall be here quite long enough to receive letters from England.

11th June. A horticultural show in the town where besides flowers and fruit prettily arranged, we saw the *beau monde* of Berne. There was a fine young woman in a peasants' dress of the richest materials and with costly silver chains. I fancied the costume was adopted as a fancy, but found that the girl was daughter to a rich farmer, and had the dignified pride of not aping her betters, a feeling not uncommon among the Swiss. At the Tuesday market, I was no less entertained by another class of inhabitants, then went to a booksellers and the bank. One of Mme Henzi's sons brought home my silver and paid his respects for the first time. He is a pleasing young man and speaks good french. Did I tell you we went to visit the bears, the tutelar saints of Berne, and fed them handsomely notwithstanding which one of their stone viceroys on the gate continues to leer at us in most insulting and comical way whenever we enter the town by the Vaudois Gate. Mme Henzi occupies the attic and third floor, other sets of people the other floors of this and the adjoining large house. To these, the lower staircase of each house is in common, and the garden to all. Nevertheless all is clean and orderly. If we are seated on the benches and even a stranger passes between us and the view, they acknowledge our presence by a bow the first time, and the passers on the road often salute us. Our cook and her friend exhibited a full Bernese costume to us. She had a little round flat crowned hat, slightly turned up at the edges, made of pasteboard dyed with sulphur of a bright yellow, moreover ornamented by a bunch of artificial roses. We should think ill of a girl so rigged out in England, but she looked remarkably simple and modest, and her poetic 'leben dir wohl' put the finishing stroke to the odd combination. Mme de Z[eerleder] called; another of the bernese patricians, she invites us to her country house to dine at one.[1]

12th June. The smart people of Berne, with the exception of a few families who are as plain in dress as they are polished in manners, are very country-town like. Mme Henzi and her daughters are dressed very simply and look well among them. Rosa is a very pretty girl, quite a belle. We learn to be early here; all the household are up before six and we before 7. Then we make up for it by going to bed at 10. Minnie sometimes consents to retire before. Either the cookery, or the heat, or something else, rather disagrees with us both, so that we are not quite so strong as might be expected from this patriarchal style of life - yet we are not ill.

June 13th. Mem: parts of letters omitted relating to the death of my dear Aunt Kirby.

Mme H[enzi] provided so many delicacies for our breakfast and tea that we have been obliged to protest that not eating is not to be taken as a sign of not liking our provisions: fancy bread of all sorts, different cheeses, delicious preserves, strawberries, cherries, mountain honey, something fresh every day. As to our dinners from an hotel, neither she nor we were satisfied at first; now we have only too much. Most things are cheap here except coach hire and wearing apparel, which latter is neither cheap nor good. We spent much more than the proportion for our two months at Paris, but it included masters and the hire of a piano for Minnie, and a good deal of expenditure for me, which will not occur again. 110£ did little more than bring us here, but, exclusive of mountain excursions, we are not living at one third the expense now. Mlle W[urstemberger] advises us to go soon to the Oberland. A female relative of hers came over a mountain there last week and the road was quite free from snow. When I hear the details of a mountain journey where we mean to go, it seems to me the difficulties are often greatly exaggerated. The guides are so weather-wise and there is so much accommodation for the immense number of travellers who pass, that those who are not ambitious of distinguishing themselves are very little likely to get into scrapes. Minnie seems to me very little altered, and always protests she would return directly if she might, though she is very well amused, and has struck up quite a friendship with Rosa who is a simple minded girl carefully brought up. Minnie is sometimes very languid but writes a great deal and improves in german. It is quite impossible to put

---

[1] Charlotte Zeerleder (1780-1863), née Bürki, was the widow of Albrecht Zeerleder (1776-1825), a Bernese patrician who had played an active role in defending Bernese interests during and after the French occupation of Switzerland in the 1790s.

in other studies regularly here. We keep up steadily our scripture reading but every thing else goes as it can. Accounts and arrangements take up no little of my time, and the hours we pass in talking french or german with the Henzis are by no means time lost. Yesterday (Sunday) it was quite a relief for me to stop the current of things and talk in English of you - thought it was a sorrowful subject but I wanted to be refreshed by allowing myself to be natural; it is such a constraint to explain things to strangers in a foreign tongue when one's heart is so full one would be understood at half a word. We were recalling Aunt Kirby's great kindness to us last summer and her letter to me at Paris. I think Minnie is really much grieved to lose her; Barham has always been one of her pleasantest recollections. This is really a charming place. I am more and more glad I came to a real Swiss town and not to an English colony. It is much more entertaining, and we see many scenes of social life we should entirely miss by being bound up with a multitude of English. The Laguerres were thoroughly kind, but these people from religion and turn of mind are more congenial.

June 12th.   Drank tea with Mlle W[urstemberger]; we set out rather late, that is quarter to six, being delayed by a call from Mme de F[reudenreich] and her sister who were very agreeable, offered us books, and pressed us to go again to the Chateau. Mlle W[urstemberger] had the feeling and kindness to ask Mme H[enzi] and her daughters to accompany us. I therefore ordered a drosky. It is not 20 minutes drive but down and up steep hills. The cottage is on a lovely spot on three sides, the most agreeable country scenes like Baylham magnified, and, on the 4th, the glorious mountains. The simplicity of the dwelling amounts to bareness, but there was a hearty welcome and a plentiful tea in the open air under a rough arbour with the vine wreathing about it and in full view of the haymakers on a lovely slope. The additions to our party were a Swiss artist and his wife, a graceful young woman, and Frederic Henzi, a youth of 17, who is learning English. The young people amused themselves with games and with the continual puzzle between french and german. We walked home down a steep descent by a lovely twilight. My journal having been broken off, I will put together several things which have been omitted on former occasions. We were much amused following the cows and sheep home from their pastures one evening. The former, (the property of the whole village), are collected by one man. They came at his call and walked soberly on, gently tinkling her bell and, as each arrived at her house, she walked in without knocking, even though the rest of the family were at supper under the same roof. In the morning they come out in the same orderly way, as the herdsman walks along blowing his horn. As yet, we have only heard snatches of *Ranz des Vaches*.[1] The sheep are by no means so sober in their proceedings, though quite as orderly. They follow the

---

[1] Melody, sung, or played on an alpenhorn, to call cattle.

34

shepherd obediently, but with all manner of antics by the way. I laughed outright to see the bounds and fantastical play of the lean black creatures. I have heard a real frog song; I could not have believed they could have made such a noise or that any creatures could produce such a dull inharmonious sound, an army of carpenters rasping boards in their sleep. One evening during our drive, we had a sight of the snow mountains reddened. As the shadows fell across the plain, the mountains were gradually lighted up with pale pink, and, as gradually, the rosy tint slanted up into the clouds and left them to their former cold blue till, as the sky glowed warmer, they stood up in it colder and bluer than ever. We were taken by Mlle W[urstemberger] to the painting room of Herr Dietler.[1] His sketches were very good, and two or three of his watercolour portraits equal to Richmond's[2] in grace and freedom, superior in delicacy and high finish. We were at dinner one day when Julie brought a note saying a gentleman wished to know if he might be admitted; the note was from Mlle W[urstemberger] to introduce Mr H. and to beg we would allow him to share a drive we were about to take with her and Rosa to see an ancient chateau. Up came the gentleman whose name I have often heard in connexion with societies for the conversion of the Jews. We were very amiable considering we were disturbed at feeding time, and expended the customary amount of extasies upon the mountains. By the way, it gives me a mental shiver to hear them extolled in guide book fashion by people who I am morally certain were computing how many zwanzigers go to a shilling or puzzling over their 'Murrays' where they were to admire in the finest parts. Chateau Worb is one of the oldest in the Canton but is now inhabited. These châteaux do not look so warlike as our castles of the same date, but this is strong by its position - an abrupt hill commanding the village at its feet. The rooms are low, large beams across the ceiling, the walls partly dark carved wood, partly covered by tapestry. All the houses, like the cottages, abound with wooden galleries where the inhabitants spend all the day in fine weather. Mlle de W., a pleasing, lady-like young woman, received us and gave us the usual refreshment, gooseberry or strawberry syrup and water; it is rather too sweet for my taste, but a very weak mixture is agreeable. The village is inhabited by very wealthy peasants who have good houses (still in cottage style) with gardens, and keep horses and cows. It was probably one of such as these whom I saw so well dressed in peasant costume at the horticultural show. We drank tea in the simplest styles with Mlle W[urstemberger] and I suspect this somewhat disappointed our English friend - it was very different from a talking party among the rich friends of the Jew's society. For my part, I was content to

---

[1] Johann Friedrich Dietler (1804-74), a Swiss painter who, after studying and working in Paris, settled in Bern in the 1830s. He specialised in portrait and genre painting.
[2] George Richmond (1809-1896), considered one of the finest British portrait painters of the period.

exchange buttered muffins for unaffected and spirited conversation. As we had the escort of Mr H. and Rodolph Henzi,[1] we did not hasten home, but enjoyed one of those charming evening walks to which nothing was wanting but silence. The public education in Swiss towns makes quite a feature in their appearance. So many times a day, the streets are thronged with lads from 10 to 20 with books under their arms, and, in the evening, they gather into groups smoking and talking.

16th June. M. Monod of Paris[2] preached an eloquent and useful sermon on 'Thy kingdom come'; his action is too theatrical for my taste. In the afternoon, we went to a meeting on behalf of the *Sociétés Evangeliques* of Paris and Berne. M.M. Monod and de Wattville spoke well. They say there is much enquiry arising among the Romanists. Whole villages, having had a stray Bible circulating among them, demand a form of worship more corresponding with it than that of the Roman priests. In one instance, this desire arose by means of one of the old Bibles with chains attached to it which had escaped burning at the revolution in France and came into possession of a peasant who could read. There is much going on which cannot be traced to any intentional human agency. Mr H. spoke in English, M. Monod interpreting and greatly improving his speech.

17th June. Went with Rodolphe and Anna to the Enghe or Lagni, one of the terraces from which there is a view of the Alps. There was a band of wind instruments played tolerably well. Came home by the Bremgarten and, as we had taken advantage of having a gentleman with us to stay later than Mme H[enzi]'s hour for tea, we had her and all her five to tea with us.

18th June. My dear Mother's letters came to cheer me and enable me to enjoy an expedition I did not like to delay longer. At 10, we set out in a phaeton to spend the day with Mme de Z[eerleder] The road is such as to hills that when our coachman was asked if he knew the way there, he shook his head and said 'but too well' and that we ought to have had 2 horses. It is a charming drive among hills and woods and picturesque villages with mountains in the distance. The roads being in a very good state, we were there in 2 hours. Mme de Z[eerleder], in her morning undress, received us with much cordiality. In true country style, we had brought her letters and provisions. She is elderly, religious, extremely well informed, and very courteous; you may guess how agreeable she was. We dined at one, in one of the alcoves in the garden, a complete Swiss dinner, only one dish of meat (cutlets) but all that is made of eggs, milk and vegetables. Mme de Z[eerleder] retired for a nap, and we were shown each to a room with a sofa to do the like. However, we both stayed in the drawing room and read.

---

1 The oldest of the Henzi boys, born 1824.
2 Fréderic Monod, (1794-1863) an evangelical minister based in Paris.

Mme de Z[eerleder] had taken us a charming walk among the hills. Her own house is perched up at a great height. We saw plainly the Fribourg range; the snow mountains were misty, but a lower range with snow upon them looked as if we could reach them in 5 minutes. We met a Cretin boy, one of 8 who are all either Cretins or deaf and dumb, although one was removed at its birth by a charitable lady who had it brought up in another village in hope of escaping the influence of association. The poor boy gave me an idiot smile and took hold of Minnie's hand; they are always pleased with notice. Mme de Z[eerleder] has one neighbour within a mile and a half, a very few peasants' cottages, and the house of her farming man near her. At one time she managed the land herself, but living at la Farneran only 5 months, she found things went wrong in her absence. In winter she lives at Berne, in spring and autumn at Zurich. A thunderstorm prevented our walk, but we had instead some very interesting conversation. These drives, besides the society we gain, give us an occasion of seeing the remote villages among the hills where the characteristics are much more strongly marked than around Berne. There was one house with three rows of galleries but that had not a barn for the upper story as most of them have. You may suppose this, together with roof and sometimes walls of wood shingles, makes complete destruction almost inevitable in case of fire. We saw the smoke of such a catastrophe yesterday, and even in these peaceful vallies there are those who set fire to their houses to cheat the insurance offices.

19th June. Rainy day, employed principally in German. In the evening went to hear the pupils of M. Mendel[1] sing several chansons, Benedictus from the Requiem, part of Mendelsohn's St Paul, and there were about 50 young men and women of the respectable inhabitants; Rosa was one. The affair was conducted with the utmost propriety and simplicity and as little display as could be in a public concert. Tickets are not sold but given to the parents of the pupils. All the élite of Berne seemed to be there. The young people performed very well; there were two fine voices. Those who had conspicuous parts were timid and the choruses were harsh, but they kept good time and, with very few exceptions, were in tune.

20th June. A little practice for the mountains. The Aar is unusually full and rapid from the sudden melting of the snow. We walked along the edge of a steep descent to a narrow wooden footbridge over the river which we crossed, and then went to a spot where its overflow, being guided artificially, rushes under our feet down some 10 or 12 feet. There we stood to become accustomed to the noise and shaking. We saw two rafts floated down from the mountains go over the fall at a little distance where it was lower. Even then it did not seem a very desirable berth for the men who

---

[1] Johann Jakob Mendel (1809-1881), director of music and organist at Bern Cathedral.

were on it. There was not the smallest danger where we were, but it was some minutes before my unaccustomed nerves could bear it without flinching, and very strange that such a cowardly person should find a sort of fascination in these roaring waters, I who hate noise and bustle, but I do delight in a mountain torrent. In the evening consulted Miss W[urstemberger] about our journey which we agreed to put off till Friday that she might join us at Interlachen on Monday. We are both really feeling the effects of mountain air now. Minnie looks blooming. She has taken spinning. I only wish you could see Julie giving her a lesson and the wheel obstinately going round the wrong way to the infinite diversion of teacher and pupil; then half a yard of even thread exhibited in triumph to me, and, during the calculation how many towels may be woven from the produce of her industry, back goes the wheel, snap goes the thread, and Julie patches it up again with all possible good humour. This is such a darling amusement that I am obliged to restrict it to rainy days.

21st June. Took advantage of a cool morning to go out and draw. By the bye, drawing is very difficult to accomplish; it is so very hot after 10. We have almost always something in view for the evening. Then we have so much writing that I do not like Minnie to sit longer over her desk in the house. Only sauntered in the garden in the evening that we might reserve ourselves for the next day's expedition.

22nd June. Rose at half past 2!!! set out at 3 with Rosa, Fritz and Gustav, and Mrs Henzi's housekeeper, for the Gurten (a high hill a mile and a half from the town). An hour's hard walking in steep rugged paths brought us through the wood which clothes its sides to the summit just in time to see the sun emerge from the hills and tint the mountains. It was indescribably lovely - the firs of a wood close by stood up dark into the sky, the herbage was a brilliant green softening into the grey mist of distance, and then the dazzling mountains seemed to come nearer than the plain at their feet. A thick white mist marked the course of the Aar into very distant windings. On the other side was the Jura and the Lake Neuchatel. We breakfasted in the balcony of a farmhouse attended by six hungry cats, and I dare not mention the number of eggs or quarts of milk consumed. At six, we descended by a longer way through woods, the morning air, perfumed by fir trees and hay, was delicious and bracing, and at present I feel nothing more than the fatigue of a long walk.

23rd June. I have not yet repented of my expedition. Went to the german church having sent Minnie with Rosa to the french. Had the more difficulty in understanding because the clergyman spoke a patois; however I lost very little. The sermon was plain in favour of missions from 'other sheep I have which are not of this fold'.[1] His dress was very strange: a broad white double frill under his collar, and neckcloth which, when he threw his head back, erected itself into a sort of cockatoo's ruff, (NB. I do not know whether this last circumstance belongs to the individual or the species), a gown made of something like black Mousseline de Laine, the breast and sleeves like those of our clergy, the shirt very short and narrow made of little flutings. The verger was as usual in bernese colours, half of him (vertically) red and half black. I have not told you of the Bâle religious meetings, I must write it separately.

Hotel Bellevue, Thun   June 25 1844.
Except in my last letter, I have always avoided mentioning plans, and present experience confirms my resolution not to dwell upon them in future. Mlle W[urstemberger] on Sunday, to my great regret, gave me the impression not only that I must wait a fortnight for her, but that circumstances having altered, she rather wished to be excused accompanying us, and I, feeling how much her going would benefit me, felt delicate about pressing her to go as she did about pressing me to delay. Then I thought it would be on the whole best to let Rodolph H[enzi] join us after two days at Interlachen, and told him and his mother so. On Monday came Col.M. who said Mlle W[urstemberger] would very much like to go, and that this was much the better plan. This put me into a fever, but I determined to hear the matter at first hand before starting on Tuesday, for which our places were already taken. The result of our conference was to change our route, cut M.H[enzi] off half his tour, and reserve the rest for Mlle W[urstemberger].

25th June. From 5 to 8 a.m. came by a beautiful road here, the snow mountains always in view as background to dark wooded hills and a rich valley. The view from our very comfortable Hotel is lovely: the Niesen[2] and the estuary of the Aar from the Lake. After breakfast, we went up a steep ascent through a wood in the grounds of this hotel, laid out in English style, to a point where we saw the Lake and snow mountains beautifully. Afterwards we drew at our bedroom window till the 1 o'clock table d'hôte when we dined with about 40 of our countrymen, women and children, and a few Germans. We are told we must never expect a separate sitting room in Switzerland without paying extravagantly for it, so we do as most others do, breakfast and dine in the public room, and drink tea in our bedrooms. While we were finishing our sketch after dinner, we heard a hollow moaning sound which I thought must mean something, and so it did, for down came the clouds and soon after the rain. The Lake was curled into

---

[1] St John, Ch.10, v.16.
[2] An immediately recognisable cone-shaped mountain on the right hand side of the Lake of Thun looking towards the higher Oberland mountains.

white breakers. There was some grand thunder and lightning, not so violent as at Tavannes, but really the variety of these storms is so interesting that I do not mind losing a walk now and then for them, and contentedly put off writing till it was over. Now the clouds are drawing up again like a thick white curtain, and the hills seem to have come nearer than ever to make up for their temporary absence. The patches of snow and the black firs stand out in such strong contrast after the rain. After about 16 rounds of dishes at dinner today, a young lady shook her head most perseveringly but in vain to make the waiters understand we could eat no more. At last she exclaimed in what was meant for french 'No mercy' - I am sure it was very sensible english. Walked into the town to purchase gum, saw the noble view of the Lake and surrounding mountains from the church yard which is approached by an immense flight of steps, and the old Castle. Lounged about the little town which is nothing but for the two currents incessantly passing through it, the Aar and the stream of english travellers. Found it was usual to take tea also down stairs, and, while we were doing so, heard a party of our fellow travellers relating their disasters in a little boat on the Lake this evening; they were thoroughly wetted and frightened.

26th June. Took a little walk before breakfast and at 8.30 went on board the steamer for Interlachen. The Lake Thun is 10 miles long. It even surpasses my expectation in point of beauty. How I did wish for you! My eyes are so deceived by the magnitude of the mountains that I always seemed to see the Châteaux and country houses as if they were plaything models. I literally could not make my eyes give me a faithful representation by all the efforts of my reason. From Neuhaus, where we landed about 10, we went in a char to Interlachen beneath an avenue of beautiful chestnuts. This place (or rather people) is most ridiculously like an english watering place: young ladies in parisian dresses flirting with young gentlemen bearing small canes, advertisements of a Covent Garden!, a luxurious table, dances and card parties here, with these fine mountains enclosing them on every side, but they brought their little trumpery world in their pockets. I would not come back if I could not choose my society and therefore keep company with the mountains who have plenty to tell me. After ordering dinner and a char for Lauterbrunnen, we went back to the bridge over the Aar to draw. Every corner is picturesque; but as there is always something wanting in temporal pleasures, here I want repose of mind. There is not time for half the beauties to be enjoyed. I do not want to have seen but to be seeing them. One recognises in these charming things the infinite benevolence which gives liberally all we can safely enjoy. Such a glorious drive to Lauterbrunnen and the Staubbach.[1] I begin to look upon stormy

---

[1] The Staubbach waterfall was one of the most famous in Switzerland. Because of its height, the water disintegrated into spray as it descended. When there was not much water or the spray did not catch the light, visitors could be disappointed.

winds and clouds as pleasant anticipations. We had a heavy shower, but then we had a vivid double rainbow where the foaming stream, the rocks and the trees seemed equally flung about recklessly. I am disappointed in the Staubbach; it is less graceful than I expected. Some of the inferior falls please me better. A minute ago I looked at it by moonlight from my bedroom. There is to my mind a strange wild contrast between the immoveable look of the mountains and the cascade creeping down for ever and for ever. The river rushes on too for ever in such turbulent haste. I found an Alpine flower quite new to me. Two girls sang us a *Ranz des Vaches* more new than pretty.

27th June. This is a roughish inn, not nearly so good as at Tavannes, but we have all we want and civil people. Only a few travellers have yet arrived, but 15 gentlemen and 2 ladies set out this morning from this place over the Wengern Alp. Coming from Interlachen, the road is in a narrow valley beside the river Lutschine, divided near Lauterbrunnen into the black and white Lutschine. We followed the latter and had afterwards occasion to observe how well each deserves its name. I rose at 5 and walked with an intelligent german lad from 6 to 8, what in Switzerland is called one hour's walk. This, however, included 10 minutes admiration of the Trimbelbach [Trümmelbach], a waterfall which is not remarkable here, but pleased me more than some grander ones. It rushes out of a cleft in savage looking rocks. I brought back quite a nosegay of new flowers and the Alpine rose blossoming in the spray of the cascade. I saw the Smadribach [Schmadribach] at a distance and rainbows in the Spitzbach and Staubbach, which latter certainly was very elegant this morning. Where it hangs off from the rock, you see the shadows creeping down the face of the rock within the folds of the white veil, and the rainbow is lovely. This fall is more than 800 feet. I bought an Alpen Stock with a glossy black chamois horn, as much for fun as for use. It was a delightful walk. I begin to feel strong in mountain air. Think of our being so enclosed by mountains that now, so near the longest day, there is no sunlight in the valley before 7. I am assured the earth is sometimes dry here, though I should scarcely have guessed it. There are such innumerable rills of the clearest water running over bright pebbles, and among rocks covered with the richest moss on banks adorned with innumerable wild flowers. One particularly attracted me, about a foot high, little silver tassels trembling on a slender stem. The inhabitants were snowed up three weeks last winter and distressed for want of provisions. I do not think I have told you of the favourite Swiss perfume, (ie) the dung hill. These elegancies are arranged with the utmost coquetry, platted like a lady's grecian tress, and made very near the houses to regale the eyes and noses of the proprietor. Moreover (would you believe it), they actually water our garden at Berne with liquid from that source, and then spread a tea table with good things close by a flower border reeking with the nauseous steam, without dreaming of its being a serious annoyance. You may see women ladling it out in all the cottage gardens. At the 1 o'clock table d'hote Rudolph H[enzi] joined us and we set out for Grindelwald in a clumsyish carriage which did by no means keep out the rain, even with all our ingenious devices of matting and carpet bags and horsecloths to stop up the frames where windows should have been. A deluge soon assailed us and sadly interfered with our view of the beautiful valley and ascent. However, it cleared up before our arrival, and we set out with a guide brought from Lauterbrunnen to see the Glacier.[1] Just as we were going, a large piece fell and discovered a fresh crevice of beautiful clear blue ice which embellished it greatly, for usually it is such a dirty mass that you would hardly take it for ice, unless you go into it, which we did, inserting ourselves into a passage where we could scarcely turn, the water dripping upon us all the while. It was quite a novelty to be so enclosed in brilliant walls which, however, looked very cold and merciless.

28th June. Set off soon after six on our mountain trip. How amused you would have been to have seen us mounted on great cart horses, the same which dragged our carriage from Lauterbrunnen, in saddles with a rail at the back, carpet bags strapped on behind, baskets and umbrellas at the side, M. H[enzi], the guide and the groom on foot. We went slower than footpace, except for one little while when the horses made an attempt at a trot, which threatened to shake all the bones out of my skin. We went to the lower glacier which is finer than the first. After clambering among wet rocks, we descended some ice steps in a gallery which was rather a tight fit. I was going down backwards, the men placing my feet, when, to my horror, I found myself on a ladder, and after a few steps in an ice cave where, to tell the truth, I should never have gone, if they had told me beforehand that few ladies ventured. However, we were repaid for the trouble and wetting by the curious sight, walls so bright, so smooth, and looking so hopelessly impenetrable, though so transparent and blue. In a little hovel close bye, we sat on 3 legged stools and dried ourselves on the hearth, the smoke going out at the roof, i.e. most of it, breakfasting meanwhile on hot milk, bread and cheese - a much more entertaining thing once in a while than a meal in some smart hotel. Our host was a worthy looking peasant. He and his daughter waited on us most zealously, and we shook hands at parting. It is hopeless to attempt any description of the pleasure I had in our beautiful road today. I could have wished for nothing more of that sort. True it is such roads I never saw, but then such horses I never rode. They climb like cats and their descent is still more admirable. Give them but time to put their noses down to reconnoitre and they are sure to find a path. Minnie's

---

[1] Two glaciers descended into the Grindelwald valley. They could easily be reached on foot from the village, a proximity which made Grindelwald a highly popular overnight stop on a tour of Switzerland

horse, I confess, put its foot once through a bridge, and tore off one shoe in a rocky hole, but such trifles, and sliding a yard or two, do by no means destroy their good character. At Rosenlaui, we went to see another glacier still more remarkable in its outward appearance, but, as the only way of seeing into the crevices [i.e. crevasses] was by mounting a high ladder, I declined. The ascent to the Glacier is fatiguing. Horses go only part of the way, and do not descend with riders. I tried for a short distance a *chaise à porteur*, which I ordered for Minnie. It is certainly a most easy conveyance. If I could but tell you what magnificent clefts there are in the rocks where the river rushes from beneath the glacier. We stood upon a bridge across it watching it foaming and eddying, then disappearing deep beyond the cognisances of eye or ear. The guide had a tumble on the wet flat stones. The poor fellow being a tailor, and not much heavier than a bit of thread blown away from a tailor's needle, could not sustain the shock of my feet sliding against his, so down we both came, but were only bruised. After dinner, we saw the waterfall and mineral baths, then remounted. It was a charming ride winding with each projection of the mountain high above the torrent which separated us from the opposite mountain, whence issued innumerable waterfalls. While we dismounted for the groom to shoe Minnie's horse, there came a heavy shower. Luckily we were close by a hovel, but the descent, always rapid and somewhat dangerous on horseback, is worse just at the part where there came another deluge upon us, so that we actually rode down, umbrellas in hand, where most people dismount, to our great credit for courage, and our horses for sure-footedness. We enjoyed the day excessively. I must not omit saying that we heard two and saw one avalanche, and heard a genuine unpremeditated *Ranz des Vaches*. At Reichenbach, we were comfortable enough.[1]

29th June. Walked from 6 to 9 for the sake of a most exquisite view above the fall of Reichenbach.[2] From the most brilliant of turf and gayest of flowers, the eye followed the retiring mountains fading in distance till the Jungfrau started from them in dazzling white with a girdle of black pines. Then we saw the fall itself. After breakfast, in a char to Brienz. Immediately on our arrival, we took horses for the Rothhorn upon the joint representation of our host and Murray that the road was practicable for them. We rode up places that I shuddered to look at as we came down, where the newly made path was so narrow that our horses hind legs often broke away the edge of the precipice. My saddle never kept straight more than five minutes after the many times it was rearranged, so I held on by the mane, frightened for myself when the horse stopped, because there was

---

[1] There was a new inn at the Baths of Reichenbach where the party must have spent the night.
[2] It was here that, fifty years later, Sherlock Holmes apparently met his death in Conan Doyle's story, *The Adventure of the Final Problem*.

not room for him to kick the flies off with impunity, and for M. H[enzi] when we went on, because he walked, when it was possible, between me and the precipice, but my worst terror was to see Minnie's saddle go round just on the narrow edge of a terrible abrupt shelf, several hundred feet high, consisting entirely of crumbling fragments from a landslip which has lately occurred, with not a bush or rock to stop the progress of an unfortunate wight tumbled head over heels into the valley below. However, we were mercifully preserved in all disasters, including that of finding two large trees across our path. The truth was it was a new path. Neither the man nor his horses had been up for two years, and he was evidently as glad as we were to be safely down again. When the road was absolutely impracticable for the horses, we dismounted at some Chalets and pursued our way on foot till I began to feel very tired. Then, having gained a steep ascent for the first time, we came in view of a little Inn among the snow, only used in the summer, to which the host had gone for the first time only that morning. We were near enough as the crow flies, but by mountain paths three quarters of an hour off and, as I knew we must walk back, I thought we should both be quite ill with the additional fatigue if there were no beds there, not to mention that I did not much relish sleeping in our day dresses among the snow. Therefore very reluctantly, I determined to turn back in the very sight of the expectant Innkeeper and his company, whom we could just distinguish to be human beings in the distance. We stopped at the Chalets to rest on our return, and made a good meal of goat's milk and cheese, cutting large hunches with M. H[enzi]'s pocket knife. There was nothing [but] bread to be had in this part of the clouds. I must tell you we have both established a character as good mountaineers, as far as our strength allows, which I am determined to push to the utmost. We saw the interior of the Chalet where the cows (who were taking their midday nap) and masters all sleep under one roof and that a very small one, scarcely separated by a partition without a door. It is very amusing to see on what intimate terms these frisky little cows are with their young masters. I saw one chase a boy with an air which said as plainly as words 'you tiresome young rogue, I'll frighten you if you meddle with me'; the boy ran away laughing. I think the cow too laughed in her sleeve, but do not affirm I saw that. No one advised us to mount on returning, so we sent off the horses and boy to wait for us at the foot of the mountain and ran down most of the way, that being the approved Swiss method. The guide took Minnie down by a short cut jumping from one grassy ridge to another. They lie in parallel lines along a great part of the mountain like ripples on water. M. H[enzi] and I went by the path taking such steps as one may suppose the flying Mercury [does] when he sets off on the expedition which he has all but begun. We found several new flowers with abundance of strawberries and wild cherries. We were back quarter before six, very hot and tired. We bathed in warm water, dined, and went to bed at nine, our usual hour among the mountains.

30th June. Went to the village church, such a noble congregation of peasants. We and the pastor's daughter were the only persons not in the national costume. Such a pleasant looking people, even the children quiet and attentive. There were three baptisms, the children swathed like mummies with very gay caps; the godmothers had wreaths of artificial flowers on their heads. The service was the same as at Tavannes. I was obliged to give the most painful attention for, in addition to a terrible patois, the clergyman delivered his sermon in a sort of chaunt which still more puzzled me. However, I did understand a very good practical discourse from Romans Ch. 3 to 12 on the duties of the baptised, the manner of fulfilling them, and the glorious promises annexed to them. We had been beckoned to a particular pew, and there came in two young ladies, one of whom reminded me of Lady E.G., but not so pretty. She gave me such a smile of welcome that I ventured to ask to look over her hymn book, and after this little overture to acquaintance on my part, she asked me after service to walk into her father's garden, (she is the pastor's daughter[1]). There we sat and chatted some time, in the course of which she told me that she and her mother contributed to the support of 6 children remaining out of 9 by keeping a magazine of the Brienz wood ware at Interlachen. This we thought would furnish a good excuse for a future visit to try and persuade her to go up the Rothhorn on foot with us. On our return, we agreed that Brienz and the peasantry were far more entertaining than Interlachen and the smart folks, and that we should like to stay here some of the days we have to wait for Mlle Wurstemberg[er], if we could get rid of our companion without offence. This we easily did; he went directly after dinner, having arranged for our remaining as long as we like *en pension*. We have a pleasant room though homely, and are well fed for 5 frs a day each. M. H[enzi] was a most useful and attentive companion; he often saved us money and trouble. In the afternoon came on a storm and the little lake was soon worked into a fury. It subsided, and we walked down the village to amuse ourselves with the goats, the churchyard and the people. The clouds were then magnificent; they became terrific soon after our return. We had such a tempest as has not been known here for 30 years. The ground was white with hailstones, many of which were an inch in diameter. It was so awful, I confess I was afraid. The wind blew off some tiles from our roof, and part of the Hotel was deluged with great hailstones. One might have thought after an hour or two of this it was over, but in another hour torrents of rain came again. I sat listening to the streaming eaves and to an incomprehensible dull sound as of falling bodies which reminded me that, a few years ago, heavy rains had brought down [a] great part of the mountain under which we were, and swept houses and trees into the lake. The lake was not a stone's throw from us on one side, and, from

---

[1] Elisabeth Körber. Her father, Samuel, had been pastor in Brienz since 1827.

the mountain, a good marksman might have thrown a stone down our chimney. The scene, by wild gleams of moonlight, was sublime, but still it was a relief when, about midnight, the tumult abated.

1st July. Walked among the cottages before breakfast to see what damage was done. All the watercourses were overflowing. The noise I had heard was the plunge into the Lake of great masses of rock brought down from the mountains. Potatoe fields looked as if they had been mown, trees down, fruit destroyed. Indeed, the poor people shook their heads and looked sorrowful, except one old man whose faith and trust seemed to make him content with every dispensation of providence. After breakfast, we went to ask Mlle Kürber about the woodwork. She recommended us, as might be expected, to buy it of her mother at Interlachen, whither her father is gone today. On his return, we are to hear about our trip. We drew for an hour and a half in the garden, then found out one of the wood workers on our return, had a most amusing dialogue in bad german, and a further insight into Swiss cottage life. Minnie begs me to tell you that notwithstanding her anxiety to return to England, she has bought a very pretty cottage in Switzerland. We are the only Ladies now staying in the house. Some Swiss dine, but the English go to the Giesbach usually. There are living here a french painter Girardet,[1] a sculptor, and a doctor, whom we see at table, and who are so lively and entertaining that, if we had a gentleman with us, I should certainly make their acquaintance. As it is, we are very snug in our own room during the heat of the day. In the evening, more rain but Mlle Kürber contrived to come to us. The Rothhorn expedition is given up; it would be dangerous on account of the earth slipping away and letting loose great masses of rock.

2nd July. After breakfast, as it rained still, we asked for some french and german books perceiving that the Innkeeper's daughter and her sister-in-law were superior sort of people and likely to have some. They brought us a very good selection, and Mlle, who is a fine handsome young woman of very pleasing manners, brought us also some very clever sketches done for her by Girardet who has spent his summers here for 7 years and sometimes the winter. He paints all day and, in the evening, amuses himself with the family, and I should think very pleasantly. Mlle speaks very tolerable french. She is engaged to a very gentlemanly-looking young Swiss doctor of law and who is also here. A deceased sister knew english, so under the peasant's dress (which by the bye is made of excellent materials), we find cultivation of intellect, good manners and a sort of kindly frankness which is very taking. The sculptor (Herr Christem),[2] though a man of talent, is

---

1 One of three Girardet brothers from the Swiss canton of Neuchatel, probably Edouard (1819-1880).
2 Raphaël Christem (1811-1880), a sculptor from Bern.

utterly deficient in tact and common sense. He does the most absurd things and relates them afterwards with all imaginable simplicity, whereupon the painter makes the drollest caricature of the whole scene. They sing Uhland's beautiful sonnets and watch the mountain varieties with unwearied interest. There seems a sort of brotherly feeling throughout the whole village. This is a sort of life I have admired in books as a charming idea of the author, but never expected to see it realized. Now I do, I strongly suspect the entertainment it affords will keep me away from Interlachen till I must go to meet Mlle W[urstemberger].

As it was too wet for any expedition on foot, we took a boat and were rowed by a girl and her deaf and dumb brother about the shores of the lake, having stopped at the Parsonage to take in Mlle Kürber. After an hour and a half, the rain drove us in. This evening, still torrents of rain, and from one place, where in the spring many acres of fertile land were laid waste by a torrent of mud and stones from the neighbouring mountains, there is now pouring into the lake a stream of mud, but I hope (as a course has been made for it) without damage. Several times in the night I heard the perpetual rain and the rumbling of the mud and stones, so that, when I got up at 6.30 on the 3rd, I was really in despair to see it going on still, the lake covered with white breakers, and the mountains with heavy clouds. We held a short consultation and determined that, as the mountains were not likely to be either safe or pleasant for many days, and as our remaining another day at Brienz would involve the necessity of waiting at Interlachen for weather and Mlle W[urstemberger], we would set off at once for Berne. The steamer was to go at 8 from the other end of the village, half a mile off at least. Our handsome hostess most disinterestedly did her very best to promote our wishes, even to insisting upon our not waiting to pay our bill for fear we should be too late. She had ordered a carriage, but, to my astonishment, we were packed into a boat and away we went as fast as 3 strong men could row against the wind. The reason for this change was that the torrents had broken up the road. I could not help saying long life to the ugly bustling steamboats, for we could not have escaped without them. We saw the Giesbach full and turbid. It looked extremely picturesque even in the rain, but I think we shall see no more of it. From Interlachen, we were hurried away with only a mouthful of breakfast, stopped at the post office and left my address for any letters which might be forwarded there for me, in virtue of which I hope to receive a letter from England which I understand crossed me on the road. At Neuhaus, found we had been misinformed about the steamer which did not go for an hour and half, so we took our little carriage on to Thun. The drive along the south shore of the lake is very pretty, but it rained almost all the way. However, it was fine long enough after dinner to enable us to take a delightful walk beyond the Chartreuse[1] which we had not seen on our former visit to Thun. I did not mention the fine feudal castle 700 years old frowning over the little town of Thun. We were in luck on our arrival at Berne at 9.30 for the first persons we saw at the post were Rudolph and Fritz Henzi on the look out for their sister, and they took care of us and our goods. As we walked home, we met Mlle W[urstemberger] who, after sending four notes to announce changes of plan (none of which ever reached me), had finally determined to set out at 5 next morning to join us at Interlachen. She is however very glad to be spared going for a few days and every body says the weather is very uncertain. I look forward to the second trip with still more pleasure than the first, and am glad of the interval to fix in my mind what I have already seen. We have both come back stronger than we went, not at all requiring bodily rest. I wrote to dear Uncle Kirby and sent it from Brientz.

4th July. The pleasure of a letter from Lady B. She says she has received but one of mine - how is that? There have been two or three destined to reach her since we have been among new scenes. Very comfortable again in our old quarters, although Julie has not come back. She had leave to go to her friends during our absence, and is engaged to another service on the 25th. Mme H[enzi] said she would see how her housekeeper liked waiting on us before she wrote for Julie, and, as 'Brunner' seems to take to us very kindly, I think we shall not have the expense of a *femme de chambre* again. We made her useful in needlework and she served us most zealously. I shall now break up our establishment here before we set off for the mountains, and, leaving my baggage ready to be forwarded, hold myself free to change my route and time as circumstances dictate. In the evening, Anna played duets with Minnie. Rosa had just returned from a tour on the mountains and, being a few days later than we were, had incessant rain and snow which the minister of Brienz had prophesied would come before fine weather.

5 July. A thorough wet day set aside our plan of going to Hofwyl.[2] We have always plenty to do on wet days but, by way of extra amusement, Minnie is to have the spinning wheel after dinner, and I am going to read English with Fritz who, by the bye, is a great favorite with me. He is a very clever pleasant boy. At Brienz, we met Gustave and 13 companions with two tutors on a pedestrian tour among the Alps. It was quite a pretty sight: many of them fine looking lads, each having a knapsack covered with goatskin, waterproof cape, and what Josiah would call a 'wide awake' hat

[1] Murray's *Handbook* described the Chartreuse as a pretty country house commanding a particularly fine view of the Lake and Oberland mountains.
[2] Over the years, the educational establishment of Emanuel von Fellenberg at Hofwyl was visited by hundreds of British travellers to Switzerland. The celebrated founder died later that same year on 21 November 1844.

with a narrow ribbon of black and red, the Bernese colours. These expeditions are an annual treat in the principal schools. The best boys are selected and the strongest among them being first tried by one day's journey. Before they set out, they learn many songs with which they recreate themselves by the way. We heard them singing; it was not sweet but they kept well together. This is a custom admirably calculated to raise a fine active race of youths, for they must endure hunger and fatigue, to bind together the inhabitants of the different cantons in brotherhood, and to make them all love their own mountains, the scene of these vivid enjoyments of early youth. I should dearly love my native mountains if I were a Switzer and can well understand a Swiss friend telling me she felt so unsheltered and comfortless in our English plains. Our nine days cost 2 frs. a day less than I calculated, and with Mlle W[urstemberger], we shall walk more because we shall be less particular about finding rooms enough and can make short stages. Horses are quite as expensive as Inns on account of the back fare.[1] Can any one tell me whether the life of Pastor Möwes has been translated into English? [2]

Berne, July 6th 1844. We spent this morning at Hofwyl with Mlle W[urstemberger]. Before we went, we saw the setting out of a funeral procession from the next house. It was that of a young woman of 23; she died of rapid decline. There is something sadly cold in the Swiss customs on such occasions. In their horror of popish superstitions, they have forgotten that, though nothing can be done for the dead, much may be done for the living. There is no prayer unless the minister is privately requested to come to the house and meet the relatives. A woman who is a public functionary arranges every particular with respect to the body and the procession. She marshals all the relatives according to the relationships, the nearest of kin being chief mourner (in this case, the Father). He stands at his own door (or the house where the corpse is taken), the others pass him one by one, bowing and shaking hands. Silently, they then range themselves in a row beside him. After, friends and neighbours, who wish to show respect or sympathy, pass in the same way, but they immediately disperse. The Coffin is placed on an open car with a canopy. It is covered with a black pall on which is placed a crown and wreath of flowers and has embroidered upon it a scull, crossbones, extinguished torch, and the car is drawn by led horses. A few relatives follow in coaches; the rest go away as soon as the car is gone. The body is taken to the grave and buried, out of

---

[1] Travellers were expected to pay the hire costs for the return journey of a carriage, an imposition which, for those not engaged in a circular tour, could double the expense.
[2] A biography of this evangelical Prussian minister had indeed been published in England: *Memoir of the Rev. Henry Möwes, Late Pastor of Altenhausen and Isenrode, Prussia, with an Introduction by the Rev. John Davies, B.D.,* London (Religious Tract Soc.), n.d. (1840).

their sight, without one word of christian hope to cheer the mourners. No women attend except the public mourner.

M. Fellenberg's plan is founded upon a valuable truth, but one which, it seems to me, must be carried out into practice by individuals and not by one person governing large numbers of different stations. He says that much misery arises from men being forced into situations for which they are unfit. Therefore he educates them not according to their parents' station but their own capacity. There are three divisions of scholars, the lowest of which learn all that a peasant ought to know, and as much as a dullard can learn. They all have exercises to develop bodily strength and activity, and all learn to sing. The first division have a finished education, but if one of them proves incapable of receiving it, M. F[ellenberg] advises that he should be transferred to the agricultural department, or, if the parents do not like that, removed. I am assured there are very few instances of discontent at the change and many are happier. The contrary takes place if a boy in either of the lower schools shows decided talent for any higher branch of science. M. F[ellenberg] began with a philanthropical idea of making more enlightened farmers, but the great expense of bringing a large extent of poor land into cultivation, and of instructing the higher classes, makes it necessary that he should be paid handsomely for these. There were boys of various nations, several English. It is a protestant establishment, but I did not hear that religion is made a prominent feature. There were girls for 10 years, but that would not do. Mlle F[ellenberg] is a very pleasing young woman. She has promised me introductions at Vevay and Naples. Mlle W[urstemberger] dined with us. Our amiable hostess at the White Cross, Brienz, has sent us two things which had been left behind and a very moderate bill; and I recommend all my friends who wish to see Swiss mountaineers[1] to go there.

7 July. On Sunday, I went again to the German church to hear M. de Watville, an excellent man who gave us a striking, useful sermon in real German which I could easily understand.

8th July. Another pouring rain, a long lesson from Herr Gelpke, and a quiet walk, after having arranged the payment of my debt at Brienz. I was amused at their way of doing business. I took the money unsealed thinking they would require to see it before they would give me a receipt, but no, they sent me back to seal it and write the sum outside, for which I chose to ask for a receipt. In the evening, we had Mme Immer (Mme H[enzi]'s sister) with her two daughters, pleasing girls who sang pretty well, another niece, Rosa, Anna and Fritz with their mother. We amused ourselves with music.

---

[1] Here, not climbers, but simply those living in the mountains.

9th July. Today I meant to have gone to Mme Zerleder but she is out, so I made a morning call on Mlle W[urstemberger], saw her mother who is a pleasant old lady, and promised to go again and drink tea this evening. I have been counting up my money to see if we can afford an extention of our mountain journey, and find we cannot. We can live very cheaply at the Hotels in the Oberland, so we need not be afraid of staying wherever we can make interesting excursions on foot, but 30 frs. a day for horses is ruinous. Our plan is - Saturday to Interlachen, that is if Mlle W[urstemberger] hears that the baptism of Lauener's child can take place on Sunday at Lauterbrunnen. She has promised to be godmother to it and thought we should like to see the proceedings on such occasions in the cottage of one of the better class of peasants. Lauener,[1] our former guide who pretended to be dissatisfied with our payment, meeting M. H[enzi] afterwards, begged him to tell the ladies he hoped they would take him on their second journey. We are already in treaty for a courier recommended by Mme B[unsen] for our journey into Italy.

Lauterbrunnen, July 13th 1844. We found Mme de F[reudenreich] very ill and therefore refused her Mother's invitation to stay to tea. We may perhaps meet her in Italy as her physician insists upon a total change of air and scene as necessary for her restoration, and she is going with her sister Mme d'A[rcamballe] for the winter. We spent a very pleasant day with Mme Z[eerleder]. There was a lady who had been *dame d'honneur* to the Archduchess of Austria, a pleasing woman, her brother, and a niece of Mme Z[eerleder]'s. We had some sprightly talk. Mme gave me a book and was very friendly. Yesterday we packed up. I have accepted Mme H[enzi]'s pressing offer to return to her house for the one night we pass in Berne, which suits me admirably, having planned differently only to spare her trouble. We part with much good will; she has been extremely kind and attentive to us. I have received a truly polite frenchified letter from M. L[aguerre] in his wife's name. She has been seriously ill. I did not expect her to reply to the letter I wrote at her request, but must feel obliged by their expressions of interest about us. This morning, according to agreement, we set off about 8 in a calêche driven by Mlle W[urstemberger]'s brother to take her up at Blumenstein on our way to Thun. By this means we saw a quite new and very pretty route. The weather is gradually clearing. From Thun to Interlachen, a delightful voyage. We only stopped to purchase some wood ware of our Brienz friend; then had a charming drive along this most exquisite of valleys here. I enjoy it quite as much the second time as the first. We have come here

---

1 Christian Lauener, born 1793, was to play a key part in establishing Wengen as a tourist resort by opening the first hotel in the village. He is not to be confused with Christian Lauener, the famous Alpine guide.

tonight because tomorrow morning Mlle W[urstemberger] is to be godmother to Lauener's child. We are to dine at his house. We have brought by way of contribution a meat pie, some cakes which Minnie helped to make, and stuff for a little frock. Mlle W[urstemberger] has brought a multitude of things so that our Lauener, who came home with us from our walk, was quite overpowered.

14th July. Minnie and I went out to prepare the usual nosegay for the Godmother, then breakfasted and went to a Mill where we were to assemble. Minnie was infinitely diverted with the little mummy-like baby, only 8 days old, and the poor little thing brought down from the mountains to be many hours away from its mother. The set of cottagers we were among were religious people and that gave them a refinement and an affectionate manner which is very charming. Lauener made a short prayer before we went to church. Relations included, we were ten persons. We tasted the spiced wine which is usually presented on such occasions. The baptism was such as I have already described. Mlle W[urstemberger] wore a veil and black gown, that being the custom among those who are not peasants. We had a very dry sermon in which all the characteristics of christianity were omitted. The mountains are a glorious temple and invite to silent adoration every hour of the day. We returned to the Mill and while we waited to have our bags fetched from the Inn, I sat and looked at the glorious view quietly and silently to my heart's content. We then set out on foot for Lauener's house which is nearly half way up the Wengern Alp, very steep and very hot, but repaid by the most delicious views. Minnie and I are both better mountaineers than Mlle W[urstemberger]. Minnie takes advantage of her agility in getting first to her journey's end, in coming back in triumph to meet us, and I of mine in walking forward alone and then sitting down to enjoy the view more than is possible when there is a necessity for minding one's steps. Mrs Lauener is a very interesting woman. She was still very weak and could not control her excited feelings. There were four other children, good little obedient things, who were tossed up on a great stone among potato bags etc. to be out of the way. It was certainly the roughest repast I ever made but I never had a more hearty welcome. We insisted upon the relations and friends sitting down to table with us, the other young godmother with feminine tact acquitted herself very well, but her brother with true clownishness could not help laughing perpetually. We were in a little wooden house with the simplest furniture, but clean. Our first dish was soup strongly flavoured with saffron; the next hunches of home fed and home cured ham and mutton and potatoes; with the ham, dried apples and pears (sweet), lettuce, good bread; then a sweet omelette made by our host himself; next toasted cheese with honey; then cream of the Alps, very thick, eaten, like sweet creams, with bread. So far, by dint of a mountain walk and good will, I got on pretty well, but when the course of good things we had provided came, I was obliged to beg off, and we all protested it was impossible to drink tea or coffee. Our plates were like painted flower pot pans, our spoons round iron ladles, knives, forks of the roughest. Every now and then our kind entertainers insisted upon taking the whole service out to wash it. After dinner, Mlle W[urstemberger] read a chapter in the Bible and part of a sermon. About 5, we started for the rest of our journey, leaving our kind hostess in tears, partly because her weak state prevented her fulfilling one of the duties of hospitality by accompanying us, partly at the thought that she should probably never see us again. These good people became acquainted with Mlle W[urstemberger] when she travelled with Mrs Fry and the Gurneys[1] of whom they retain an affectionate remembrance. After stopping a little while at a cottage, we were accompanied a great way by a noble looking woman and for some distance by others. A boy blew an Alpine Horn and echo returned the most exquisite sound, 'notes by distance made more sweet';[2] I cannot imagine any thing of mere sound more perfect than this voice of the mountains. It required strenuous exertion on the part of our guides to get me away from such music, though I was anxious to be at the top by sunset. It is a new delightful sensation to be wandering among these magnificent mountains, enclosed by them on every side, and often for a long while without seeing a human habitation or a human being. A small party may easily lose sight of each other, and that without the least danger, for the horse path is almost always a distinct guide. We arrived at a little wooden house yclept Hotel! de la Jungfrau about 9. It is directly opposite that mountain so that we saw two avalanches from the windows. You may guess we were very tired with our long walk, too tired to eat, so we went to bed in rooms far worse furnished than our servant's, but very clean.

July 15. At quarter before 4, I awoke my companions to mount a small hill behind the Inn and see the sun rise. We all set out but only Minnie and I reached the summit. My alpenstock did me good service in the descent for we were quite alone. It is a beautiful sight to see the light creeping down from the tips of the mountains, but I think what is gained by the ascent is hardly worth the trouble to those who saw it the evening before. (Inserted note: one peak quite black by contrast with the snow white). At breakfast arrived our three horses with the other Lauener who went with us over the Sheideck, and was pleased that we asked for his horses again. I can only repeat that nothing can be more enjoyable than riding among the mountains. The Wengern Alp is wilder than the Sheideck. We heard another Alpine horn but the echo not so fine, more avalanches, ate strawberries at a chalet, and decked ourselves and horses with flowers. We

---

[1] These well-known Quakers met up with Sophie von Wurstemberger in Switzerland in different years: Elizabeth Fry, the prison reformer and sister of the Gurneys, travelled in the Oberland in 1839, the Gurneys in 1843.
[2] From poem by William Collins (1721-1759) entitled *The Passions, an Ode for Music*.

had to pass over a sloping piece of hard snow, a very ugly place I thought, and expected to dismount as a Lady and gentleman did who we met just then. However, our guides would not let us, and it was rather a nervous business, though I did not go into hysterics like the poor Lady who had only to go on foot. We dined at Grindelwald. The glacier we had seen before and therefore only went a little round that we might pass close by the lower one. Our horses being heated and tired, and the men also, we rested 20 minutes on a table land near the summit of the Sheideck. The horses grazed, the men lay full length on the turf. Mlle W[urstemberger] and I sang together and separately, and Minnie ran wild. Our halt was so agreeable to all parties, that we made it a little too long and were very nearly benighted, which in such roads is no joke, for both horses and men need to see well to pass safely over roots of trees and slippery stones. We did not arrive at the little hut-like inn of Rosenlaui till after nine. It was worth while to see the quiet stars come out one by one, and the mountains ghastly on the light side and black as ink on the shadowy, hearing, in the gloom of overhanging trees and silence of all living things, the everlasting rushing of the stream. We were excessively tired and very gladly retired to our little sheds. We had a long discussion to find out whether we could go over the Grimsel, but horses are so expensive that I decided to give up the pleasure, thinking Mr H[egan] would prefer my spending the money differently, unless indeed he could see Minnie springing about with a pair of rosy cheeks which would do credit to any mountains.

July 16. About half past 6, we set out on foot for the Rosenlaui glacier. We had so much admired it before that we wished to see it again; it seemed, if possible, more beautiful than ever. This time we went upon the glacier by steps cut in the ice. Rather a nervous business to look down into these immeasurable deep blue crevices and feel your footing so very insecure, but the men are so skilful that, unless people are foolhardy, there is little danger. Then we went up a ladder to look into another which was not at all dangerous. After breakfast, we mounted and came, partly on horseback and partly on foot, down the most lovely descent to Meyringen where we are now waiting for dinner. Rosenlaui is to my taste the most beautiful valley we have seen. We had a very pleasing christian man as guide at the Glacier. He insisted upon walking all the way down to the Inn with me. We had quite an interesting conversation. It occurred in the course of it that I said we had been told ladies might safely travel in Switzerland without a gentleman. He was charmed with that mark of confidence in his country folks. A very hot and fatiguing, though beautiful, ride to Meyringen where I felt glad to have resisted bravely the temptation to go over the Grimsel, considering the threatening weather and the failure of our strength. Our favorite horse guide is a bit of a rogue; after all though, he is a pleasant clever fellow. He made us push on over the Brunig during the heat of the day under the pretence that we might be benighted on a very bad descent, when in fact we arrived between 6 and 7 taking it very slowly, and he gained his end which was to return that night to Meyringen. The Brunig is a wooded mountain. In ascending, there are pretty views of Thun. On the other side, the inhabitants of Lungern have spoilt their valley by draining half their lake and converting it into meadows. It is a romantic place but, after the Wengern Alp, we are dainty and expect more magnificence where we have such rough travelling. We had walked part of the descent but set out again to see a little of the village. Our horses were standing at the door so Minnie undertook to plait the tail of hers to the infinite diversion of the villagers who collected round us. We were in fits of laughter at the imperturbable gravity with which Minnie continued her task in spite of the poor animal's twitchings to gain undisturbed possession of his own fly-flapper. Just as it was done, his master came out and declared he should go with his tail plaited to Lauterbrunnen in remembrance of the 'little one'. The children were so astonished at the transaction that they followed her about to gaze. The costume is different here; women wear on their chests a large stiff heart-shaped piece of embroidered stuff, sometimes ruffles at the neck and elbows, the hair all pulled back from the forehead and plaited with strips of white or red calico fastened at the back of the head by large ornamented pins, about the size and shape of table spoons, stuck in by the handles, so that the two bowls nearly meet; some have a piece of stiff white lace, like butterfly's wings, which can serve no other purpose than show and effectually prevent all shelter for the head. We are now in a popish canton and see signs of it, (ie) beggars, images of saints, crosses and prettily ornamented churches.

17 July. Set off soon after six in a char. At Saxlen, we stopped to see the skeleton of Nicholas von der Flue, a real saint in great repute in this neighbourhood.[1] It is, like several other parts of skeletons we have seen, a most disgusting object; the bones are surrounded by gay clothes, narrow ribbons bound round them, upon which a multitude of jewels, some real, some false, are fixed. Jewels mark out the eyes and nostrils, eye brows and beard. His hermit's dress is also preserved. At Sarnen, we were received with a sort of friendly hospitality at the rough little Inn (Schüssel). Mine hostess sat with us during breakfast, accompanied us sightseeing, and presented us with nosegays at parting. We saw Landenberg and the Rathhaus, interesting from the connexion with Swiss history.[2] The richness of these vallies is most remarkable, such luxuriant verdure, magnificent walnut trees, pears, apples, plums laden with fruit and growing

---

[1] Nicholas von der Flue, 1417-1487, patron saint of Switzerland, soldier, turned judge and finally hermit, but one to whom many turned for poltical advice.
[2] On the Landenberg stood the castle of Heinrich von Landenberg, the Austrian bailiff. The castle was allegedly destroyed by a popular uprising in 1308. In the Rathaus of Sarnen is to be found the Weisses Buch, the oldest document to contain a description of the creation of the Swiss Confederation.

with all their might; flax, hemp, and white poppies are also cultivated. At Stanz we saw the atelier of Dershwander,[1] a young artist of great promise, whose paintings adorn several churches in the neighbourhood and would do credit to a Royal Academy exhibition in London. He has spent two years in Italy, and seems to be quietly working for such encouragement as the genius of popery affords. The church is very handsome, dark and white marble well carved; here also are interesting historical remembrances. There is something of individuality and romance in Swiss history which greatly excites my sympathy. You cannot think how amusing it is to be out of the beaten track of English travellers; it is almost the difference of being in another country. In England and France, the village Inns are almost sure to be bad, not so here. One now and then meets with an Inn in some remote place fitted up *con amore*, where the host is independant of his gains by travellers, and very likely a magistrate of some consideration, as at this place Beckenried. We are in a very pretty salon fitted up with beautiful wood work, a good piano, in short, well furnished, close upon the beautiful lake of the four forest cantons (Lucerne). Our host is absent, his daughter is accomplished and agreeable. We are very fortunate in coming here just at this time, for we are all over-tired and the weather is rainy. We went out in a little boat to see the shores of the Lake, and went into the church also. There is quite a flavour of Italy here and even some Italian words in common use.

18th July. At four (a.m.) o'clock, we found it was much too cold and rainy to cross the Lake in a little boat before 5 to meet the steamer, so we determined on another expedition, and set off between 6 and 7 for the monastery of Engelberg in a high valley under the Titlis mountain. It is a lovely drive; at the end as much of a scramble for a carriage road as our previous paths for horses only. The usual Swiss scenery: snow capped mountains, wooded hills, precipices and a rushing stream. Unluckily we did not arrive till noon, an hour too late to be invited to dine with the Monks! Mlle W[urstemberger]'s father was well known to the Abbot who received us most graciously with an old man's fondness for women and children. His rooms are quite luxurious, adorned not only with pictures, but with all manner of drawing room nicknacks. He showed us a very complete collection of Swiss medals, quite a history in metal, very tiresome to my companions, but not so to me who like to see contemporary representations of great men and events, however rude. At any rate, it was the old man's hobby of 40 years, and we could not cut short the exhibition. We were then committed to the guidance of the sub-prior who seemed very good natured but somewhat childish in his appreciation of the smart clothing, plate and

---

[1] Melchior Paul von Deschwanden (1811-1881), a painter born in Stans who specialised in church painting and who, in his field, had influence throughout Switzerland.

jewels of the monastery, and in his complete ignorance of what points were likely to be most interesting to strangers. I asked to see one of their rooms. He showed us his own two apartments, a most comfortable batchelor's lodging. In the library, I asked to see some ancient manuscripts. He seemed to have some difficulty in reading the old printing of the Latin, and smiled at my question whether any of the monks were great readers. In fact, the vacancies were not in the shelves appropriated to 'the Fathers', but in those of general literature. Minnie was delighted to walk upstairs and down in a real monastery among live monks or 'monkies' as she calls them by way of affectionate diminution. Neither Abbot nor Sub-prior spoke french. I could understand the former and he me tolerably. He greeted me with a pun when he heard my country. I had come (he said) from Engel (ie Angel) land to Engel-berg. The sub-prior spoke such a patois I could not make it out and Miss W[urstemberger] said he seemed very ignorant. Everything gives one the idea that they lead an indolent, comfortable, old batchelor life. Young men are educated there. We dined at an Inn, not only Swiss but like the one at which we breakfasted in Gräfenort. It had that air of 'well to do in the world' which belongs to the dependancies of rich monasteries. All along the valley are signs of superstition, of opulence and of laziness. At breakfast, there was no butter but cheese from the monastic pastures celebrated for its excellence, and, to make it taste the richer, we had it toasted. I was thoroughly frightened coming down the steep winding descent by the edge of a precipice. Our coachman was so tipsy he could scarcely walk, but the horses were sober and, knowing the road, behaved like rational beings instead of their master.

19th July. Again a rainy morning, so we took our ease and are really not sorry to have a little repose in this comfortable 'Albergo del Sole'. When I was tired of writing and, moreover, a little indisposed, I asked for a history of Switzerland which our hostess borrowed of the priest for me, and I lounged on the sofa to read. Minnie has been writing, playing and drawing, Miss W[urstemberger] by reading. There is a Balois family here, but only the ladies sit in the salon. The church is much ornamented, but I believe it is only a foretaste of what we shall see every where in Italy and therefore do not particularise. Our host is organist. His son has been playing to us this evening and also M. Bernouilli who is more master of his instrument. The house is almost full. People walk in and out and do as they please, but leave us in quiet possession most of the time, and we have not wanted a hearty laugh if it were only at mine hostess's little dog who, when asked what the lazy women of Unterwalden do, in the slowest and most deliberate way turns head over heels.

20th July. Still rainy. We congratulate ourselves that we are not in a hurry and are in a cheap comfortable lodging. We amused ourselves as yesterday. There were fine gleams between the times of the steamer's passing up and down the Lake. At last, between 6 and 7 a.m., our bags were actually put into the little boat when the clouds alarmed me, and I determined upon staying. Long before the boat reached the steamer, there was a pelting rain, so we rejoiced to be sheltered. Among the inmates, there was a Balois family Bernouilli related to a philosopher of that name of some note, themselves intelligent and pleasing: father, Mother, and a daughter who was a little older than Minnie. We agreed to play at a game like 'my Lady's toilet' and we actually cried forfeits like great babies, but not, I think, like simpletons. Minnie's diversion was excessive at M. Bernouilli's ineffectual attempts to screw up his mouth for whistling which she had imposed upon him. The preceding evening, we had played at making verses.

21st July. At last we were rewarded for our patience, a lovely morning, and we set off by the early steamer to church at Lucerne. It was a great pleasure to hear our own animated scriptural Liturgy. I never valued it so highly as since I have compared it with others. I have heard many excellent sermons in french and german, but always missed our prayers. Our morning preacher, I concluded, was a tractarian, from his mystification about baptism.[1] It was a clever sermon. The congregation took a spirited part in the responses and singing. The morning preacher is resident, but the evening one was the appointed minister, and as he said very little in his sermon, I have very little to say about it. Afterwards, we went to call on a friend of Mlle W[urstemberger] who has a lovely place near the town. It was a glorious evening. We only regretted such an one should happen on Sunday when we would not take out horses or men. The mountains were all in a red glow.

22 July. A fine day for the Rigi at last. We set off soon after six in a lumbering coach with the slowest of drivers, but as it was open and the view along the lake was lovely, we bore it with tolerable patience, though we wanted our breakfast long before we had it at Küssnacht. Goldau is most melancholy, a waste of rocks and dried mud where in 1806 stood a flourishing village. Though grass and even trees have grown on the greatest part of the ruins, there is a large tract left which brings it before you as if it were of yesterday.[2] I do not know whether the inhabitants have been stupified ever since, but those of the Inn are the slowest I have met with.

---

[1] The tractarian movement, initiated in the 1830s, sought to revive traditional values and beliefs in the Anglican Church. In contrast with some dissenting groups, tractarians affirmed the importance of baptism as an essential spiritual experience in the life of a Christian.

[2] The landslip of 2 September 1806 destroyed the village of Goldau and caused the Lake of Lowertz to flood with the loss of some five hundred lives. *Murray's Handbook* gave a detailed description of the tragedy, and British visitors were much moved by it.

We saw the chapel on this spot where Wm Tell shot Gessler.[1] At last we set off with two horses only - as it is not a long or fatiguing ascent, we thought that would do. I walked first for an hour and 10m., then the others. We came to an assemblage of peasants and others who, in a rustic senate, were choosing their chief herdsman and other public officers. We dismounted to watch the proceedings. There were short speeches, then a show of hands accompanied by a merry laugh. Several Capuchin friars, in their long brown habits, black hoods and beards, were there. They looked dirty, coarse and impudent, very odious indeed. The peasants in their best, various beautiful costumes, some smart frenchified people and travellers. When the legislation was finished, they amused themselves by running races and leaping for small prizes. We arrived early in the afternoon in the long low wood house at the Rigi Culm, secured our beds, and dined with an English family, evidently of the aristocracy, a father, 2 daughters and a niece, as we guessed. Then we loitered about the summit of the mountain and a curious scene it was: a panorama taking in almost all Switzerland into France, Italy and Germany, the desolation of Goldau, the magnificence of the snow mountains, the peaceful Lakes (we saw 13) and then .... the perpetual ringing of the hotel bell announcing fresh arrivals two thirds of whom were turned away. There were 300! persons there that evening: many slept on straw, some sat up all night, guides and grooms slept in the stables, at least those who arrived early enough to get shelter for their horses. This was a curious assemblage, more English than of any other nation, but a Babel of tongues it was. A horn was blown to give notice of sunset and bring out the folks in all various stages of dinner, some with hands full, and some with mouths full, and the newly arrived very empty indeed. We were very fortunate in the weather: it was a lovely evening. When the sun was down, there was an immense table d'hôte. We just looked in; it was like a beehive, both in buzz and warmth. At 9.30, we succeeded in obtaining tea, but found people showed a somewhat rude impatience to get us out of the room because (as we learned at last) 7 ladies were to sleep there on mattresses, one of them being at least 60 years old. We took compassion on her and gave up one of our beds, so Minnie slept on a contribution from our beds in our cabin which was not high enough to allow me to dress my hair without rapping my knuckles against the ceiling. Such a racket there was till late at night, and such a grinding of coffee and making of rolls for the morrow.

23 July. At 3.30 the Alpine horn was blown in the passage to wake the sleepers for sunrise, and, at four, there was the same turmoil as in the

---

[1] The final episode in the conflict between William Tell and the Austrian bailiff Gessler initiated by the latter when he required the Swiss to bow to his hat on a pole and Tell had refused. Tell's victory over his adversary represented for the Swiss the triumph of individual liberty over foreign tyranny. Even before arriving in Switzerland, many British visitors would have been familiar with the legend.

evening. The sun rose splendidly, the mountains and the clouds upon them became of a lovely pink, the shadows and reflexions were most beautiful. We could distinctly count the 13 lakes, but for a description, see Murray. Those map-like distances give me the vague dreamy pleasure of all great spaces, but then there must be time and quiet for one's mind to float along to the furthest horizon. On this occasion, all was bustle to ascertain what we *did* see. The sharp mountain air oppressed my breathing, but strengthened me so that I am no worse for my full share of walking down a very beautiful descent - we had only one horse between us. Once, finding my footing insecure and my head giddy when there was no one within sight but a peasant coming down loaded with milking utensils, I asked him to let me put my hand on his arm, to which he most cheerfully consented, and we had a pleasant chat till my companions and the horse came up. We are at Weggis dining and waiting for the steamer. From Weggis to Fluellen, we enjoyed the beautiful Lake which becomes wilder towards that end. There are so many windings and bays that we often seemed enclosed by mountains towering one above the other, sometimes sloping down to the water's edge with rich verdure and trees and a village nestled among them, sometimes a steep rocky shore. Mlle W[urstemberger] had been very anxious I should not see the classic ground of Swiss history in bad weather. Now she was content on that score, but she and Minnie execrated the steamer with its comfortable awning which, to say the exact truth, did a little intercept the view. I forgot to mention a curiosity we saw on the Righi. It does not belong (it is true) to Switzerland but to France, as Mlle W[urstemberger] discovered to her great comfort. *It* was a woman, travelling with its husband, dressed in boy's clothes, a brown cloth tunic hardly reaching to the knees, leathern girdle, black pantaloons, man's boots and hat, but a woman's collar, cuffs and hair hanging in curls. At first I thought it was a boy, but our guide said, with a strong expression of contempt, 't'is a woman.' Then I saw its face was too old for the size. Its husband was similarly dressed; both had poles. They are known in the neighbourhood and seem rich people. Its face is not disagreeable, though rather hard. It was also on the steamer with us afterwards and first all the gentlemen went to see it in the bow of the vessel; then upon their report most of the ladies went to gaze. When it went off in a little boat, there was quite a rush to the side of the vessel. On the steamer, we also met for the second time a pastor and his bride, M. Fuetter; they were known to Mlle W[urstemberger]. They were going our way and, as they were pleasant young people, we agreed to take a carriage together from Altdorf to Andermatt on the St Gothard. We had a pleasant evening drive to Amsteg through a valley much resembling that of Interlachen.

24th July. Set out at 6.30 for the Devil's Bridge. Of the most wonderful road, I attempt no description. (I forgot to mention a walk through a romantic narrow valley full of waterfalls and where some manufacture was carried on which we took in the evening from Amsteg). We ascended the *winding staircase* among magnificent rocks which not only look as if they would fall and crush the passer, but now and then fulfil the threat. We passed over a boarded part of a bridge where the snow beneath us was more than 10 ft thick - the remains of an avalanche which had fallen during the spring and, a fortnight ago, when it was melting fast, carried away part of the bridge. (Pencil note in margin: A few days later, these boards being supported merely by frozen snow, gave way with a carriage upon them). In other places, men were clearing away the remains of land slips. Notwithstanding the perpetual recurrence of such accidents, the road is in excellent order, so many men being employed upon it. Carriages are actually drawn over the mountains. The bridge scenery is magnificent; we saw it to great advantage with the rainbow lying on the foamy abyss. Then we walked through the hole of Uri, a tunnel cut in the solid rock, to the miserable filthy place Andermatt, where we dined and sketched while our horses rested. We came down the road at a quick trot. Every time the zigzacs brought us to the verge of the precipice, we could not help shrinking as if we were certainly going over. The solid boundary stones look such pebbles compared to the overhanging rocks. We reached Fluellen an hour too soon for the steamer. Thence we had a delightful voyage the whole length of the Lake to Lucerne. If I were not an Englishwoman, I should like to be a Swiss. At Lucerne, we could not get comfortable places in the diligence, and Mlle W[urstemberger] made a bargain with a return Voiturier to take us the 56 miles to Berne in one day in a capital carriage with one pair of good horses for less money than our places by diligence would have cost.

25th July. Rose at 4, notwithstanding the hard work of several past days, to see a Lion cut out of the living rock, after Thorwaldsen's design, in memory of the Swiss guards who were cut to pieces in Paris in defence of Louis 16. The sculptor is a Swiss, Ahorn.[1] It is very beautiful. The noble creature's attitude, dying on the broken shield of fleur-de-lis, is quite touching. We returned by the church and another of the bridges. I forget whether I told these are long, crooked and heavily roofed, looking like tunnels. In the angle of the sloping roofs inside are triangular pictures representing scenes in Swiss history, in the lives of the Saints, and in Bible history. I could not persuade my companions to admire the valley of Entlibuch as they ought to have done. They would persist in comparing it with the magnificence we had left, till they went to sleep, and left me to enjoy the quiet beauty present without reference to the past. At Langnau, we saw a magazine of cheese, 700 being one tenth of the proprietor's stock, some 4 feet in diameter, and very rich. The peasants who make them in the

---

[1] Lukas Ahorn from Constance had sculpted the Lion Monument between March 1820 and August 1821.

mountains are well paid. Left Mlle W[urstemberger] on our way at her grandmother's and arrived at Rue de l'Isle with no other disaster than the loss of Minnie's cloak in an unaccountable way. Mme Henzi and Rosa are at Rolle, but the housekeeper was most zealous in our service. It was refreshing to have a quiet night in our comfortable room. Moreover, we made a bargain with our Voiturier (a most unaccountable person like a smart courier with a tinge of the brigand) to take us at a cheap rate to Fribourg at three o'clock, so we were not hurried, but enjoyed our letters. Mlle Fellenberg wrote to tell me that Mme Dufour would receive us after the 27th at 55 frs. the week, the two. She also told me that two of her intimate friends had passed a winter there and been perfectly satisfied. She has given me a letter to Mme Couvreu at Vevay, and promises one to Dr Macartney at Naples, and to some one at Rome. I heard nothing from Mr Gaussen[1] and, as it would not do to remain at Berne during Mme Henzi's absence, I thought we could not do better than establish ourselves at Vevay for at least a week, and, if we find it as agreeable as every one promises, for a longer time.

26th July. Left Berne with regret; we have experienced so much kindness there and had so many enjoyments. We all 3 agreed we should like nothing better than to set off for the mountains again together instead of separating. Mlle W[urstemberger] and I have determined not to lose sight of each other, though we are both too busy to keep up a close correspondance. She is a right good creature with much cleverness and acquirement together with a simplicity which is extremely attractive. The poor housekeeper was really in tears at our departure. Fritz has made up his mind to come to England, and Anna only dares not hope for such happiness. Well, there we were, poor wandering birds, turned out of our temporary nest again. I do not take leaving even new friends a bit better than before, but feel less timid in being left to myself, and very coolly established myself at the Zähringer Hof,[2] a good hotel, where we have a pretty good room.

27th July. Lionized ourselves about Fribourg and its promenades whence there are beautiful views. The remarkable bridges are seen from our hotel.[3] Went into a church to see a painting by A. Caracci and was coming out quite disappointed supposing I had seen it and that there was only one good figure in it, but, being a little incredulous as to its genuineness, I ventured to address a pleasant looking Capuchin friar who, when he found I could

---

[1] Louis Gaussen (1790-1863) had played a leading role in creating the Evangelical Society of Geneva and an allied School of Theology. He was well known to and supported by British evangelicals. His advice had been sought over possible lodgings in Geneva for the two ladies.

[2] One of the two hotels in Fribourg described by Murray's *Handbook* as 'good'.

[3] The two suspension bridges of Fribourg, completed in 1834 and 1840, were much admired at the time for their length and height.

speak German, accompanied us into the church and showed us the real picture, so sadly destroyed that I had overlooked it among a multitude of bad paintings, but full of expression and grace in what remained. It is a dead Christ and the Marys. He spoke of that, and of the one good figure in the other picture, like an amateur. After dinner, we went to hear the organ; it is delicious.[1] I never heard such an imitation of the human voice and very rarely a voice half so fine. At first the noise was rather overpowering. We are contriving to hear it at least once again. Here also we saw another *It* in nearly the same dress as the former, accompanied also by a man. We both remembered so distinctly the former *It* that we were certain this was not the same. Perhaps as the strong minded women like to 'wear the breeches' metaphorically, the strong bodied women like to do so literally.

28th July. Heard a very good German sermon and stayed after looking about us in the Cathedral for another performance on the organ. In the evening took a guide and saw the old fortifications and a little valley enclosed by rocks called 'le bout du monde', in which there was nothing remarkable, except the sound of water rushing along within an impenetrable looking wall without the least external sign of the natural tunnel.

29th July. A hot diligence journey to Vevay. We had disagreeable company with whom we would not dine which so affronted the landlord at Bulle that we could get but a couple of eggs to eat, and were treated with great insolence. I repented of my economy, though it was right to retrench as we had spent so much upon horses on the mountains, which I cannot find in my heart to grudge. It procured so much pleasure and advantage to us both, without the lasting evils which would have been so very likely to arise from walking too much. Our present sejour is cheap and, as I am afraid most of the Genevese are at their country places so that we shall gain no society there, I am disposed to remain here for a while. Mlles Dufour are 3 old maids, not any way remarkable at first sight. Our bedroom looks upon the most beautiful part of the Lake which is, this morning (30th), deep blue. We set out after our early breakfast to take my letter of introduction to Mme Couvreu but, meeting her carriage, we learnt she would not be at home till tomorrow. We therefore gave the letter with my card to the coachman. Then we walked through the vineyards to a country house whence there is a beautiful view. The stone walls and dusty roads encircling the vineyards are very disagreeable, but the vines are pretty, such a bright green and loaded with grapes. Among them towers a fine plant of Maize of which Polenta, the national dish of North Italy, is made. The blossom grows almost as elegantly as rice, and there is a pretty tassel of green or red filaments from the extremity of the scheathe [*sic*];

---

[1] Murray's *Handbook* described the organ as one of the finest in Europe,

mattrasses are stuffed with the husks. At 3.30 we took a boat to visit Chillon. I was disappointed - it requires accidents of light and shade to make it picturesque. We saw it too clearly in broad daylight. However, landing there, seeing the dungeons, the ring to which Bonnivard was chained, and all the material for exercising tyrannical cruelty, could not but rouse some interest, even in this hackneyed place.[1] The trap door, by which prisoners in the act of worshipping an image of the Virgin were let down into the lake, dwelt most on my memory. The pillars are covered with celebrated and ignoble names.[2] The Lake was so calm our sail was almost useless, the water bright, reflecting the minutest objects. We also landed at Montreuil [Montreux] and mounted the steep hill to see the fine view just when the setting sun was reddening the mountains. We saw Clarens also. Our row home was charming - first the tints of a clear sunset showing off the picturesque bays and headlands, then starlight, and then a brilliant full moon, placed us in a lake of silver and diamonds. I never saw any effect of that sort more beautiful. Our three hostesses were with us and we all enjoyed it extremely. By the bye, they are well informed women and have mixed in good society.

31st July. Was awakened at 4.30 by the roaring of winds and waves, the blue lake crested with white foam and showed a different beauty from that of last night, but not inferior. We walked into the town to see the fair and buy ribbon for my bonnet. There we watched the lake dashing about like the sea at Brighton in a moderate wind. We sat to enjoy the scene on the terrace of a magnificent house which Mme de Couvreu's brother has nearly finished as a town residence for himself and his mother. After an evening walk and tea, we work all together and read aloud a french story.

1st August. Made an attempt to sketch but rain drove us in. Tried to get an Italian book; there was but one in the town and that a bad edition. Saw a fine stormy sunset from the Terrace of St Martin's Church.

2nd August. Went out to draw. Mme Couvreu called. She is quite a gentlewoman, but her manners struck me at first as somewhat haughty, as if she was quite tired of being teased with strangers. However, she became more sociable afterwards. We are going to drink tea with her on Monday. In the evening, saw a very beautiful country seat called Hauteville. Every such place here has a lovely view - they need not intercept each other.

---

[1] Hackneyed through the publicity given to the castle by Lord Byron's poem *The Prisoner of Chillon* which was usually explicitly recalled in the journals of British travellers as they passed by. The text of the poem could be bought in Vevey thereby allowing travelers to read it within sight of the castle.
[2] Presumably referring, in particular, to Byron's name, though it is doubtful that he himself carved it.

Remember always I do not pretend to give you guide book information - it would take too much time. You must read 'your Murray' - it will contribute greatly to your information and pleasure as it does to ours.

3 August. Went out to draw and buy a travelling dress for Minnie, the old blue having been demolished on the mountains. Saw the marble works in the evening.

4th August. A letter from M. Gaussen proposing our going to Mme Wolff's house at Pré l'Eveque, Geneva. I have a letter from Mrs Morton to Mme W[olff] so that will do very well. We shall probably go on the 12th, thankful that our path is everywhere so comfortably made for us. This likely to be a quiet part of my journal, we are nearly stationary at Vevay. We went to morning service on Sunday at a church in the neighbourhood, our own Liturgy, a congregation of about 40, a young Irishman officiated and gave a tolerable sermon. In the evening, we went to a little Chapel in the Hotel des 3 Couronnes and, arriving a little too soon, sat on the delightful Terrace. These Swiss Hotels are charming places, greatly preferable to boarding houses for luxury, but much more expensive. I do not think I ever told you that up to the present time, the only night we have slept in Switzerland out of the sound of running water was at the top of the Righi.

5th August. Went to draw a little while, but had to return early and see a staymaker for Minnie to make up for Mme Bourgagnet's deficiencies, to the great disgrace of the celebrated Parisienne who could not fit such a figure. As we returned, the lake looked inviting, and I remembered I could not give Minnie a treat next day because we were engaged, so we arranged for a boat to take us after dinner to the mouth of the Rhone and land us at 7 at the other end of the town to attend a missionary meeting. We had a delightful row, the flat reedy land through which the muddy Rhone hurries into the lake; quite a repose to the eye, and gives fresh zest to the glorious mountain scene. We were sorry to come away. The only interesting part of the meeting was that conducted by M. Bouss,[1] but it is pleasant to join christians in a foreign land in a good work. There seemed a true spirit of charity among them. We returned in country style by the light of a lantern; the worthies of Vevay only light their lamps now and then.

6th August. Half expected a letter yet knew there was barely time. Sat a long while drawing on the terrace of La Tour. I have now discovered what has hitherto interfered with my full enjoyment of this lovely place - I am presented by recollections of Rousseau, Voltaire, Lord Byron, and every place brings their names up. It is really detestable; they have each defaced

---

[1] Possibly the evangelical pastor Ami Bost (1790-1874).

the beauty of the scene by associating with it some vice dressed up in false colours. Yet it would all speak of purity and nobleness and truth if men would listen, instead of pretending to interpret when they do not understand its language. I was driven to such extremity by my vague notions of indignation when Clarens was pointed out to me that I had half a mind to read the *Nouvelle Heloise*[1] thinking there must be some good notions in a work so many people have admired which would drive out my suspicions of evil. However, I found a better way when I want subjects more of this earth than the grand thoughts such scenery suggests, that is to remember the brave struggles these rugged crags have witnessed for civil and religious liberty, and the patient charity now working in many a shadowy valley. It is well I have vented my spite to you that I may be the more amiable this evening. We are going to Mme Couvreu who has politely offered her carriage to convey us and we are glad to be spared a hot walk. I ought to mention that our kind hostesses insisted on having an English plum pudding (a very successful imitation) in honour of my birthday. Mme Emma Couvreu and her family pass the summer with her mother (likewise Couvreu) at her Chateau Burier whence there is a most exquisite view of the Lake looking on St Gingough, but although we were sent for early to enjoy the grounds, we could only see from the terrace the approach of a storm which kept us in the rest of the evening. The time passed very pleasantly however. There is a tone of earnest piety among the elders of the family which inspires confidence, much information, and perfectly polished manners. Mme C[ouvreu] is a charming old lady full of vivacity and kindness. Mme Emma is handsome, clever, animated, perhaps rather severe, but gives me the impression of a person to be depended upon for truth which inclines me to forgive the harshness. M. C[ouvreu] the husband, seems a straight forward sensible man, less brilliant than his wife.[2] The brother is so quiet I heard but little from him. They seem all of one mind and are the benefactors of the whole neighbourhood. They live very simply but comfortably. We had a table covered with all varieties of delicious fruits, cakes etc. at tea time. The daughters, girls of 15 and 17, are pretty (one beautiful) and well bred, the son was at school.[3] There was a widower with his daughter, a picturesque half Italian girl of 17, who conducts his household, a lady from the neighbourhood, Mme de Souza, whose loss of property and of parents have compelled to seek her own living - she is at Burier till she can find a situation - and a German lady, governess to the girls. We had a good deal of pleasing conversation on

---

[1] Rousseau's famous, and in its day highly popular, novel which was published in 1761. Its heroine, Julie, lived in Clarens.

[2] Jacob Frédéric Couvreu (1791-1864) had married his cousin Emma (1802-1851) in 1821. The latter was much involved in good works in the neighbourhood and had played a crucial part in creating a refuge for young girls opened in Vevey in 1829.

[3] Edouard, b.1824, had been a pupil at Hofwyl between 1833 and 1839. In 1844 he was a student in Stuttgart.

religious subjects - there was no peculiarity which made it difficult to join with them. Minnie and the young people were very sociable over some prints. At ten o'clock, it was raining and pitch dark. Mme Couvreu insisted upon sending us home as she had done the Frenchman and his daughter. How the coachman found his way without lights is a marvel, but we arrived safely.

7th August. No letters. I begin to fear you must have kept to my first address and I must wait till I get to Geneva. Returning from our evening walk, we saw magnificent clouds among the mountains and a thunder storm which has been going on until now, the 8th. A pleasing note from Mme Wolff expressing her satisfaction at receiving friends of the Misses Morton. Mme Couvreu speaks very highly of Mme Wolff and of the society we are likely to meet at her house. After debating and endeavouring to reconcile the conflicting interests of purse and pleasure, we have decided upon going to Mme Wolff on Monday next, there to arrange our further journey. It is provoking to have received Emma's intimation about Dr and Mrs Ryan when we had left Thun for the 3rd time - every time we could have called. In fact, we most likely dined with them without knowing it. I think I looked at the stranger's book there, but many people do not write their names till their departure, and some omit it altogether. I will answer Emma's kind letter soon. A rainy day. We had only a little walk in the evening. In the afternoon, read *Notre Dame de Paris*[1] aloud with Mlle Dufour, and worked.

9th August. The only persons we knew in the stranger's book were M. and Mme D'Arcamballe and Mme de Freudenreich who have passed on their way to Naples where we hope to see them. In the afternoon, walked to call on Mme E. Couvreu who was dining out, but we saw her Mother, the gentlemen and the rest of the family. Our short intercourse was a pleasant little peep into the interior of a Swiss family of the highest class. I fancy there is material to make friends of in this family, but we pass on.

10th August. Packing and accounts, plenty of the latter for I only this morning received the reckoning of our tour with Mlle W[urstemberger]. We have had a quiet lounge on the Terrace of La Tour. I have not told you that a great part of this Chateau is habitable; there are some tolerable pictures and two rooms full of ancient curiosities in each of which sits a figure as large as life clad in mail, peaceably employed, one in dining, the other studying an old black letter book of devotions. There are various relics pertaining to Swiss History. Our kind hostesses seemed unwilling to part with us. I could willingly stay but that we should then have too little time at Geneva. If any one wishes to spend some time cheaply in a lovely

---

[1] Novel by Victor Hugo, published in 1831.

place, being content with homely ways, they cannot do better than come here. The rooms are pretty good and the hostesses upright, friendly people, much respected in the neighbourhood. In the afternoon, it rained, and we were obliged to content ourselves with working and reading *Notre Dame* till we came to a part so disgusting and so blasphemous that we unanimously resolved to read no more, only wondering it should have been recommended by those who ought to have had a purer moral taste.

11th August. Sunday in the morning English service at St Martins. In the evening, an excellent exposition in french from M. Bouss, of the 7th Chapter of Isaiah. The view he took was new to me, perhaps it is to you. The excellent practical lessons would be too long for a letter, but the general view was this - God, long suffering with Ahaz, commissions Isaiah to encourage him by a promise that his two most powerful enemies should be overcome. Ahaz being incredulous, God further offers him a sign, but Ahaz is so far from confiding faith that he rejects a miracle offered by God himself upon a pretext of not tempting God. The 13th verse is an indignant exclamation at the obstinacy and unbelief of men, and God refers to a sign, already given, which should surely come to pass, verses 14 and 15, adding that in such a space of time as would suffer for a child[1] to come to the knowledge of good and evil, the land which Ahaz abhorred should be forsaken of both her kings, as we learn from History it was.

12th August. A letter from dear Anne in which she did her best to reconcile truth and my pleasure. Still I did not like to hear you had that nasty influenza, although you told her you were really better. I hope I shall soon have a letter, but I have no right to expect you should always be well any more than I am. Lately I have not been quite right but have begun to take my prescription again and also to be better for it. Our kind hostesses and the good natured Rosette accompanied us to the place of embarkation and took an affectionate leave. The day was fine. We saw Lausanne and the beautiful shores to advantage, yet it seems to me that the view of Mont Blanc from the Lake is inferior to that of the Alps from our house at Berne. We arrived at Geneva about 2 and came on to a good house in a garden looking so still and snug among the trees that it is quite reposing. There is nothing to remind one of intending to go further. We have two small but cheerful rooms, the very same Miss Mortons occupied 17 years ago. What pleasant dreams I shall have! M.Wolff is a respectable looking old gentleman, Mme W[olff] very pleasing and motherly. There are here a Lady and little girl, a young American Clergyman (Mr Cheever, now well

---

[1] Note inserted by the writer: 'It is the child either Immanuel or the child mentioned in Chapt. 8.'

known in England as an author),[1] Dr and Mrs Speare with daughters and son, the latter a student of medicine in Paris, where his parents live with him.[2] Mme W[olff] was up part of last night attending the accouchement of her daughter who has a fine boy and is doing well.

13th August. Find we have missed seeing Mme Henzi who was at Geneva on Saturday and left Rolle yesterday. We went to enquire for letters yesterday evening and saw something of the town. Dinner is at 3.30, breakfast at 9, tea at 8.30, all public, but quite like a large family. This morning, we have been a longish walk to see Fanny's friends, Miss Cracrofts - they were out - and to call on Mr Gaussen who was in his study, so we did not see him, but his mother and sister who gave us a friendly reception. I must tell Maria more about them when I have time, and Miss Morton shall hear about Mme Wolff. Poor Minnie has descended even below the titles of "scrap" and "individual"; she is but half a one, for the clerk of the steamer proposed to take her at half price without my hinting at such an indignity or having any intention of passing her off for under 12 yrs. Yesterday evening, I had only a little walk with Mme Wolff when she came late from her daughter. This morning, 14th, we have been wandering about the town to find a cloak for Minnie and materials for two pairs of slippers, one for Father, the other for our little godchild. We are induced to undertake this work because Mme Wolff has proposed that Mr Cheever (the American) should assemble the English visitors for family prayer, and we had this day a specimen of waiting for late folks very likely to be repeated - so we mean to turn the odd minutes to account. On our return, we found Dr Malan[3] who had come to call upon us. He is extremely prepossessing in manner and appearance. He entered into a long conversation on religion with us, especially with Minnie. It was very striking to her and I trust may be useful. We are going to drink tea at his house this evening. Afterwards came Mr Gaussen and his sister, both very friendly. In the evening, in spite of the rain, we went to the service in Dr Malan's chapel. He took the beginning of the 12th Chapt. of Romans as his subject and his first remark I thought singular and beautiful. He said 'how unhappy we should be if God had not pointed out any way of showing our love and gratitude to Him in this life, even though we were assured of

---

[1] George Barrell Cheever (1807-1890) published his *Wanderings of a pilgrim in the shadow of Mont Blanc* in New York in 1845. A British edition appeared a couple of years later.

[2] Dr Thomas Charlton Speer (Miss W. spells the surname wrongly throughout) had married Catherine Templeman in 1817. Their son Stanhope was born in Boulogne in 1823 and achieved some measure of fame in 1845 when he became the first to climb the Wetterhorn. Later he practised medicine in Cheltenham.

[3] H.A. Cesar Malan (1787-1864) had established his own chapel in Geneva in 1820, after breaking away from the mainstream Protestant church. He established links with the Scottish Presbyterians.

eternal happiness.' We then went to the house. Mrs Malan is somewhere among the mountains for the benefit of her health. The party consisted of 3 daughters about 18 and 20 and 13, Mrs H. Malan, niece of Mr Baptist Noel, Dr H. [Malan] and Mr Ceasar Malan, 2 young men names unknown, two Miss Brooks of Yorkshire, travellers, a gentleman with them, Mr Cheever, and a protestant minister of Pesth, deputed by the Queen of Hungary to obtain information from the Vatican and other libraries relative to the first introduction of Christianity into Pannonia,[1] in opposition to the claims of priority set up by the papists. He talked Latin with Dr Malan and German with his son, so we had four languages going on round one table. It was a pleasant party and we were so dissipated as not to return till 10.30.

15th August. Cheered by a letter from you. Minnie says I was not half so content as I ought to have been; however, I do not doubt you are getting well. Pray tell Mary that when I heard you were ill, I quite reckoned upon her kind attention. I am glad and thankful that you are better, but it cannot be pleasant to hear you have been ill. I was not afraid of being forgotten on the 6th.[2] I expected to have your loving remembrance and your prayers. We have had only a short cold walk for it has been very rainy all day, so that the proposition of a fire after dinner was joyfully received, so that we sat and worked in the drawing room most of the afternoon. Conversation very insipid unless we can talk french with Mme Wolff. The only one really congenial with her is Mr Cheever who cannot get on well in french, and she does not speak English.

16th August. Rain again. The gentlemen are driven to desperation. We began by transacting some business in the town and now have plenty to do at home. In the evening, we took a long and pleasant walk to see the junction of the Arve and Rhone. It really exceeds description, the dark blue bright rushing Rhone disdaining to mingle with the slow turbid Arve. There is a line where the two rivers meet corresponding with the advancing or retreating rocks which form the bank of the Rhone.

17th August. Fine at last. We sat an hour on the rampart, a public walk whence there is a charming view of the Lake and the Jura. In the evening, another walk to see sunset on Mont Blanc - it was lovely, but I think I still prefer the Bernese Alps. We saw the same exquisite rose and violet tints I have before described. Others of the party accompanied us both times. Last night, a Revd. Mr Croft [3] returned from Chamouni where he had had almost incessant rain and scarcely seen anything. Two ladies and two gentlemen introduced by Dr Malan this evening.

---

[1] A Roman Province in the middle-Danube area, falling mostly in today's Hungary.

[2] Miss W.'s birthday.

[3] Rev. Thomas Croft, canon and archdeacon in |Canterbury.

18th August. In the morning, at the English service, the Bishop of Cashel[1] preached a good practical sermon but not remarkable for eloquence as I had been led to expect. At 5 we went with Mme Wolff and the 4 Irish to hear Dr Malan. Afterwards Minnie and I had a nice tranquil stroll in the quiet little garden paths, then we sang *Agneau de Dieu* with Mme Wolff. The event of the day was your thrice welcome letter; it brought good news even earlier than I had dared to hope, and came at the time of times as you will find out as you read on. The weather looked so promising that we proposed starting at 6 next day for Chamouni. I was reminded that my passport must be signed for Sardinia[2] but having sent it at Berne to be viséd for Italy expressly to save trouble and delay, I concluded it was all right, but, taking the precaution of looking, discovered to my annoyance that they had made me pay for a passport to Interlachen of no use, done no more. In future I shall not so easily believe gentlemen can transact business so much better than Ladies. The consequence was to put off our journey.

19th August. The morning was so lovely it seemed a shame to lose a whole day, so the result of several little billets doux which passed between me and M. Wolff before we were dressed was that a Char was ordered for 10.30, by which time M. W[olff] obligingly promised to get the proper signature. However, my passport must be sent back to Berne before we go into Italy. We could come no further than St Martin's tonight. We had a beautiful drive, saw the cascades of Maglan and Arpenaz. There is a change among the flowers since our last Alpine tour. What strikes me most now is the profusion of Barberries, a shrub covered [with] orange berries close to the stem, another with most beautiful red berries as large as cherries, the autumnal crocus, a lilac cyclamen, and the winter cherry. Mont Blanc looked majestic as we approached, though a few clouds hung round him. I have no patience with Fanny's 'zigzags'. I have a great mind not to admire Italy to spite her. It was glorious moonlight when Minnie and I stood on the balcony of our room looking across the bridge and a river at our feet and the valley rich in foliage to the glistening mountain. All was silent. What is it which makes silence seem part of the grandeur of these majestic mountains? We were too much enchanted to feel our weariness, but the prospect of a hard day's pleasure tomorrow drove us to bed.

20th August. Set off at 6 in a little vehicle like half an Irish outside car, right merrily, through a most romantic lovely country, and breakfasted in a rough way at a little Inn at Servoz. Soon after quitting, one of our horses fell, but we were not endangered. The road looks tremendous for a carriage of any sort, but it is pretty often traversed as you may guess from the fact

---

[1] Robert Daly (1783 – 1872) had been consecrated Bishop of Cashel in 1843.

[2] Chamonix lay in Savoy, at this time one of the territories of the Kingdom of Sardinia.

that the first evening we were at Chamouni 24 chars arrived, and the second 20. The country is so wild and fine, how provoking I cannot make you enjoy it. As we entered Chamouni, we heard there were neither beds nor guides to be had, it was so full. This coming also to the ears of two Englishmen!!! who had already had the satisfaction of 'doing' us out of our turn for breakfast, they set off on foot by a bye path to get there before us, (the Chars are not allowed to pass one another), so, as we knew that chance was gone, we went straight for a guide and, by good fortune, the only remaining one was one of the best. In half an hour, (ie) at noon, we were on Muleback, attended by a couple of active intelligent guides, on our way to the Montanvert. The narrow mule path is absolutely crowded - every ten minutes you meet travellers. It is no joke passing: sometimes there is not actually the width of two mules' bodies, the feet of the outer one are but just on the edge. Then, when they come down without riders, they are not so polite as might be wished. One knocked me down, happily against a mossy bank and I was no worse. Minnie gave me a little fright: she was sick for a few minutes, but it appeared to be only the consequence of eating heartily after fasting too long, and she soon went on as merry and active as ever. Our mountain experience made us quite heroines; here, where so many make this first attempt, we were greatly praised for courage and activity. At the little Pavillon by the Mer de Glace, we dined - you must look at the book for a description. I do not admire the glacier so much as that of Rosenlaui, but all around is gloriously grand. We walked on the glacier without any difficulty, having the hand of a guide and the iron-pointed pole, in the use of which (by the bye) I have become expert; it quite takes away my giddiness. Among other people whose names we knew, Dr Roget[1] was at the Mer de Glace. There is a crevice [i.e. crevasse] through which you look down upon a torrent rushing between crags of Ice; it is curious and terrible. These crevices always make me shudder. We ventured to ride down all but a little at the top that we might not be too tired to visit the Cascade des Pelerins close bye another glacier. It is very remarkable; the water falls into a basin of rock so narrow and deep that it rebounds and shoots up many feet into the air forming in the second descent a beautiful parabola. We are not excessively tired, though we had but one mule between us. One considerable addition to the pleasure of our evening return is the moonlight, on account of which I was desirous of taking the trip this week. The variety is so charming when the rosy tints fade and the silver glitter gradually lights up. When we had begun to arrange matters in the room appointed for us, we discovered a huge pair of boots and a case of razors. Seeing that those articles did not belong to our toilet, we called for an explanation. The travellers who had quitted the

---

[1] Dr Peter Mark Roget (1779-1869) was on a tour of the Continent with his two children. His son John Lewis Roget wrote an account of the trip, parts of which were published in Roget, S.R. (ed.), *Travel in the two last centuries of three generations*, London, 1921.

room had returned, but as we had another pretty good room, we did not complain. Not only were the Hotels full, but every bed to be had in the village was occupied. There were 160 with us at the 'Union'.[1] It was so droll to see two long rows of people, chiefly men, looking ready to eat one another, and almost all playing with their spoons as if to appease their stomachs with a sound belonging to eating. It was impossible to serve the 8 o'clock table d'hôte punctually, and the various groups of ladies, who preferred tea at their separate tables, had plenty of time to observe while they waited for hot water. We had a letter for Mrs Wanchope, a very lady-like woman who was staying at the Union with her son and daughter and Mrs Forbes, while Professor Forbes made observations on the glaciers.[2] Also, the Speare family followed, so we were not wholly among strangers, but we had little time to speak to anyone.

21st August. We were off soon after six with 2 mules and 2 guides for the Col de Balme. We had taken bread in our basket so, after one and a half hours march, we stopped at a Chalet and breakfasted on that and goats' milk and rye bread six weeks old. We were so cold, though wrapped in our great cloaks, that we were glad to dismount and warm our feet. Minnie had a run. We were shown into a long low room of dark wood, very comfortable looking. In a recess, a boy was in bed, but he awoke and dressed himself without being disturbed much by our presence. The view from the Col de Balme is magnificent. The prints will give you a wrong idea of it. All I have seen dress it up to look picturesque which it is not. Consequently Minnie does not like it. I could gaze upon the scene for hours, but, having only a short time, I looked with hungry eyes to bring away a distinct impression of that amphitheatre of snowy mountains and savage rocks. While we were on the summit, there was what the guides call a *coup de vent* which shook even the little low house where we were dining. I could not stand against it and sat down on the turf. We were above the beginning of perpetual snow and I gathered gentianella with one hand and a snowball with the other. To my taste it would be worth all the trouble of the journey from Geneva to see that view alone if the road were ugly - instead of which every step is charming. We ventured to ride down the deep descent to Trient, then mounted again by the Tête noire, quite a different scene. Before, we were going over a ridge, with a steep descent every way, from which rose again, on more than nine tenths of the circle, higher mountains, Mont Blanc being one. Every other object was lost in

---

2 The *Hotel de l'Union* was one of the best inns in Chamonix and much frequented by the British.

2 Professor James David Forbes of Edinburgh had established himself as the leading British glaciologist of his day. He spent several summers in the 1840s in Switzerland making observations and taking measurements of glacier movement. On this occasion, he was accompanied by his wife (née Alicia Wanchope), her brother and her sister-in-law.

their immensity; the very wind seemed nothing to their steadfastness. In the pass of Tête noire, you skirt the mountain looking down a rocky precipice interspersed with trees upon a luxuriant valley and rushing torrent. The Val d'Orsini [Val Orsine] is every thing that is smiling and delightful, snug among these awful mountains. We made a little detour to visit a picturesque cascade, where we sat on the turf while our guides gathered wild currants and raspberries for us, and the mules grazed. I must say it was a great luxury to be as it were alone and yet protected, not obliged to talk except now and then a small political or statistical discussion by way of being civil to the guides who are very chatty. They are a set of fine fellows - almost every body speaks well of them. They are quite polite, and always on the alert to render little services. The mules are very large. They certainly go up and down more quietly than horses, but they are terribly rough on level ground. I was glad to get down sometimes to rest myself, but learnt to place confidence in them, even when they persisted in letting my feet hang over the precipice. We had some milk on our way home for which we were obliged to pay extravagantly. The inhabitants are sadly spoilt by strangers, begging and extortions every where, no patriotism, and popery by way of religion. The peasants are much less interesting than our friends of the Oberland; I do not mean merely the choice ones Mlle W[urstemberger] knew, but those with whom we made acquaintance by ourselves as we tried to do at Chamouni. It was beautiful moonlight when we returned, having walked or ridden 33 miles in 14 hours. So much beauty I never saw in any one day of my life; the remembrance of it is a treasure laid up for future enjoyment. We had some misgivings as to weather, but parted with our guides agreeing to start at six next morning if possible, but Alas! Alas! at 5.30 on the 22nd began a quiet determined small rain. Our guides looked melancholy and could not find in their consciences to say more than perhaps it would be fine in the afternoon. Now our purse said we ought not to stay beyond Friday, and a rainy day shut up in our small room, or in the great Salle which was already most disagreeably crowded, was no desirable thing, so, grieving at the disappointment, we determined to come away at once. His Sardinian Majesty's servants are a set of rogues: in spite of the tariff, none of the chars would bring us two to St Martin's unless we paid for 3 places or took a stranger. I consented to the former evil, but the head waiter brought a respectable-looking middle-aged man with a request that I would allow him to take the 3rd place. I began to expatiate on the smallness of the Chars while I looked at his physiognomy. That being satisfactory, I allowed him to come. After some packing, we arranged ourselves and set off in the pouring rain. Our companion was very chatty. He turned out to be a little Dutchman from Haarlem, spoke excellent french, and was violently Buonapartist and anti-English. His name I did not ask. At St Martin's, he had paid for his place in the diligence, but politely gave it up to accompany us further. We procured a tolerable carriage to Bonneville, where we dined, and meeting Mr C[heever], he offered to carry tidings of our probable arrival an hour after him. However, we could get nothing but a little char whose driver made a point of passing every thing on the road, so we arrived first and took the good old gentleman M. Wolff by surprise. The rest of the party were out on an excursion. He received us most hospitably and we had a lively evening between tales of travel, music and drawing. Mr. C[heever] draws very well for an amateur.

23rd August. The Irish ladies seem gentlewomen and quiet, amiable people; the sons are somewhat odd. Mr Cheever became quite sprightly today. We had some animated talk at dinner; the company was better assorted than before. Letters etc. It is a great disappointment not to see Fanny P. I wonder if her friends are still at Morny [Mornex]; they have not called. A Mr Wilson is added to our party. Mme Wolff knew him before. He is said to be a religious man. We had a little party last night, Dr and Mrs H. Malan, Miss C.M[alan], the Revd M[alan] and two Miss Agnews (or some such name) English. There was nothing very entertaining except a history of a Swiss lady and gentleman whom our Irish companions visited with Mme W[olff]. They are living upon a very small income at the foot of the Jura, and, having no children, devote themselves to good works beyond their family circle. Their house is a sort of asylum for all who want one. They receive an increase to their circle very simply, merely making the difference that if more are to be maintained upon the same income, each one (themselves included) must be content with less. The Swiss I have met with are truly hospitable. On Saturday the 24th, we went to visit Mme Brochet, Mme Wolff's daughter, and her very young son. She is a pleasing woman; baby was asleep. On our return, we found the Spear party had arrived, having had a wretched weather at Chamouni since we left them.

25th August. We heard a very eloquent discourse from M. Adolphe Monod;[1] he is however a little too rhetorical for my entire satisfaction. The church was crowded to excess and the heat almost too much for me. In the evening we heard MM. Verneuil, Monod and others speak extremely well about Deaconesses. If I had not been already convinced that such an institution is fully warranted by scripture, I think their reasoning would have convinced me. Mr Wilson said his objections were removed.

26th August. Your nice letter rejoiced me; it does not surprise me that you think a quiet drive occasionally does you more good than any thing else; I only hope you will continue to take whatever suits you best, and just recollect a few of my lectures when you are disposed to say 'it is not

---

1 Adolphe Monod (1802-1856), French protestant pastor who had studied theology at Geneva in the 1820s, and who between 1836 and 1849 taught theology at Montauban in France.

worthwhile'. I received your letter written upon Mrs Wood's and one since hers - did I omit to mention them? It was a great shame, for I should have been very anxious if they had not come, and was delighted to have them. My mountain trip has strengthened me this time. Today the Irish party have gone to Chamouni and the 3 gentlemen to the Oberland. I am sorry that 2 of them do not return. We have been drawing this morning, and now I must let out my gown for I am growing fat. A walk in the evening.

27th August. Father's note to apprise me of the arrival of our woodware. How quickly it came, it was dated the 23rd. Thank him for it. I hope you will be entertained by the contents of the box. They are really exact models - the utensils carried by the little herdsmen and women and the Chamois hunter are quite accurate, as also the buckets which are the shape constantly used for carrying milk, water, etc. I have a beautiful chamois which I bought afterwards, but the real horn on top of my Alpenstock was lost by one of my guides. We called again to hear about Miss C[racroft]s. In the evening, we had a tête a tête walk. Dr Malan has been absent a few days to fetch a son dangerously ill with epileptic fits. Mr Wilson told an occurrence which took place lately, and, I think, to a friend of his. Mr A., travelling in Italy, received much kindness from a Jesuit and expressed a desire to show his gratitude in any way which could be pointed out to him. Some time after, in England, Mr A.'s attention was attracted by the extraordinary resemblance of a man working as a mason to this Jesuit. Upon closer inspection, he was convinced of the identity. The man avoided him, but Mr A. seeing him in such an inferior position thought the time was now come for showing his gratitude and persisted. The Jesuit then told him that the greatest favour to him would be to take no notice, and not tell any one who he was. It is supposed he is one of many who have long been suspected to be [in] England disguised. There are many tales afloat about the disappearance of papists suspected of an inclination to protestantism. I think, however, they must be received with some caution in a place where neighbourhood of the two persuasions embitters hostility.

28th August. Several of us were a little ill this morning, probably the combined effects of over fatigue at Chamouni and change in the weather - it is now very cold. However, with Mme Wolff and Miss Spear, we rode and walked to a very lovely place belonging to a Mme de Sellon. (I think they must be related to Lady B.). We saw Mont Blanc in a fine rosy glow. While we sat in a little summer house, Mme Wolff took out her french Psalter and, at her request, I read aloud two Psalms - such an employment harmonised well with our enjoyment then. I sometimes hear scripture quoted at table in a manner which seems to me not sufficiently reverential and not judicious as to the effect produced on others.

29th August. Another quiet day, only a walk in the evening. Another arrival, a young lawyer Mr Adolphus Stockfleth, what a name!

30th August. Just such another day and walk which increased the inflammation about the top of the windpipe which the east wind always gives me. However, it being fine weather, Mrs W[olff], Miss S[pear] and the german (Mr Stockfleth) went with us.

31st August. Went in the evening to see a house Mr Brochet [is] building for his family. We two with Mme W[olff], enjoying unrestrained conversation, stayed out too late. We saw the place where Servetus was burnt[1] and the house where Felix Neff [2] lived.

1st September. We heard a most excellent sermon on the Lord's prayer from Mr Lawrenson, the English clergyman. My cold was so bad, I did not go out in the evening. Minnie went to Dr Malan's with Mme Wolff.

2nd Sept. Wrote a german note to Caspar Shenkel and spent the rest of the day in sneezing and weeping. In the evening, a young lady came. Other folks worked and talked. I sat in a corner.

3rd Sept. Wrote for Divoto the *Vetturino* Fanny recommends. He is gone from the Couronne; most likely we shall get him. I had rather have an Italian, but Mme Wolff tells me she can recommend both a travelling servant and *Vetturino* of excellent character. Yesterday, the lake was furious with the north wind. The steamer was forced to land at some distance from Geneva and came in only this morning. I had enquired for M. Peschier; he came today, but I was out. In the evening Mrs Murphy and her party returned from Chamouni delighted and quite excited beyond their usual placid natures. Their arrival disconcerted a mountain expedition planned amongst us who remained, but, as the 4th was a fine day, I thought it a pity not to do something, and proposed seeing Ferney (Voltaire's chateau), Coppet (Mme de Stael's). Mrs Speare said she had never been in a tone which showed she would like to join us, so I asked her and her daughter, and we four took a carriage. Ferney is much dilapidated, though inhabited, and is now to be sold. If such a man could have had a cheerful mind, one might suppose there was much enjoyment in this comfortable moderate house and pleasant grounds commanding a beautiful view. There is one arcade, which was a favourite walk with Voltaire, where openings are cut in the foliage that he might peep upon the mountains as he walked

---

1 Servetus, Spanish theologian, burnt alive in 1553.
2 Felix Neff (1798-1829) well-known Swiss evangelist, ordained as a Congregational minister in London in 1823, and who worked mainly in France.

and mused. Coppet is still inhabited by Mme de Stael's family. It is a pleasant handsome place. We were told at first that no one could see the house as Mme de Broglie had friends staying with her, but, having had a hint from Mme Wolff that a little management might do something, I talked over the old servant who shewed us the grounds and prevailed on her to take in our cards with a request which was granted - we had only to wait till the rooms were vacated. A very intelligent woman showed us the apartments Mme de Stael occupied, in one of which there is a very striking likeness of her: a great coarse negress-like woman but so full of character, that there needs no assurance of its being a correct likeness. She lived solely for her pen and society, cared nothing for the beautiful scenes which surrounded her, and never walked in her own grounds. She usually read in bed till eleven, then had three women to dress her at once by way of expedition, always wore a turban and some rich dress (very good taste for her style of person), but gave herself very little trouble about the matter, breakfasted, wrote and paid visits till dinner at 6, after which she suffered nothing to interfere with conversation; she would not have a billiard table. Physicians said she died of over-excited brains and want of exercise. She liked a good table. Here again was a rich gift of intellect but neither wisdom nor happiness. Our drive was very beautiful. In the evening, we went to Dr Malan's chapel where there was a meeting preparatory to a national fast which is to be observed this day 5th. The protestants and catholics could not agree to fast on the same day. In fact, the taking in of popish territory seems to have been a great source of discord in Geneva. The townsfolk have already split into innumerable sections. Plymouth brethren increase these troubles by their fractious conduct. Our Irish companions are quakers - their dress left the matter doubtful. They call themselves 'friends', though they do not call us 'thou'. We took a saunter before dinner, and, in the evening, went with Mme W[olff] to a religious meeting. It was very crowded and so hot as to make me feel quite uncomfortable.

6th September. Josiah's birthday; probably he was not at home to receive my letter, but when he does, he will see I did not forget him. This was the day fixed for a long projected excursion to the Salève, a neighbouring mountain, and the bridge of the Caille.[1] At quarter past 5, looked out and, thinking the weather promised well, l called Minnie that we might be ready to breakfast at 6 as agreed. Soon after came the maid to say the ladies had decided the weather was too cloudy. I growled out one of Töppfer's [2] stories of an Englishman who vowed he would not set off while there was a

[1] The Pont de Caille was a new suspension bridge, completed in 1839, which crossed a ravine just south of Cruseilles, a small town half way between Geneva and Annecy.
[2] Rodolphe Töpffer, a teacher in Geneva, took groups of pupils on walking tours of the Alps, and published accounts of these under the title *Voyages en Zigzag*. Descriptions of British travellers regularly featured in them.

cloud as big as his plate. The carriage was countermanded, and the young men went to bed again. In half an hour, Minnie heard Mme W[olff] in the adjoining room say what a fine day and she entreated me to let people know, so I tapped at the door and said 'look at the blue sky'. The hint took, people began to think it was a fine day, the carriages were ordered again, and every body was to be ready for breakfast as soon as possible. At 7 Dr S[peare] had a fit of dyspepsia and thought he could not go. His wife, though wishing very much to go, did not like to leave him, one carriage was exchanged for a smaller, the Dr had a cup of tea, was better, did not like to be left behind, and begged half an hour's delay. His wife did not like to disarrange the party again, I did not like the good-tempered woman should be disappointed and stoutly insisted upon having the two Landaus, at any rate that there should be no hindrance on that score. The two young Murphys were missing at breakfast; they had never been called the 2nd time. A young lady, who was to accompany us and had been put off, was sent for again. At last, we thought we were ready, Dr and all. One of the carriages was small and closed; the men spent some time in opening it. We got out of the gate. Mrs Murphy remembered that she had forgotten something. She ran back, and we waited till she returned breathless. We were fairly off a little before eight. After driving 3 miles, our coachmen, who were stupid surly fellows and had poor horses, declared they could not go the road Mme Wolff wished - it had been disused several years; so we had to take a much longer route. However, the day turned out delightful. The Dr. and his wife were pleased that they had come, and all went well. We were 13 in the two carriages, very closely packed inside. Arrived at the foot of the mountain (it is 1300 feet above Geneva). Dr and Mrs S[peare] and Mrs M[urphy] declined ascending and were to wait for us in the carriages a little further on. We visited a ruined convent on our way, and had a fatiguing hot ascent which, however, did not distress Minnie or me. Misses Cullimore and Speares were most overcome. We were rewarded by a charming view at the top over Lake Annecy. We sat on the turf, drank from a fountain, and ate the rolls we had brought with [us], but the rogues of young men who had carried Mme W[olff]'s bag helped themselves by the way, and we were calling out for more. It was observed we might have a most beautiful walk all the way down the mountain to La Caille; what a pity the carriages were not ordered to go on there. Mr Stanhope S[peare] good-naturedly volunteered to go back the way we had come and meet us with the carriages and the rest of the party at the bridge, and M. Stockfleth accompanied him. We had a lovely walk over a terribly rough path. The bridge is iron, and suspended, at a much greater height than the Menai, over a rocky ravine traversed by a stream, which looks (where it trembles over the rocks) like a plaything from the bridge. All the young gentlemen and some of the ladies went down this steep ravine to see sulphur baths on the stream, so we had a hot walk up the other side. On arriving at the little inn, there was a rebellion on the part of the young gentlemen when they heard that all our provision amounted to a cake or two. They vowed they would have dinner, so when Mrs Murphy and I arrived (I had stayed behind with her that she might not overheat herself in the ascent), we found the whole party commencing a vigorous attack upon mutton, poultry, and especially wine and water. We had really a very fair dinner and a very merry one. About 6, our slow coachmen were ready. They contrived to get 5 francs more on some pretext of post dues, but admitted that if we had dined where they wished us, we should not have paid it. The evening was delicious, only somewhat hot for those who were 6 with great cloaks in a small carriage. As we approached Geneva, one of our horses cast a shoe, another delay. We arrived a little before eleven, having had a very pleasant excursion, notwithstanding the list of troubles which I have related as a specimen of the difficulty of conducting a scheme in which so many are concerned. The moral of the tale is do not encumber yourself with too many people in travelling, especially not with valetudinarians, and the axiom, despotism is extremely agreeable to the despot and not disagreeable to the subjects when it is tolerably mild.

7th September. We were all disposed to be extremely sedate today. Your welcome letter. It had long been proposed we should take a little boat to see Mont Blanc at sunset from the Lake; this just suited our languid state. Mr S[tanhope] Spear insisted upon rowing his sister and our two selves alone. We enjoyed it extremely for an hour and half. The scene was quite exquisite; the repetition of the purple, pink and yellow hues on the calm Lake produced such harmony in the brilliance, especially when viewed with the head laid down close to the water's edge. By the way, how is it that some views are so much more beautiful seen in that way [than] by looking up?

8th September. We had an excellent sermon from Mr Lawrenson, and received the sacrament. In the afternoon, heard Dr Malan.

9 September. On the 9th after dinner, I walked with Mme Wolff to call on M. P. whose family she knew. We were ushered into a room full of people and children. I was introduced to his sister and began to ask about her brother. She pointed to a gentleman opposite, grey-haired, tolerably stout and with features so rounded from what I remembered that I could not identify him at all till he smiled. Then I recognised the expression of a countenance. He was equally puzzled about me, but the moment I mentioned Mrs D., he remembered us all and enquired with much interest about Louisa and the rest. I was on the point of making a great blunder for I thought Mrs D. had told me he was married, and Mme Wolff said so too. Therefore I took it for granted that the children who were playing about him very familiarly were his, and did not know to the contrary till Mme W[olff], who had walked a little way with his sister, told me he was not

married, but was living with his brother and sister upon the small fortune he had gained in England. He is going in a few days to Havre, if not to New Orleans (I forget which), with his little American Nieces on the way home. The children all busy about him as the little D.s used to do.

10th September. Today Minnie and I visited the Hospital. The sick seem well attended, though more poorly lodged than those in some of our great establishments of that sort. There is a protestant Chaplain, but priests are allowed to visit the Papists. There was a *soeur de charité* there whose appearance was not very prepossessing, but the grateful affectionate look with which she was welcomed by a poor man who had just lost his leg showed she had gone on a kind errand. A thunderstorm made us afraid of going to the Dahlia show, which we went to see this morning (11th). They were very fine. We saw also some other flowers and fruits and the cemetery. Our Irish friends left us this morning for the Oberland on their way home. We parted with mutual regret and exchanged addresses that we might have some prospect of meeting at London or Belfast. Will you procure for me a little book written by Miss Cullimore but without her name; you will like to read and I to have it – *Future Days*.[1] There have just arrived a Miss Maclean who had been here some years ago, her Aunt Mrs McInnes and a cousin. A wet afternoon. We worked and read in our little salon.

12th September. The museum, only pictures and statues. Some of the former were good, a storm among the mountains by Calame,[2] some pleasing landscapes, one purporting to be a S[alvator] Rosa was at least a good copy, and other pictures of which parts were good. In a very old one, the adoration of the Magi, full of absurdities, there was nevertheless a most lovely and intellectual expression in the infant Saviour.[3] A rainy evening. Miss Maclean played some Scotch reels in a very characteristic agreeable way.

13th September. We went a morning expedition to the grounds of M. Tronchin and to a chalet where he charitably receives poor people in a state of convalescence for a very small sum. There is a charming view. Mrs McInnes' party took a Fly and Minnie rode there with them. On our way home, we visited Diodati, Lord Byron's former residence. How little real

---

[1] *Future Days, a series of letters to my pupils*, London, 1844. The introduction indicates that the unnamed authoress had been 'for the last fifteen years one of the heads of an Establishment for Education.'
[2] Alexandre Calame (1810-1864), Swiss painter of the Romantic School who specialised in mountain landscapes.
[3] One of the scenes from an altarpiece painted by Konrad Witz for the Cathedral of Geneva in 1444.

happiness could he have had there. He has left a bad reputation here. M.M. Spears and Stockfleth returned from the mountains with plenty to relate.

14th September. We have had a nice *tête à tête* walk which we agree has its peculiar charm inasmuch as we may loiter to look at a flower or catch a lizard without troubling anyone. Today we sat a long while looking upon the Rhone. There has been a most distressing occurrence in Geneva this morning. One of the floating sheds on the Rhone for washerwomen foundered and almost all the women were drowned. As we passed, they were seeking the bodies, but we did not know what had assembled the crowd. There are generally about 30 women in each of these sheds which are kept up at the expense of government and a small rent is paid for the liberty of going there. We took another little stroll in the evening.

15th September. Again disappointed of hearing M. Gaussen's catechism so we heard Mr Burgess of Chelsea[1] at the hospitals. It was a sensible sermon. In the afternoon at Dr Malan's.

16th September. We went on the edge of the Lake to sketch the rest of our day as usual.

17th September. A letter from M. Feder to tell me that Divoto could not reach me at the time I proposed leaving Geneva and that, unless he brought travellers, the expense would be very great of coming to fetch us. Having, in the meantime, heard that Wm. would come, I think that increase of expense unnecessary, so I spoke to a Voiturier today recommended by Mme Wolff who is to let us hire a calêche (I shall see it today) and pair of horses with an experienced driver who was in the habit of conveying Mme de Stael between this lake and Italy. We take all our luggage, start on Wednesday, and expect to be at least a fortnight in reaching Genoa, for which we pay 500 frs, all extras included (there are many): 10 frs for each Sunday or other day of rest on which, however, we have liberty to use the carriage for short journies, 5 frs a day *bonne main*, 48 frs each a day for board and lodging at the best Hotels. We have a regular contract signed by both parties. I can dismiss the driver and his equipage when I please, or keep him on to Rome if Divoto should not be at Genoa. Feder writes very respectfully of Mlles P. and C. and hopes he shall do justice to their recommendation when he has the honour of receiving us. Mme W[olff] will give us introductions at Naples and Rome to a General and a Clergyman and Mme Calandrin, sister-in-law to M. Tronchin, a great man here, will give us one at Florence and at Pisa. Minnie has received Mr H[egan]'s letter to the Marquis Litta. We were glad to hear a good account

---

[1] Richard Burgess (1796-1881) had become rector in Chelsea in 1836. He had previously been a chaplain in Geneva and in Rome.

of all the B. party. After dinner the young men proposed rowing us on the Lake which was acceded to, and we had a very pleasant hour's row surrounded by loveliness and grandeur. The only drawback was that, as there was some swell on the water and young S[peare] would have a little narrow boat to go fast, his mother was frightened, yet would not get into the safer boat to be rowed by the young Dutchman - so she was left. Mrs W[olff] and Dr S[peare] had a *tête à tête* and we three young people went in the other. We sat still and very sober - therefore there was not the smallest danger. It is a cheap amusement with amateur rowers. I paid 31/2d for our half of the boat.

18th September. Today your welcome letter with its pleasant news. We went with Mme W[olff] to call on the Revd. Mr Adams and his wife. He is an American minister of some celebrity. Unluckily, he was not at home, but we had an opportunity of seeing M. Merle d'Aubigné who has a very agreeable countenance.[1] For the 2nd time, I went the round of the hotels in search of Dr and Mrs Ryan, having seen at church persons we met at Thun whose appearance corresponded with Emma's description, but we could not find them. We saw letters at the Ecu addressed to Mr G. Babington, so he is expected there on his way. In the evening, came on a thunderstorm which lasted till 5 this morning, at which time we were to have been called for our expedition to the Voirons, a mountain trip which takes a long day. But there was no embarrassment of decision - there was a mass of hailstones remaining at 9.30. We shall not be at Genoa before the 9th.

19th September. Notwithstanding the storm, the air was so oppressive, we quite crawled along in our morning walk. In the afternoon, rain again, so that we were obliged to have a carriage both going and coming from M. Gaussen's at the other end of the town. We spent a very agreeable evening, the family are so clever and pleasant. Mlle Gaussen, the daughter, about 21, is a very interesting intelligent girl and speaks English beautifully. The bad weather disappointed us of M. Merle d'Aubigné. There were Mr and Mrs Adams, the former pleasing, the latter shy and awkward, talking in the American slow way, Mr Whitmore, their relation, an elegant young man for a Yankee, and Mr Cordés, Pasteur, who seems as good as gold. There was some highly interesting conversation. M. Gaussen has a great deal of general information and a very clear and lively way of imparting it. It is not improbable we may see more of the Adams party. They were to decide on Monday whether to set out for America or come here for a few weeks to practise french speaking before they follow us to Rome. Mr Whitmore is

---

[1] Jean-Henri Merle D'Aubigné (1794-1872) was founder of an independent College of Theology in Geneva in 1831, and is best known for his five volume *Histoire de la Reformation du XVII siècle* (1835-53).

very anxious to find a companion to go into Italy, but I did not offer him the 4th place in our carriage.

20th September. The weather quite put an end to our expedition to the Voirons. We only strolled about and went to see our carriage horses and coachman. We were persuaded into choosing a heavier calêche than the one we first fixed on, one inducement being that the luggage goes on springs. The horses are large and look strong. The coachman, Louis, has a bright good-natured face and is not too old which I rather feared hearing he had been 20 years with his master. A lady sent a proposition through Motta for the vacant seat. I declined.

21 September. Fanny's letter telling me that Wm. had set out on Monday [16 September] without my address, so I posted down to the Messagerie, left a note for him there, and another at the post office. We sat on the Ramparts. It was a most oppressive day. Packed the great trunk and settled accounts that we might be more at liberty to lionize our companion. Mme Wolff sent her manservant to meet the Bâle diligence in the evening, though M.[Wolff] said it was not possible he should arrive so soon.

22 September. Went to the English church in the rain; came back ditto. To Dr Malan's in the afternoon. Sent again to meet Wm.

23 September. Still no Wm. I shall soon be so much the Mamma as to begin to be anxious if he does not arrive tonight. Rainy.

24 September. No Wm. We sent last night and went this morning to meet him. It is quite clear that even if he comes tonight, we cannot set off at 7 tomorrow. We failed to see the Library and saw the hydraulic machine which supplies the town. It looks terrific from the force with which the turbulent Rhone moves the immense wheels. The condensed air, by means of which the water raised by the wheels is forced to a higher level, is supplied by chemical agency.

25 September. William came, looks well, and has enjoyed his journey. We start at 12 - we were just setting out for a walk after breakfast when there came a note from Wm to say he was at the Couronne and ready to start, so I changed our route to go and see him. Found there was really no reason on his part against our going at once but this reason for it, that if we delayed a day, we should spend Sunday in a dull place among the marshes. I therefore bestirred myself and, to every one's astonishment, we got off without disasters or forgets at 12.30. Now fancy us if you can in a good roomy calêche which would very well hold five 'Grandpapas' and 'Mammas', generally on the back seat, but sometimes changing with Minnie, or putting her in the third if there is any spinal reason (for instance,

if she wishes to have a comfortable nap). Murray,[1] the baskets and the cloaks occupy the spare room. The provisions go in the pockets. You must know none of us are inclined to starve, so I laid in a stock of chocolate cakes to be eaten dry. We replenish the bread basket wherever good rolls are to be had, and we can always buy fruit on the road. Our heavy luggage is on springs and well covered behind the carpet bags, quite dry under the coach box. Our carriage can be opened or shut in three minutes. What are pannels in front of our coaches, are glass in this, so we see a great deal when it is shut. Our coachman is nearly qualified for the fat boy in Pickwick; he is such a tidy little pincushion. He seems disposed to be specially good-humoured when he likes, and very determined to do as he likes. He begins at the end of the 2nd day to patronise us with a benevolent air. We have a pair of clumsy cart horses which never seem to go quickly, yet they do their work well. Our plan is to breakfast at six, start about half past, dine in the middle of the day while the horses rest, and, taking care to arrive before 7, drink tea and go to bed at nine, so we have all our travelling by daylight, yet avoid the heat of noon. I have brought away from Geneva the remembrance of much kindness, especially from Mme Wolff who was quite affectionate to us. We became almost intimate with the S[peare] family, their straightforward way and good nature compensating for what was unpleasant in their manners. We have again reason to be most thankful for the kindness we have been permitted to receive, and if I part with regret, still it has been a good thing to have interchanged so much good will as would make it a pleasure to meet again. Now for our fellow traveller. He is so unaffected and good humoured that we are as much at home as if we had been acquainted these 100 years. I keep up the 'Mamma'ship, but the dignity of grandpapa has been repeatedly forfeited by most juvenile bursts of laughter. He looks older than he is and his presence adds greatly to the respectability of our appearance. We evidently pass for Mamma and her two children. He is quite desirous of learning Italian, and we are to begin to speak it as soon as we reach Domo d'Ossola. I allow the time till then for our better acquaintance. I had a nice little note from Mrs P. and shall send her at least a message when I have time to give Fanny the trimming she deserves. We set out in the rain and saw but little of our route, dined at Thonon badly, and could get no further than Evian where we had comfortable rooms; however, I could not sleep.

26 September. A fine day. We were off about 6.30, and soon had the carriage open. A beautiful drive all day. I snatched a sketch at Monté [Monthey] where we stopped a quarter of an hour. Then we both took one while our dinner was being prepared at St Maurice where we fared very well. We are boarded by our coachman which makes us observe how we

---

[1] i.e. Murray's Handbooks.

are treated. Afterwards, we stopped to see the fall of the Sallenche,[1] and walked on to a grand gloomy ravine whose whole breadth was filled up by a little river along whose banks we scrambled a little way. With all this, we arrived at Martigny before six. Just now, we heard a most wonderful hurly burly of drums and all sorts of discordant noises. As it continued a long time, I began to think the Valaisan war had broken out again and the insurgents were coming here, but soon learned its more peaceful origin. It is a custom here when a young widow marries that she should give drink money to the batchelors of the town or be serenaded thus. One has refused this tribute and has therefore been saluted nightly for a month with this uproar.

27 September. We were called up at 5 but not off much before 7. It was then cold and damp. We were glad to wrap up in our cloaks, and even to walk a while, to warm ourselves - the sun is so long in descending into these vallies. We go along beside the Rhone, with a wall of mountains on each side. Almost as far as Sion, the valley is marshy and wretched. I saw horses grazing where the grass was not visible above the water. Abundance of cretins and goitres. Rich autumnal tints are beginning to embellish the country. There was a new feature in our day's drive: so many small hills like mountain tops tumbled down into the valley and crowned with picturesque churches or chateaux. We allowed ourselves half an hour's sketch of a beautiful scene. The Valaisans were sowing the wheat which is to be cut the beginning of June and gathering their grapes. Yesterday, we thought we had made a great bargain of a good lapful of grapes and peaches for 4d. Today, we did better. Seeing a man pressing grapes in the vineyard, we asked if he would sell some. He said they were not good enough, but we got out to see and ask questions, and selected 12 bunches of what we should call fine Muscatels. We offered to pay, when the man said, 'Madame' would not hear of such a thing pointing to a Valaisan lady and little girl who were seated knitting among the vines. She spoke very politely to us saying she wished we would stay to have some gathered from the heights which were much better. They do not put any sugar to the wine used by the common people. We dined at Sion at 12 Table d'hôte. Made a purchase of a yard of calico to serve as table cloth for our lunches. You must know we are in a fair way of trying the grape cure, we devour such quantities of fruit. Then we went into a church. At Sierre, we strolled on and, as our custom is to ask questions, we began to talk to a pleasant-looking woman who was beating out hemp seed. She offered to fetch us some plums, absolutely refused payment, and wanted us to take a plateful. Mind you look for the prints and description of Sion - it is a most curious

---

[1] This fine waterfall was known by the name Pissevache, a name which offended the sensitivity of some British travellers who consequently renamed the fall after the mountain river which provided the water.

place. We sketched at Dompierre. Arrived at Turtman about 6. We went to see a cascade near. It is a fine sheet of water and is so surrounded by lofty rocks that one felt alone with the rushing waters, as if it had been a living thing among the silent crags. The village looked picturesque in moonlight as we returned. We all consider ourselves to be wonderfully comfortable and only wish our respective friends could see how we enjoy this lovely country.

28 September. Set out a little before 7, the valley still swampy and the mountains magnificent. I did not enjoy them so much, having a headache. We arrived at Brieg, our dining place, at 10.30, but did not dine till the late hour of 11.30. Our only companion was an enthusiastic young German making a pedestrian tour, but before we left came two ladies whom we have met at Martigny and Turtman. They pity us for turning out at 6.30 and we exult over them - they were too late for the cascade, and today they must have passed the finest part of the road in the rain where we were able to walk. We are now safely housed at Berisal, a rough little inn but clean, on a woody knoll looking down precipices and up to the snow most sublimely. Everything here is on such a grand scale - forests of tall pines thrown down by avalanches look like straws scattered about. We met many droves of cows and goats coming down for the winter, and the gusts of wind preceding the rain reminded us what the road must be in stormy weather. Louis said he had come across in a traineau when the snow was 13 feet deep and it required the exertions of 10 men to keep it in the middle, as any slip would have sent it over the precipice. He says he has passed twice in the snow and never desires to try it again. We are quite as well served as when we ordered for ourselves, though we had not a good dinner today.

29 September. Sunday among the mountains. We awoke somewhat refreshed, though I had a rheumatic headache caught by traversing, in wind and rain, from our dining room to our bedroom, by a bridge across the road connecting two parts of the house, which was covered, but not enclosed, and then an open gallery. Minnie was made ill by the smoke of our wood fire; Wm. only escaped by retreating; I only suffered in my eyes. Our former acquaintances, who also came here intending to stay Sunday, are a Mrs Tate and her daughter from Hampstead. We were the only guests in the little inn, and they begged to share the room with us, so we had a merry Saturday evening recounting our adventures. Next morning, soon after we had breakfasted, they came down and, as we had previously determined, we asked them if they were members of the the Church of England and would join our social worship. We read the Liturgy together, sang a Psalm, and read one of Dr Arnold's sermons with which they and Wm were much delighted. They are late diners and we early, but as we were disposed to eat together, each gave way a little and we fixed three o'clock. Meanwhile, we

3 sallied out for a walk. The scene was still and majestic. I cannot describe it, but its influence sank in like dew. However, we could not enjoy it long for the rain, and we returned. Soon after, Mrs T[ate] and her daughter came in dripping, though they had taken refuge in a cowshed. In the evening, we again united in our church service. How amused you would have been to peep at us all five sitting round a large open chimney, in the low wooden room, with a blazing wood fire, and using much coarser utensils for tea service than your servants do. Our bedrooms were very cold; we were glad of all our wraps. But people were very civil, and we all agreed that the Sunday among the mountains was a very pleasant day. It rained heavily all night, and, on the 30th, we were fully satisfied that we were above and in the clouds. They were careering about magnificently, though Minnie irreverently compared the breaks in those below us to the cracks in a bason of gruel which has stood all night. You may suppose we had our carriage shut and ourselves well wrapped up. Still the cold and damp penetrated, the gloomy grandeur was enhanced, but the beauty sadly diminished, and distant view we had none. One object took fresh beauty from the mist - where the road passed under a cascade, the sheet of water we looked through was like a veil of silver thread. It was really laughable, in connexion with our previous remarks upon Fanny's depreciation of Switzerland compared with sunny Italy, that the first steady sunshine broke out just as we passed the cross which marks the summit of the pass. We made bold to visit the Hospice and were kindly received and invited to dinner by Father Barras. Louis, however, did not approve our accepting the invitation, seeing that we might be kept two hours at the custom house, and that the latter part of our road is shamefully out of repair. We saw the apartment for strangers, the refectory, and a beautiful St Bernard dog who came bounding out with a deep toned bark. At Simplon, we dined and contrived to set off early to reach the custom house before our fellow travellers, because we knew they had prohibited books, and might occasion our having more trouble, whereas we had nothing to hurt them. However none of us were annoyed. They examined Wm.'s trunk and one of ours slightly, not detaining us half an hour. Our drive all the way down was enchanting - such gorgeous colouring of autumnal tints added to grandeur of form. We lingered in that gorge of Gondo, getting out to walk several times, and only grieved to leave it. I believe we were all too strongly impressed with the beauty we had left, to hail any change with delight, yet it is a striking and lovely change to this fertile valley. It seems still a dream that I am in Italy, but a dream full of interest. I could lean out of the window half a day just to catch indiscriminately all the novelties which float by, without giving myself the trouble to look for more. Indeed, I have seen too much today. And then we never have a moment's quiet. We are so very merry between our interjections, and we work so hard at the concoction of Italian sentences. My first oration was about a washerwoman. The girl could not but smile, though she understood. We

had delicious figs, grapes, peaches and pears brought for tea, at which we worked perseveringly for a while, till we sent for Louis to clear up our ideas about visiting Lake Orta, which we have virtuously declined as it would take a whole day. We are now at Domo d'Ossola. We had four horses up the Simplon, and always went foot pace. The vines along part of the Lake of Geneva were trained in the beautiful way we have since seen in Italy - whole trunks of trees with branches support festoons so luxuriant that, at a small distance, they seem living trees in full foliage.

October 1st. Arona. After our first specimen of the comforts and discomforts of Italy, we set off on our beautiful drive to Baveno. It is indeed a new country to me; everything is so graceful, the landscape is so prettily dressed in full costume, not even necklace or bracelets omitted, and the charming campaniles! I am afraid I shall grow as devoted to them as Clara or Fanny are. We did not get out of the carriage except to be ferried (carriage and all) across the Doveria, and, arriving at 12, immediately engaged a boat to take us to the Borromean Islands. The lake is perfectly enchanting here. We indulged ourselves with a peep into the upper end of it, and were cruelly hurried, though we gave 4 and a half hours to little more than some get through in 2. That must excuse our not criticising Isola Bella. I suspect I might have found out something trumpery in it if I had had time for anything besides enjoyment. We all think the Pescatori the most thoroughly picturesque: such flowers, such perfume! All the while, we could scarcely take our eyes off the lake, flowering stalks of aloes 14 feet long; but the lake! with its colours and its forms models of beauty. We had a shower which wetted us but little and added greatly to the beauty of the scene. You will not wonder we were too late to get to Sesto tonight, and had to travel one and a half hours in the dark, but it does not matter. Minnie had a comfortable nap on my shoulder, and we are in a very good inn. Two specimens of Italian manners: I left my parasol at Domo and, when I was about to write for it, found it had been forwarded free of expense by the courier of Prince Doria. Now the reverse. I neglected to bargain with the boatmen first. Consequently they cheated me, employing all sorts of appeals to justice, humanity and vanity in their glib Italian which I could combat but lamely. When we went away one of the men came forward to wish me good bye most affectionately, as if we had parted on the best possible terms. We have men to make up our beds here. One came through our salon while we were at tea with an armful of sheets. We have agreed in future to forswear the decoction which goes by the name of tea here and keep to fruit, bread and milk. Poor Minnie is thoroughly knocked up though she slept an hour and a half this evening. Wm. is also gone to bed, and I suspect I only sit up because I am too excited to sleep. Really a wet day would be a benefit. People are perpetually amusing themselves by scribbling over our passports which at least procures the commissionaire half a fr. At Arona, tired as I was, I had scarcely an hour's sleep, from fleas. I shall be continually tormented.

2 October. We are all quite glad not to have too much beauty today. Indeed, I can scarcely prevail on my companions to admire anything. Again Doganas and passports, but no incivility and little delay. The beauties of the road today were ruined castles and sometimes mountains, much of it was nothing more than fertile. Oxen treading out corn, the threshing floor in the open air in the corner of the field, winnowing with the spade, were illustrations of scripture which interested me. Cartloads of grapes, men carrying clusters of them between two, on a thick stick, women with red handkerchiefs disposed like veils and bare legs. The countenances of the men are often very handsome, but at once cunning and passionate. All these differences amuse me. Louis observed it must be a bad year for silkworms, there were so many leaves remaining on the mulberry trees which border the road. Otherwise they would have been gathered by the peasants who keep the worms. At Varese, we had a complete Italian dinner - some things very good, others very bad; among the former, fungi. The waiter attempted to cheat in giving change, but Wm. frightened him into refunding. Minnie and I looked into the church. The handsome clock tower here, as elsewhere, is separate from the body of the church, which is also handsome. There was a pleasing picture, the adoration of the infant Saviour, among many bad ones. At dinner, a man and woman played the violin and guitar to us. As Wm.'s head ached, we soon dismissed them.

3 October. Como, for noise, dirt and fleas, exceeds imagination. The latter bid fair to drive me into a brain fever by absolutely depriving me of rest. Nothing sends them away - hitting half a dozen in half an hour makes no perceptible difference. The Comese keep up laughing, shouting, and coming in from their boats till past midnight. At 2, cannon are fired to announce the steamer from Lecco and, at 4, begins all the clamour of market boats arriving. The town is very prettily situated and has all the air of being the centre of a rich and populous neighbourhood, notwithstanding which I saw five churches in a ruinous state. There are innumerable country seats on the richly wooded borders of the lake. This morning, we had intended going in the steamer to Bellagio, sleeping there, and coming back tomorrow. Wm. was 3 minutes too late, so we deferred till the afternoon and went meanwhile to see the cathedral and Church of St Fedele. At noon there came on a violent wind which frightened us, so we agreed to take only a quiet drive and wait for tomorrow. I think the rest was good for us all. Certainly it was for Wm. who was rather bilious and overtired, but it occasions our sleeping three nights in this noisy flea trap. Address with my christian name at full length.

4 October. Today I am somewhat better, for the plague of fleas was abated last night, and there was no market this morning. By way of compensation, however, our next neighbours amused themselves by setting up most inhuman screams about midnight. Before 8, we were on board the steamer, having determined upon the advice of an English lady to go the whole length of the lake instead of stopping to see some statues. The lake is most lovely and varied, the day was beautiful, with rather a brisk wind, mountains reaching quite down to the water's edge, luxurious looking palaces, perpetual windings of the shores, snow mountains in the distance, the water sometimes the clearest warm green, sometimes bright blue. You must suppose these made beautiful pictures. We regretted not having arranged to visit Pliniana[1] from the representation an Italian gentleman gave of it, and hereby recommend my travelling friends to disembark at Torno for that purpose. I thought the steamboat a capital opportunity for getting an Italian lesson gratis. Therefore, besides the aforesaid person who addressed us, I entered into conversation with two Italian ladies and their respective husbands. For a wonder, we were the only English on board. After dinner and a long rest, Minnie and I sauntered out, looking again at the Cathedral and Volta,[2] and amusing ourselves with the people. When we meet, I will tell you what a gentleman our Louis proved.

5th October. Left noisy dirty Como where we were ill served except at dinner. Louis volunteered to take us by the longer route through Monza, being the most interesting. For about three quarters of an hour, we all stood up in the carriage exclaiming at the lovely view of the Alps as we crept along the hills. Then, by dint of unceasing enquiries, we found our way by a detour to the ancient Lombard church of Galliano, now turned into a barn. Even I, albeit no antiquarian, felt a lively interest in contemplating the very inscriptions and frescoes, not to mention the architecture, which had delighted the eyes of christians in the 4th century. Moreover, the great saints of this neighbourhood happen to be my particular favorites, St Ambrose and Carlo Borromeo. We clambered about and peeped and scratched, to the infinite amusement of a troop of ragged ciceroni, and the consternation of Louis who began to despair of getting to Milan that night. At Monza, we saw the cathedral founded by Queen Theodolinda in 588. For a description of the curiosities, see Murray who was very useful here and at Milan. We should not have seen all if Wm. had not stuck to his 'Murray' and called over the inventory. Although we arrived at Milan early, we could not get in at the two principal hotels, as there were multitudes of other travellers driving about in all directions on the same errand. We thought it best to come at once to a second rate hotel, 'Pension

---

[1] A villa close to the lake shore which got its name from the intermittent spring described in a letter of the younger Pliny.
[2] Piazza Volta.

Suisse,' upon Louis' recommendation. We are obliged to pay for coming in such a crowd, but are tolerably well off, and the people are very civil. Moreover it is such a comfort to have a decent woman about one, instead of men and an old hag as at Como. After dispatching our letters, we enquired about the prospect of an English service for the next day, and, looking over the visitor's book for the name of the clergyman who was to assist, we found that of Dr and Mrs Ryan to whom I immediately sent my note and card. She came, and was very friendly, delighted to welcome a friend of Emma's.

6th October. Wm. had a bad headache, and I did not like to leave him to feel desolate among people of a strange tongue, so I asked Mrs Ryan to take Minnie under her protection to the service, and stayed with him. I forgot to mention that my first impression of the Cathedral was that it was all ornament outside and wants massiveness to make it grand. This idea does not lessen on further inspection. I cannot partake the admiration of my young companions for its exterior, but I exceedingly admire its interior. We went in by twilight on Saturday evening; those lofty arches looked noble, (*note in margin*: but the beautiful roof is a painted show). After dinner, Minnie and I walked up and down the Cathedral half an hour listening to the fine organ. Dr and Mrs Ryan and sister went early on the 7th. We hope to meet again at Florence. In the morning, among other matters of business, we had to write to the Archbishop of Milan a note which we took to his palace, and saw his pictures. In the afternoon had a carriage and went to see that most exquisite of pictures, Leonardo da Vinci's last supper. It is most affecting. It seemed to bring me into the very presence of Christ in the days of his humiliation. The idea constantly present was how altogether lovely is that character which can inspire such a representation to our outward sense, so touching and so grand. The painting is dreadfully injured, almost obliterated in some parts, in others worse, for it is repainted, but the head of our Saviour is one of the most perfect. This was altogether one of the greatest enjoyments in the way of pictures I ever had. We were a long time in its presence, partly alone, but when others came, they seemed over-awed, and, if not silent, talked in a low voice. We saw the church founded by St Ambrose. It interested me much to see several memorials of the venerable man. There is also a magnificent altar. We have seen several of these splendid things, rich in profusion of gold, silver, and precious stones. I care very little about them and, if I were not afraid of missing something curious, I should leave the Sacristans who are eloquent in praise of their wealth, and wander about pleasing myself with the general effect of the architecture. We saw the church Sta. Maria delle grazie and then drove to the very handsome triumphal arch. It so happened that we saw the marble against dark purple clouds and the bronze horses illuminated by flashes of lightning. Minnie and I bought each a silk gown, having been told they would be cheaper at Milan than elsewhere - so we had to work hard to make them into petticoats.

8th October. The Cathedral. We visited every detail, the silver chapel in which Carlo Borromeo is buried, and then mounted the roof amidst groves of pinnacles and a crowd of statues, almost all remarkably pretty, but the whole thing is too filagree for my taste. I admire the interior extremely. From the roof, we had a most glorious view of the Alps, especially Monte Rosa for which we had long looked in vain. Minnie and I then took a warm bath. In the afternoon, Minnie and I drove to the Brera,[1] not knowing it was closed at three. We consoled ourselves by going again to the Cenacolo.[2] We had previously taken Mr H[egan]'s letter to the Marchese Litta, but he was at his country seat 24 miles from Milan, so we gained nothing.

9th October. Minnie and I made a grand exertion to be at the Brera by 9 and were rewarded by seeing some very pleasing pictures. We had put off our departure till after our dinner at noon, to await the Archbishop's answer to our humble request to see the Certosa.[3] The answer was that permission must come from the Bishop of Pavia to whom it was too late to apply. I consoled myself with the idea of seeing at least the church, but no, when we arrived, we found that only Wm. might go within the brass rails which part the middle aisle from all the rest, so we could only peep through doors at the Altars and squint at pieces of legs and arms in the pictures on the sides. We, and the ladies of another party, were thus excluded by a late regulation, and I leave you to guess the comments we made. The Certosa is the most gorgeous thing I ever beheld, but far from the most interesting. I have not much taste for Mosaics and such costly difficulties. The front is like a large inlaid cabinet; the old part of the exterior behind pleased me. The road goes all the way beside the canal bordered by trees, through a flat country, so that, adding the circumstance that it has been more or less rainy and foggy from the day we left Como till we came at noon on the 11th in sight of sunshine and the Appenines, we do not any of us think much of the beauty of Lombardy.

10 October. Spent the morning at Pavia seeing the Cathedral, of which part is blocked up in process of enlargement, and the rest not beautiful, except the tomb of St Augustine and a picture by D. Crespi, Adoration of the Magi. You must know we have all somewhat a horror of *Valets de place* and such like guides. Wm. is furious against them. However, on enquiring if the tumble-down place could possibly be the entrance to the Duomo, a

---

[1] The famous picture gallery of Milan.
[2] i.e. Leonardo's *Last Supper*.
[3] A Carthusian monastery largely built in the fifteenth century.

bright little boy constituted himself our guide, and was so intelligent that he actually won upon us to accept his services for the rest of our walk. The Italians as far as we have seen are universally most obliging in such matters, even when not paid. They will come out of their shops and accompany us a long way, but we are tormented by clamorous offers of hired service at every place of public resort. Looking on our way at the odd old church St Michele (of the 6th century), we went to the University to see the Malespina Gallery containing some good pictures, and instructive from being chronologically arranged. A very polite curator took much pains to show many curious things, Parmeggiano's pocket sketch book, specimens of the earliest engraving on wood in Germany, and on silver and gold (Nieli) in Italy. We came in torrents of rain to Voghera, and found that, in the hurry of repacking after the Dogani[1] had visited us, my carpet bag had been left exposed, and was wet through. I had a pan of charcoal and dried what I wanted for the night.

11 October. Felt very cross at being awake at 5, having had very little sleep several nights from fleas. However, we set off before 7 in a wet fog, and travelled all day in the most execrable road you can imagine; being the great road, in a level, I do not believe the carriage rolled 6 yards from morning till night. From Novi, where we dined, we had a third horse, but it was a wretched creature and the boy was stupid, so at last Louis, out of all patience, sent it back. Once we came to a dead stop behind six waggons of which the first was stuck so fast in a deep rut that 8 quadrupeds of various sorts, and as many bipeds, could not move it for a long while. I believe if Louis could have reached any tangible representative of the Sardinian government, he would have thrashed it with exquisite satisfaction. He looked affectionately at his horses and said 'They try to trot but they cannot'. 15 horses to one cart on two wheels! The country becomes beautiful again - our favorite mountains and torrents and cascades, but all on a small scale and, as yet, rather dreary looking. We left Ronco in a mist which cleared off in time to let us see the blue Mediterranean between the mountains and then a fine view of this beautiful Genoa. It was quite a home sight to see the waves and the Union Jack fluttering in the harbour. Then there was Josiah's letter and one from Anne and Clara to delight me. It is a terrible long time since I heard from you. Saturday, we strolled through the town, bought Vasari,[2] and chose a carriage for our further journey. Sunday went to the English service, peeped into the Cathedral, saw Mrs and Miss Tate.

---

[1] i.e. customs officers.
[2] The book by Giorgio Vasari (1511-74) on the lives of Renaissance artists was acclaimed when first published in 1550 and has been reprinted through the centuries since then.

Monday, 14 October. The banker's Dr Roselli called, a most pleasing gentlemanly man. He is going out with us tomorrow. Made our bargain for Fanny's prince of *Vetturinos* with his brother. Minnie and I made purchases. We are charmed with Italian politeness; we have met with no exception yet to the most obliging conduct. Reverse: cheating, fleas, mosquitos (we are speckled all over), beggars, noise, oh, such a din. We are half way up to the moon, and have a fine view of the harbour. It is so pretty, I am nearly crazy, so good bye. We are (14th) more and more charmed with this beautiful city, and regret we have not more time to bestow upon it, but I think spending much time on the road is hardly consistent with the advantages expected for Minnie, and expences are enormous in the large towns. 14th, afternoon. We took a boat to see the town from the sea. We had first a most amusing scene with the clamorous boatman: Wm. in his tall hat standing with imperturbable serenity among their vociferations. The men we chose afterwards declared they would strike Wm.'s name off the list of English because, when we were outside the first jetty, the wind setting in from that side, there was more swell than his stomach could bear, and [we] were obliged to turn back within the harbour and visit the ships. We had also a whimsical political discussion with our men who considered Englishmen as brother sailors. Afterwards, we saw the splendid Church Annunciata, brilliant with gilding and marble. Then Minnie and I shopped. We are very independant and want no valet.

15 October. Went to the silver workers before Dr Roselli, and then went with him to the Palaces Brignole, Rosso, Balbi, and in all of which there are interesting pictures. We had only too little time to examine them; there is a month's work only to read them, as it were. I am delighted with the works of many painters whose names I never heard before. The great charm and wonder of the day was a medallion *basso relievo* by Michael Angelo, heads of the dead Christ and Mary, most affecting. I could not look at it so long as at the Cenacolo; it was too distressing. There is the whole history of a life of suffering beneath the calmness of death. Dr Roselli was most kind and increased my pleasure by talking Italian. We returned exhausted to dinner; indeed, Wm. left us before the 3rd palazzo. It is hard work to be excited all day and worried all night by mosquitoes. We are all speckled as if we had the measles, but poor Minnie is deplorable. She has now gauze curtains all over her bed and says she sleeps in a meat safe. 10 o'clock, thunder and lightning raging without, which I hope will cool the air here. Such a terrible noise all night: a tropical rain, banging of doors, shouting of sailors securing their ships.

16 October. At 11 came our true knight Dr Roselli again, and took us to the churches of St Stephen and St Ambrose - in the latter was a charming Assumption by Guido, the church of Carignano, from the cupola of which we have a delightful view of Genoa. Then to the Ducal Palace and that of

the Pallavicini, where there were fine pictures. We also saw several other views and gardens. After dinner, we sallied forth to see one more picture in the Goldsmith's street (very pretty), and to provision ourselves for the journey. On our return, we found your welcome letter and also one from Mrs Y. inviting us to her villa near Leghorn and proposing we should take into our society at Rome and as travelling companions thither a Mr B., a young man travelling for health, and his uncle. I should be happy to visit her if we passed through Leghorn, or she were at Pisa on our arrival, but our agreement with our Voiturier is made to Rome. The other proposition I do not entertain for a moment; we three are perfectly contented and not disposed to try experiments.

17 October. Started with the super-excellent Jean Baptiste Divoto, who is not at all the sort of person I expected. He is a young man with a countenance as simple as a Swiss peasant and very good-natured. He looked all smiles when we spoke of *La granda Signora* and showed us her testimonials among many others. Our carriage is as good as the last, except that it does not open, which is now of less consequence because we do not go through defiles. We have three horses, though we pay for only two, but our bonny greys are rather small. Are you tired of expressions of admiration; you must tell me in your next if you are. At present, I shall describe, because I think you have not such full descriptions of Italy as of Switzerland. Fancy our road, constantly up and down along the shore, which is scolloped out into a succession of bays and coves, great and small. Sometimes we rise over the ridge of a mountain, sometimes we are near enough to the sea to be wetted by the spray, then among groves of olive trees to the mountain tops. The colour of the trees is a dullish pea green, more like sallows than anything we see in England, but they have a light soft feathery look, and the old stems are twisted into picturesque attitudes. Mixed with these are pines, tall slender black Cypress, golden chesnuts, figs and mulberries, hedges of the great aloe, vines as usual, country houses of all sizes and colours dotted all over the mountains. For some miles, the whole air was perfumed with orange flowers. We went to see the orange groves of a villa on our road, and could not resist buying oranges fresh from the trees, though very dear. They had a good flavour, but were neither so juicy or thin-skinned as those brought to England. You should have seen with what zeal Minnie stuck her thumbs into one in remembrance of Father's indulgence. Now and then, the rocks go down into the sea, which today was bounding over them in fine style, and it had such a lovely colour. Sometimes there was an old castle or a pretty village on the water's edge. In short, there was a succession of beauties all day long, finished by a glorious sunset. I was so very tired I wished it would leave off being beautiful, but I could not leave off being delighted. As we are now quite among rough Italian inns, we do not attempt tea at night, but, when it is cool, have vermicelli soup and, when warm, fruit and bread with cheese

instead of bad butter. There is a great deal of lacemaking here; it is good but coarse. The country people make the fig trees look very miserable by stripping them of their leaves to give to cows. We are at Sestri.

18 October. Started just before 7 after the unsatisfactory breakfast we often get in Italian inns. For 2 or 3 miles, we had the same lovely scenery, and sea views as before. Arbutus and stone pine added to the list of trees. Then we went quite among the mountains, less dreary than those of Switzerland, but also far less grand. All day long, we travelled up and down, skirting the higher mountains, till the last ridge brought us within view of the fine Gulf of Spezia. Divoto advised us to mount a neighbouring height where *la grande Signora* had sat to enjoy the view and draw. This latter, we dared not do having, both of us, sore throats, and there being a cold wind. We did not see the view to advantage for the sky was very grey. We also heard that two of our three pretty horses had had the honor of dragging *la grande Signora* and her friend. We thought they wagged their tails in rather an intellectual way as if they had been used to *bel esprit* society, so we adorned their foreheads, not with bay, but with mountain pinks. At Sestri, our beds looked clean and, after a very successful flea chase, I hoped for a good night's rest - greatly needed for I had not enjoyed one for ten nights, but, alas, except two short dozes, I passed the whole night killing gnats, and rose very miserable indeed. The beggars are intolerable - almost all the population are shameless impudent beggars. We give as much at the inns as in France, Switzerland and Piedmont where they were thankful. Here people always grumble, which annoys me excessively. I always felt afraid of having done injustice, but I must get over that and be prepared to answer the smiling politeness with which Master and servants wish us *buon viaggio*, having done their best, unsuccessfully, to cheat us. One of our horses fell lame and we left it here. The road was beautiful a great part of the day. We crossed a ferry in a wretched old crazy boat, and, for want of a single plank, were carried a few yards by the half-naked savages who ferried us. Guess how the young ones laughed to see me, their first victim, snatched up, cloaks and all, while I was meditating 'how shall we get over'. We walked over a long piece of bad road out of compassion to our little nags. At Carrara, we immediately ordered a car to go to the quarries. There came a small black skeleton pony between two long poles on which were fixed seats. We had a chair to help us climb in. When we were seated in front, Wm. and the *Valet de place* behind, there was some danger that one light pony would be taken off his legs, so it would be down men, up poney. However, a boy came and sat on the shafts. Off we went helter skelter over huge blocks of marble into ponds of mud washed of[f] by passing through a running stream up to the horse's body. However, by good luck, we were not shaken out of the car, and our teeth were not shaken out of our heads. We had just time to perceive we were in a wild beautiful defile when a pouring rain began. We had the courage to alight

and scramble up to one quarry. It is very curious to see such masses of marble of all shades from the purest white to dark grey. Veins of marble streak the mountain's side and look at a distance like snow lying in the clefts. It is a wild looking place and a wild people inhabit it. The oxen, who are employed in bringing down the blocks, appeared to use such violent efforts one might think one journey would kill them. We should have enjoyed wandering about and seeing more quarries, but a deluge of rain rendered it impossible. On our return, we were obliged to order in our bags and get dry things. We saw one atelier of a man who had worked under Sir F. Chantrey.[1] All the sculpture worth having was far above my purse. We were no little diverted at our equipage on leaving this place: two big oxen were harnessed before our horses, the driver sitting on the yoke between their necks with his face to their tails. So they drew us up the mountain, and we came down a bad road at a famous pace. I conclude because, as Divoto intimated, it was a bad neighbourhood. We are at a wildish sort of little inn at Pietra Santa with the wind howling around us and preventing our having a fire. We have agreed to help one another gnat hunting and, in the intervals of writing industriously, we are very merry. Oh! the horrors of being devoured by gnats and fleas in spite of passing the night hunting them.

Sunday, 20 October. Very rainy at intervals. We had our social and private reading and prayers, and took two little saunters through olive groves, the air being most oppressively hot.

21 October. From Pietra Santa to Pisa where we arrived at 12.30, and immediately set off for the Campo Santo, a very beautiful cloister containing a collection of frescoes most ancient and curious, some sculpture ancient and modern; among the latter a *basso rilievo* of Tobias by Thorwaldsen. This building, the Baptistry, the cathedral and its Campanile, which is the celebrated leaning tower, stand altogether on a green on the edge of the town and are a very interesting group. We went to dinner and then returned and ascended the tower which is neither dangerous nor difficult, I think. From the very top, we saw the sun go down into the Mediterranean. On our way home, we went a long way on the banks of the Arno and across it to a pretty little church close by it. The river with its two bridges (one of very pretty arches), churches and towers, altogether make a very picturesque scene, and, (heightening the effect) as we watched the moonlight glittering on the stream, we heard the sound of deep voices chaunting the *De profundis*, and a funeral procession with long flaring torches passed us. Hotel de la Victoire was so very comfortable that it required all our resolution to set out on the 22nd, but we went first to see

---

[1] Sir Francis Legatt Chantrey (1781 - 1842), one of the most famous British sculptors of his day.

the Duomo which contains pictures and sculptures which interest me extremely. I wished for more time. I do not admire the interior as a whole and the exterior not at all. The leaning tower also does not please me. In the Baptistry is a most beautiful sculptured pulpit, and the font ornamented with parian marble, but the most charming thing was the exquisite echo of the Sacristan's fine voice, which was nearly equal in power and clearness to the echo from the Wengern Alp. Surely Milton must have heard this, he talks of sounds 'sweet as from blest voices uttering joy'.[1] The sound comes with too much calm dignity for earthly joy; there is something graceful in its approach. Pisa is a clean pleasant-looking town. We are in the country of straw workers; women and children stand plaiting at their doors. At Spezia, there were as many lace workers. We are in a rough inn at Empoli waited upon by a man who looks as if he had just come in from the plough, and a couple of boys for chambermaids, who declare that Minnie and I can have but one bason between us because there is not another in the house. They thought it quite unnecessary we should have plates for our bread and butter. I have forgotten to leave *your end*, you shall have it next time; also to ask for Mr S.'s address which is of the less consequence as we spend so little time in Florence. We hope to dine there tomorrow.

23 October. We are so very dismal in this charming Florence to which we looked forward with so much eagerness. We came under an evil star from a filthy inn at Empoli, where the host was saucy because we gave no more than was right. Just here, of all places, Minnie left her watch. Think what a consternation we were in! the last present, a 40q watch and chain. We had decided upon taking post horses and going back direct from Florence, Wm. kindly offering to go with us. He could not go alone, because he does not yet speak Italian. However, we have persuaded Divoto to go, and are very anxious for the result. It is a most wretched rainy day. We are just under the dripping eaves, looking down on a small square court surrounded by the high walls of the hotel, and ornamented solely by 5 holes of a gutter. Wm. is gone to live with his cousin. We dined at 12 and, being both oppressed by dullness, resolved to go in the rain and enquire for letters, which we did not get (I did not expect any so soon). Then we found out Mrs R[yan]'s address and, to save our future time, we went there in a little chariot. She was poorly and could not see us, but we were all the better for the exertion. We both look as if we were just recovering from small pox. Divoto is a hero. He walked straight upstairs at Empoli and took the watch from under the pillow of the bed which had not been touched since Minnie left it. She is shocked, you should know it: 'what will Mrs W. say' and begs I will tell you she is very sorry and hopes never to be so careless again. I can bear witness she was more frightened at the inference which

---

[1] Paradise Lost, Bk. 3, l. 347.

might be drawn from her forgetfulness than concerned for her own loss. Of course you will not tell tales.

24 October. After settling with our good *Vetturino*, we made our bargain for staying in this hotel where we are tolerably comfortable considering that, by every body's account, Florence is crowded with strangers. Wm. came in introducing his cousin Mr Morgan, a kind simple-mannered old gentleman who loves a long chat dearly, and is most willing to be our guide. There was a deluge last night, and it has been raining all day, but I was determined to do something, so we went to get some money, and then to Mr S.'s to ask Mrs Schmidt's address. After dinner, we agreed to meet in the Cathedral in which, and in the Baptistry, we sauntered some time, but it was too dark to see any thing to advantage. We went into a Bazaar, came home wet, and had a long talk with our gentlemen. This evening, Mr S. called. His face is prefaced by a long red beard. I should have been puzzled even if I had recollected his former appearance. Of course, he did not recognize me. He told me Mrs S. has just lost a child, is residing at Lucca. He said Mrs S. would be happy to see us but did not like speaking English. I said I would be happy to see her and speak Italian, but shall wait for her to call first.

25 October. Our beaux came and we went to the paradise of pictures, the great gallery of Florence, the Tribuna.[1] Like all other terrestrial paradises, it was disappointing. Mr M[organ] wished me to have a general view of the galleries and to admire the *Pietra dura* before we were absorbed in the pictures. Therefore we did so, all the while secretly panting to get to the Raphaels and the Venus.[2] Well, one cannot see the pictures for the statues, nor the statues for the pictures. I am not in raptures with the Venus, lovely but, to me, insipid. I like the knife grinder and the wrestlers better. I cannot possibly enumerate all the pictures admired. There was an exquisite Madonna by Raffaelle and Sybil (Guercino). We saw 4 small rooms today, besides a glance at the gems, and were glad to rest. After dinner Wm. went with us to the church Sta. Croce where are some good things, but we had no sunlight to brighten them. Then we went to Mr Morgan's and chatted some time with the old gentleman. We are glad to amuse him, both because he is so kind to us, and because he is just now suffering a most vexatious loss of property. Tomorrow, I dispatch letters to secure apartments and a servant at Rome. It is quite appalling to think of all the multitude of pictures I have to see and most of them of such a style as I cannot pass bye, as I do Dutch interiors, in spite of Minnie's earnest representations of their artistic merit.

---

[1] The Tribuna was the best known room in the Uffizzi and contained both sculpture and pictures.
[2] The Venus dei Medici.

26 October. Directly after breakfast, we went to the gallery again, having appointed to meet Wm. in one of the corridors. It is so amusing to see how hard he works at acquiring a taste, and the fun is that he begins at the beginning of the art, which is by no means the easiest for a modern. He stood so long between Murray and some hideous old Giottos (forgive me Fanny) that Minnie and I were forced to leave him and, when we had done our contemplation of the statues, to refresh ourselves in the Venetian school. On our return, we called at the Post and found your nice letter and Aunt Kedington's. They were a great treat, the more because unexpected. I had gone more in hope for Minnie than myself. We came home and feasted on them before dinner. Afterwards, we went out alone shopping. Very daring was it not. I bought a very supple fine Leghorn[1] for 24s and 2d; no doubt I ought to have had it cheaper, but it was a pretty good bargain for me. Gloves are cheap and bad; the fighting about prices is disgusting. I know there is nothing to be done with a grave face, yet how to manufacture a grin when I am annoyed is a puzzle.

27 October. Waited 2 hours for the gentlemen to accompany us to church, not knowing the hour or the place. At last sallied forth alone, and arrived when the sermon was half over. Hurried home to dinner and ordered a coach to take us to the afternoon service, after which we walked to Mr Morgan's fearing he was ill; but no, they were late themselves, and willing to believe we did not expect them. We gave them a good scolding and sat chatting a long while afterwards.

28 October. Went to the Pitti gallery, saw some charming things, but were turned out at 12 because it was a saint's day. To our great dismay, Friday is a whole feast day, shops and galleries closed all day and at least half Saturday, and we have decided to go on Monday. Went again to the Duomo, and then to a respectable french shop, quite a treat not to be obliged to bargain.

29 October. Again to the Pitti. After staying as usual between 3 and 4 hours, Minnie and I made desperate efforts, by asking and running after all sorts of curators, to get permission to copy, but the director, who alone could give it, was not in Florence, and the time consumed in obtaining it would have been all our time except those unlucky saints' days. Our various tastes are amusing. Wm. inspects the old things which he thinks it his duty to admire, especially gems and tables, beautiful things, but as the pictures and statues are so far more beautiful, we only condescend to give them a glance. After dinner, we drove to the Cascina, a sort of Hyde Park to Florence. The hills and the river, the pines and cypresses with various

---

[1] A straw-plaited hat named after the Italian port (cf. p.9 & n.).

picturesque towers in the distance, make it a very pretty scene for the fine folks. Mrs Ryan called. Mr Morgan met us on our return and spent the evening with us.

30 October. We were at the gallery before the doors were opened and had a good study in the Tribuna before it was filled. After 4 hours, we despatched some notes to Rome and returned in the rain, but determined not to lose time so (being left to ourselves) we took a coach, bought some things, called on Mrs Ryan, and went to see a beautiful statue (by a Mr Power[1]) which is going to England: a captive Greek girl; it is very graceful. Among the wonders I see here, my taste very often revolts at first, yet, upon examination, follows pretty well in the beaten track. Only you will be surprised to hear that I admire Guido, Correggio and Carlo Dolce much less than I did, and have taken into favour quite a new race whose names I never heard in England. Fanny would be quite satisfied with my admiration of Fra Angelico, who does the most comical stiff things in the world, but so full of beautiful expression that I overlook all imperfections.

31 October. To the Pitti again where we had the impudence to try and copy in pencil without permission. We drew for an hour without interruption. Indeed I was so far from my model that I think the guard did not find out what I was doing but told Minnie she must not do it without permission. When Wm. joined us, we went to the Academy of Arts and saw more pictures, most of them old and curious. There was a head said to have the features of Savonarola, by his friend Bartolomeo. I have only just begun to realize that this is Florence, where so many men lived and so many transactions took place which interested me long ago. I have been in a bustle ever since we have been here, and have not thoroughly enjoyed any thing but the paintings and statues which we have made our daily study. Then it has been cold and rainy, so that our eyes were either devoted to the inspection of puddles, or we were in a coach from which, in these narrow streets, we can see nothing. After dinner, we went to the Boboli gardens adjoining the residence of the Grand Duke. There are most picturesque views of Florence from thence, but we were too late to see things to advantage.

I leave out two days to send my letter before the English papers give an account of the inundation. Days omitted: 1st November. We went to the Cathedral to hear the music on All Saints' Day; it was nothing particular. Then we went with Wm. and Mr Morgan to Fiesole, a hill about an hour and half drive from Florence whence there is a beautiful view. It is covered with Villas, the valley of the Arno and the towers of Florence below, and

---

[1] Possibly the French sculptor Jean-Baptiste Charles Emile Power who exhibited in the Parisian Salon between 1863 and 1870

the Appenines all around. The house is pointed out where Boccacio laid the scene of his *Decamerone*. There are, on the summit, most interesting records of times before the Romans, Etruscan, the old walls of the city, an amphitheatre of which enough remains to show the circular form of three tiers of stone benches and the narrow stairs leading to them, the den for wild beasts and the hole through which they were fed. There is a very ancient church, the remains of a pagan temple. Another thing that interested me was talking with a family of peasants, friends of Mr Morgan's faithful servant Giovanni - the only opportunity I am likely to have of seeing the agricultural peasantry of Tuscany in their homes. Their manners and countenances were open and pleasing. They gave us beautiful sweet scented nosegays. In the evening, it poured with rain, but we were engaged to drink tea at Dr Ryan's. As Wm. did not go with us, I engaged a Valet. It was well we did, for we were driven to the wrong house and found ourselves in the open court of a strange place in a deluge. Our Valet succeeded in bringing back the coach. We arrived safely and had a pleasant evening. Mrs R[yan] is a kind energetic little woman. She and the Dr and his sister seem to have the greatest regard for Emma and a reflected good will for all her friends. There were staying with them Captn. and Mrs Burton and their daughter, an elegant girl who played very well. They gave me a recommendation for a singing mistress and for Pianos at Rome. There was also a very pleasing girl, Miss Bartholomew, and her brother, and a Mr Hewit just returned from Greece.

2 November. There was Mass for the dead in all the churches for 8 days. We went to the Cathedral thinking to hear fine music, but it was only middling. The priests' black dresses looked very gloomy without anything of solemnity, from the careless multitudes loitering about. In the rain, we went to see Mr Morgan's sketches, and in the afternoon to S. Marco. It was so dark with rain we could scarcely see any thing, but we pored over a Missal beautifully illuminated by Fra Angelico. At S.Lorenzo, we had the mortification of hearing that the sculptures of M. Angelo were not to be seen on holidays and we had not light for anything else.

3 November. When we rang for breakfast, we ordered a coach to take us to church and learnt, to our astonishment, that it was impossible to pass the streets. We are at the side of the hotel, our windows commanding only the inner court. The front is separated from the Arno only by a road paved with large flat stones, without footpath, and barely wide enough for two carriages. There is a parapet about 3 and a half feet high from the road and very much higher from the river in its usual state, perhaps 18ft. The hotel is raised three steps. Little more than 100 yards on the left is the old bridge, two thirds covered on both sides with houses. The whole concern looks very rickety. Opposite, the houses are on the water's edge. From the old bridge, the ground slopes down past us to another bridge about an eighth of

a mile distant. Now if you can form a clear idea of these localities, you may have some notion of the view we had from the front door. The street was under water many feet on the left, and as far as could be seen on the right, the Arno, one mass of yellow mud, raging and rushing past, continually coming over the parapet, carrying with it trees, beams of houses, a cart, mattresses, chairs, tubs, animals, and, as we looked up, at a shout from the crowds assembled wherever there was a foot of dry ground, there came whirling past the woodwork of the Suspension bridge. While it continued to rain and the river continued to rise, the prospect was by no means pleasant. If the old Bridge had given way, we were in imminent danger that the shock would have knocked the house about our ears, though we were not so deep in the water as the hotels below. Their ground floors were filled and, of course, the kitchens. They received their provisions in boats in the next house but one. Here, the water only just reached part of the ground floor. When we went down to look at the frightful spectacle, a very pleasing Polish lady, who spoke good french, invited us into her front room. Her husband was terribly frightened. They had packed up to leave this hotel, but there was no telling where we should go to be better off: half Florence was under water. We saw the river break down the front of a cook's shop opposite and walk in at the windows of a Palace. It added to the melancholy effect to see ornaments and various utensils on the half broken walls and floors. We comforted one another, exchanging visits with the Poles. We read our service etc., and went to bed with no little anxiety, though the waters had greatly subsided.

4 November. The river still going down, we prepared for our journey, though in doubt whether we could proceed, when poor Divoto came in with a long face. The carriage had been nearly covered with water and could then be approached only by boats. The horses had been got out 'naked' as he said, by dint of much exertion, but the harness left, some men and horses having been drowned on the spot. Of course, we decided to stay, especially as, till the arrival of the Roman courier, we did not know if the road was practicable. It is almost the only road by which any thing has arrived. Being brave folks, we and our Polish acquaintances went by the back way to the Galleria where Wm. joined us with a dismal account of themselves. They had six feet water on the ground floor and saw nothing in the street but horses swimming and boats or rafts. Mr Morgan was also afraid of wanting provisions and did want water, all the wells being filled with mud. In all lower parts of hotels and houses, provisions were spoilt, the inundation was so sudden. It seems the custom in the large hotels that each head waiter of a story should cater for the visitors in his division and have a separate kitchen and store room. Our *cameriere* brought in our usual abundant dinner with an air of exultation saying that no body else dined so well as his charge for they could get nothing but from boats. We immediately offered to send away half our dinner but we could only prevail

on him to take one dish. He was determined we should feel there were advantages in being so near the moon. The public granaries were under water; soldiers were set to grind wheat in handmills for the poor. Mrs Ryan told us she let down a hook to get a leg of mutton from a boat. The town is choked with mud. It still rains, but the danger seems past. The night was tolerably fine and the waters were going down fast, but on the 4th it began to rain again as hard as ever. Notwithstanding, as soon as we could procure a coach and send it for Wm., we set off to the church Sta Annunciata. It was a very striking sight. The building is very richly ornamented. The beautiful marble pavement had been deep in water and was still wet and dirty. Hundreds of people, mostly poor, were kneeling upon it, some probably of the sufferers by the inundation. I liked to see this immediate acknowledgement of a superintending providence, but Alas! in one place a man was selling candles to be burnt before the shrine of the virgin, in one corner a priest was receiving money for rubbing little rosaries on the tomb of a saint, and in another they were offering prayers for the dead. The whole scene was so full of the deep interests of human life that I turned away unwillingly, even to see some very fine frescoes in the cloisters. Then to Sta Maria Novella, beautiful and curious pictures here also. Then to the tombs of the Medici to see those magnificent sketches in sculpture by Michael Angelo, Night and Day, morning and evening, and a Madonna and child; this latter charmed me, the form astonished me. I made the echo of the vaulted roof repeat the great man's praises and longed to have two hours quite alone without the pleasant old *custode* looking tired of my admiration and musing. We went to enquire about the Ryans knowing they were in a low part of the town. They had not actually suffered more than the alarm of seeing a torrent of mud rushing for hours down the street. Their house was about 4 feet under water from the ground floor. They saw a poor man taken from a window opposite drowned in his house. They exclaimed so vehemently against our going next day that they shook my resolution. Next, we made two attempts to cross the broad pavement to the Palazzo Vecchio, but we should have been wet through in half a minute, and I did not like to keep men and horses out. The river was rising again rapidly. We had a long chat with our Polish acquaintances, watching it from their windows, and had decided against going next day when Wm., on the other side of the water, was frightened about staying. Among the contradictory opinions, it was difficult to decide, but every one agreed that the road to Rome was practicable, and common sense told that within any time sufficient to dry the roads, Florence must be terribly unhealthy from the stench of mud, if not also distressed for provisions, no carts being able to come in from the country, and the mills having been demolished. The river continued to rise till 7, but did not get over the parapet again. We hear terrible accounts from Pisa and Leghorn. A poor woman here going to Mass slipped down in the mud and was suffocated. We decided to start next morning.

6 November. Having provisioned ourselves, among which a bottle of good Marsala procured by William was one of the most useful, and taken all sorts of precautions, we set off about 8.30. On getting into the carriage, we found it still very wet, not a door or window would shut properly, and there was an odious smell of stagnant mud. Off we went amidst smiles, bows and good wishes, but soon came to a standstill. After going over immense heaps of mud, we stuck fast. The soldiers employed on the road told us it was impossible to get on, but it was equally impossible to turn. Horses were tied behind and flogged to pull us back to no purpose. At last, we three, with the assistance of the bystanders, made a leap over the mud and walked some way from one hillock to another, while our horses were unharnessed, and men extricated the carriage. We went down another street almost as bad, the women calling to us from the windows 'you are going to your deaths'. By dint of great exertions, we got through, and out of Florence, after which there is no great difficulty on the road. The tremendous rain began again. Of course, it was impossible to keep it out of the carriage, or out of our carpet bags, but Divoto pushed on, and we arrived at Poggibonsi at 3.30, drenched. We soon had a good fire, and you would have laughed to see how fussy Minnie and Wm. were drying our things, and what a blazing fire they kept amidst all sorts of wearing apparel. Wm. says he exhibited a great deal of *dry* humour on the occasion. At all events, we were merry, and, so far, are glad to be out of Florence. We had miserably dirty rooms, were haunted by vermin of every description, and, after a wretched breakfast, started at 7 with the cheerful anticipation of just such another entertainment for the next night.

7 November. In which we were not mistaken, for besides the usual delectables, we have the misfortune to be on the road with three families who have ordered beds a week before. How I will make your hair stand on end with a faithful account of these detestable Italian inns! At Sienna, we saw several interesting sculptures, frescoes, and inlaid pavement in the Cathedral, and, in the Academy, a whole school of painters utterly unknown to me before, who have much merit as to expression and, the later ones, of drawing. They require not merely to be seen, but to be studied. One has not half the pleasure to be obtained from these ancients without dwelling upon their works long enough to identify oneself with them in some sort, and have the novelty of living in the old world. I have several times been struck with the two very different expressions of the Italian peasantry, one, such as we generally call an Italian face: dark browed, cunning, passionate, with handsome regular features, the other less handsome, but remarkably innocent and affectionate, a different simplicity from that of the Swiss, more child-like and docile, less quiet and reasonable. We have been rejoicing in a fine day, and, having had the carriage dried three days with braziers, it was a little more tolerable. The

country to Sienna is hilly, richly wooded, and has picturesque little towers or convents perched on the top of the hills, but it wanted sun to light it up, and we wanted spirit to enjoy it. From Sienna, it is dreary to Buonconvento where we stop the night. I have neglected to send my letter from Sienna, which I regret, as it will occasion a delay of some days. We are all so longing to get to Rome that I hardly think we shall look at any thing else on the road, but oh! fie, for shame, I verily believe a vehement desire of being comfortable has much share in our eagerness for the 7 hills.

8 November. All the way to La Scala, where we dined, we rejoiced that it did not rain, but our joy was all over then - we had a tremendous storm of wind and rain all the rest of the day. The road almost like going over downs in England, but shorter hills. You may imagine how wind rushed upon us quite unprotected by any sort of fence. It seemed as if we must be blown over, and, to mend the matter, in attempting to shut the window (which shuts like a door), it was dashed into fifty pieces. Luckily the wind soon ceased to come on that side, and we were busy sopping and mopping at the other. We are to have a taste of Italian weather since floods come when we are on the banks of a river and wind when we are on the mountains. Our *vetturino* is very obliging but too soft by half. He says any thing to please, but does not stick to it. We have been hoping to get to Rome in five days exclusive of Sunday. Now he tells us it is impossible, and we are impatient. This is such a strange scene, just as if it had rained huge blocks of stone, and so dreary, scarcely a cottage, hill after hill, the road winding about so that you may see pieces of it before you miles before you reach them. Radicofani - the inn is a strange place, a huge old palace with immense galleries supported upon black arches, passages like large halls, large lofty dreary unfinished rooms through which the wind howls piteously. Here again Milord had all the best rooms (Lord Fingal's family),[1] but we had a good fire in Wm.'s room and got on tolerably well. Our windows looked upwards to the village at some little distance and, beyond that, to the ruined castle of a robber knight.

9 November. We were anxious to start early to get to a good inn at night, so at 6.30 we were in the carriage, starving with hunger (Milord had eaten all the good provisions), but not with cold - we had taken such precautions with wraps. It continued to rain violently at intervals with a stormy wind. We came to a torrent so much swoln that it was doubtful whether we could cross it. Divoto chose to wait till Milord's carriages came to try it first. Men on the other side threw stones into it to show its depth, and, true enough, it did look formidable. They asked if we would have oxen to pull us through. After a furious altercation between these men and Milord's

---

[1] Arthur James Plunkett, Earl of Fingall, b.1791, had married Louisa Corbally of Co. Meath in 1817. At the time they had eight children.

people, a pair of oxen, harnessed to a sort of timber drag, pulled Milor's three carriages and luggage van through. You may fancy what a scene it was, all three men and horses (they harness 6 or 7 to one carriage) waiting on the brink of this turbid angry torrent; every one looking anxiously for the success of the first experiment, for the large stones carried down often break carriages in the middle of the stream. However, it was successful. We all passed, separately. We had made preparation for letting the water pass easily out, if it came in to our carriage, by taking up the carpet and tucking up ourselves and every thing else above the seats. However, as the carriage is hung very high, very little came in. We were fearfully jolted, but got safely through to Ponte Centino. This is the entrance to the papal states, where we should have undergone a vexatious searching but for our *Lascia passare* for which I had written to Torlonia from Florence, so here we had no trouble, but took refuge from the pouring rain in a wretched hovel of an inn, and had the satisfaction! of hearing that 10 horses were wanting to go on, *none* there. Of course. Milor (who was also travelling with *vetturino* horses) would have his 8 first. Before we could get to a decent resting place, there was another torrent to be crossed, three times as wide as the first - which was likely to be increasing every moment by the continual rain. Divoto said we had better get our dinners here and rest the horses. The former we accomplished with immense labour of jaws and much philosophic determination to satisfy our stomachs, without asking any questions of our palates, but the old cock's last crow seemed still vibrating in our ears while we were eating him. At last, horses came, Milor's train started. I did not much like being left behind, thinking that in any real disaster, their men would have helped us, but Divoto is very chicken-hearted. His private opinion was that they could not get over, and he wished to wait till their additional horses returned. However, after waiting till they would have been back if they had not got over, we insisted on starting. Notwithstanding the good woman told us in the accustomed phrase that we were going to death, we knew we should stay to be tormented and that what others could do, we might. We passed safely through the torrent which was less formidable than we expected. Acquapendente looked wretched, and there was plenty of time to get on at least to Bolsena. The situation of Acquapendente is very pretty. It was fine enough to allow us to walk a little up the ascent, beautiful rocks interspersed with rich trees, cascades, and picturesque though ruinous-looking buildings. This dreadful malaria country! It is so melancholy to go miles and miles in a fertile country without seeing a habitation, except such as are ruined and deserted, and overgrown with moss and grass. Besides, everything was soaked where we passed. About 5, we reached Bolsena. As the weather and the season made it dark very soon, we intended staying there if possible, but desired Divoto to enquire about additional horses first. The rooms were dirty holes with a horrible smell and the only place where we could have a fire was a common room filled with all sorts of rabble. We could not tolerate this, but, on ordering Divoto to proceed, found there were no horses, so we had to go on with our tired ones, and pick up others as we could. On the road, we passed some curious basaltic rocks, but had neither time nor light to examine them. We then met 2 horses, tired also, but they help[ed] somewhat. When it grew dark, Divoto tried to light his lamps, but his matches, like his unfortunate self, had been so often drenched that they had lost all their fire. I had my patent light in my carpet bag which we dragged, tumbled out its content in the dark, and accomplished the light with some difficulty from wind and rain, I being in fever all the while for fear of robbers, since this road is a favourite haunt, and we had left such tidings of ourselves and our defenceless state at Bolsena. Soon, one of the carriage lamps went out which I remedied by one of my Genoa wax night candles which did very well. After two hours of travelling, in the fidgets, we arrived at Montefiascone. Imagine our delight in being ushered into clean rooms and served by such a brisk waiter that it seemed as if the fire which blazed up the moment we asked for it must have come from his fingers' ends. He brought an armful of large bulrushes to make a blaze. We agreed to have a second dinner, being quite hungry enough. Here we spent Sunday very comfortably.

10 November. Divoto spread all he could, down to his scanty wardrobe, in the sun. After reading, we took a walk. There is a very pretty view of the Lake and surrounding country. The town and its cathedral and large monastery are picturesque, though, on a near view, shabby and dirty. On the 11th, we found ourselves so early at Roniglione that we determined to get on to a solitary inn, Le Sette Vene, and gain half a day in Rome. It poured again. We arrived with my carpet bag drenched and Minnie's somewhat wet (Divoto has no contrivance). The place was crowded. We could get access to no fire but in the common room, and we could not well take out our night things to dry in a perfect throng of gentlemen, couriers, priests, monks, soldiers etc., so, after supper, being no longer able to endure the noise and smell, we went to bed (to the outsides of our dirty beds), consoling ourselves with the hope of Rome tomorrow.

12 November. Rome indeed! About 11, it cleared up. St Peters and the Castle St Angelo presented themselves in yellow vapour, soft but bright, a very beautiful midday effect. I have not been yet, and certainly was not then, sufficiently at rest to realize the fact that I looked upon Rome of the heroes, of the martyrs, of the Pope. We had not much delay at the customs, but drove to the Hotel d'Allemagne where we had pretty good apartments, but rather dear. The remainder of that day, the whole of the next, 13th, and part of the 14th, was occupied in looking for apartments, and finding those of the people mentioned to us, who were likely to be most useful. Capt. Allen, an acquaintance of Wm.'s through Mr Morgan, was a great help. Torlonia's brother received us with much civility, and gave us cards for

different things, among others for the apartments we have taken. Signor Modetti was most willing to serve us, and Miss D[ouglasse] and Dr.P[ollock][1] gave us valuable information. The latter would have gone house hunting with us if it had been necessary. The number of apartments we saw was very great, but the number of stairs we ascended to see them passes my arithmetic, almost every flight having its own particular puddle or puddles by way of warning as to the rest of the dirt we must expect to meet with. We decided on one dwelling at 12 o'clock on the 14th, and so effectually bestirred ourselves that we provisioned ourselves, got our servant packed up at the Hotel, and dine at home at 5. Now you will wish for a full description of our abode. We are about the middle of the Corso, the fashionable place for shopping and driving about from one end of Rome to the other, in a street between the Corso and the Piazza di Spagna, which is the English quarter. We are only 3 doors from the Corso, just out of the noise, and should be very quiet but for a blacksmith's opposite. There is a carriage entrance under our drawing room to the staircase, which will be useful on rainy nights. We have a first floor consisting of two large light cheerful bedrooms for Minnie and myself, a small anteroom, adjoining our maid's bedroom, where she sits and works, and which serves as housekeeper's room and pantry, a drawing room, in which, by the bye, we take all our meals, 41 by 25 of my feet and more than proportionately lofty, having two tiers of windows, the selling of Joseph and other scripture histories painted on the windows, so that the room requires a terrible quantity of light, but not so much fire as one might expect. You will guess we did not wish for so grand a room. Then Wm. has a small sitting room and bed room on the other side of our drawing room. In all, 10 windows facing the street, an entrance where we keep our wood, and the use of a kitchen. The furniture is not at all grand, but clean, especially the carpets and beds. We have plate, linen, crockery and lamps, plain but whole, and plenty of them. Our landlady is a respectable widow who occupies, with her servant, the remaining rooms of this floor. We hear she has been used to good society. She speaks very good Italian. To go on with my journal before I forget it, Miss D[ouglasse] kindly invited us to spend the evening of the 14th with her, thinking we should not be provisioned, but, as we were very tired, we declined.

15 November. Went about finding shops and choosing baths with Signor Modetti. Wm. was determined not to see sights till next week, but my impatience was too great for such delay, so Minnie and I took a coach and went to St Peters. The approach delighted me; it is magnificent. The interior disappointed me in producing no feeling whatever of awe or solemnity. It is grand in size and rich in decoration and not looking for any

---

[1] James Pollock and his cousin Miss Douglasse feature regularly in the journal and, at the end, join the three travellers in their journey from Rome to Venice.

thing sacred in character. It gives pleasure as a most beautiful sight, but not elevating. The Castle St Angelo pleases me. It seems a symbol of Papal dominion, majestic and weighty from its great extent, but not strong or offensive like our northern fortresses where each little tower, besides contributing to the whole, seems ready to do battle on its own account with a vigour not depending upon union. I returned, glorying in having seen St Peters without Murray. It was quite a relief to be in happy ignorance, instructed only by my own eyes and ears, with such general recollections as come naturally, enhancing the charm of every thing in this interesting city.

16 November. We called on Helen (the family of the lady called by this name was at that time in political disgrace and we did not mention in letters anything likely to bring her or ourselves into trouble) who had called on us, on receiving our cards. She took us to hear more pianos (we had already heard 20). We found a very good new grand at Strohm's for 6 scudi a month - the men of greater celebrity charge 7 for those hardly so good - so we agreed for it. In the evening, we drank tea with Miss D[ouglasse], met Mrs Hayward, Lady Belcher[1] and Dr Grant - a very agreeable evening. Miss D[ouglasse] seems to me quite loveable.

17 November. There wanted only a quiet Sunday to make us feel settled here. There was not much animation in the manner of performing our English service, but nothing unpleasant. Mr Hutchinson[2] gave us a useful sermon; there was none in the afternoon. We went into the vestry where there is a good lending library from which I took a book.

18 November was the dedication of St Peters; we went. There were the Pope's red and yellow guards, and a procession of bishops and cardinals. Cardinal Mattei performed the service, most of which was chaunted by the Pope's choir. The voices were very good, but, except one or two solos, I did not think the music was fine. We stood immediately behind the Swiss guards, and saw and heard very well. Certainly the procession and the lights added much to the splendour of the view down the middle aisle. In the afternoon, we drove with Miss D[ouglasse] and Mr P[ollock] to see the Coliseum and other ruins in its neighbourhood. It was only a general view, and all I have to say at present is that it interested me extremely.

19 November. We had our gowns fitted by Mme Clarisse and did several other things equally tiresome and necessary.

---

[1] The wife of Sir Edward Belcher, a naval officer who had been knighted the previous year for services in the Chinese war.
[2] Rev. James Hutchinson, the Anglican chaplain in Rome between 1837 and 1850.

20 November. We three went together to the Coliseum, wandered about the galleries, and brought home a nosegay of the wild flowers growing there, which I cherish.

21 November. To the Vatican to see pictures only and try to get permission to copy. One day, we called on Mrs Collyer who had stated by note her inability to call on us. Met the husband of our Polish acquaintance, but because this is a deceitful world where it is held imprudent to trust anyone, I dared not call on her, though much prepossessed in her favour.

22 November. Again to the Vatican for the permission towards which I have made one step in getting a letter from the British consul. This day and Tuesday, we had Italian lessons. Took a charming drive with Miss D[ouglasse] and hunted for a singing mistress.

23 November. Again a drive with Miss D[ouglasse], and found the singing mistress who is a pleasing little person but very dear for Rome. I forgot to mention that, on the 22nd, Dr Grant paid us a long evening visit, made himself very agreeable, and spoke most kindly of Fanny. If you show Fanny my letter, she will explain things which I mention only shortly. Helen has no news to send; nothing has transpired.

24 November. A quiet Sunday. It is very cold but constantly fine all day ever since we have been here. I am so vexed that I forgot the right time to write to you for the 13th. My letter was begun with that view, but wishing to let you know we were safe in Rome, put the other intention out of my head. No need to say I thought of you and dear Father. You see I have no room to comment on your letter though I have written as shortly as I could.

25 November. We had still the same business left which prevented our going early to the Vatican to draw, so we went to a tower on the Capitoline where we had a fine view of the 7 hills. The Sabine hills are covered with snow and Soracte[1] had a glittering white tip. We looked along the Appian way; the ruins charm me mightily. We are very comfortably housed, and like our servant much. You shall hear more particulars next time.

26 November. In the morning Sig'ra Garofalini, then the staymakers, then we set off to the Vatican with our letter to the Majordomo who, being altogether a Major, told us we must wait till Friday for our ticket, but, in the meantime, we went into the rooms of frescoes and oils to see which we would choose and where there was room for us. I am more and more charmed with the Communion of St Jerome by Domenichino, and still feel that the Transfiguration by Raffaelle is by no means the finest picture in the

---

[1] Mountain visible from Rome.

world to my taste. The foreground figures are perfect in my eyes, not so those of the Saviour, Moses, Elijah and the disciples. We called on Miss Douglass, and Mr P[ollock] walked with us to leave cards for Genl. Ramsay,[1] to whom I had a letter from Mme Wolff. In the evening came Monsig're Alberghini,[2] paid us a long agreeable visit, and was most kind in offering us assistance. He spoke affectionately of Fanny and hopes to see her in Rome again. We declined going to the Sistine on a Sunday, and he very kindly offered to get us tickets for a funeral service on Friday. This put us in a fuss about dress. We had been making enquiries about the propriety of having black for ecclesiastical ceremonies, and determined to procure it, not thinking it right to omit a courteous compliance with the customs of the place, even if (as English) we could creep in without. The matter of dress makes my pocket groan, but I do not think it would be fairly doing my best to have all the advantages we can from our sojourn here if I did less. Mr Pollock came to accompany us to see the Coliseum by moonlight, but, as he had not succeeded in engaging the moon, it was put off.

27 November. Set off directly after breakfast to Mme Clarisse, ordered very nice black watered silks for Minnie and myself with the etcs., which we are to have tomorrow night. Miss D[ouglasse] has lent us proper veils. After lunch, to see a picture by Mile (an Irishman) painted for Prince Albert, Naomi and Ruth, very interesting. Soon we were joined by William and Mr P[ollock]. The latter tried to show us the studios of three artists, but the day being cloudy, they were not at work. We then went to the studio of Gibson, the sculptor, where we saw his pretty things, and his brother who does not exactly come under that description.[3]

28 November. Signora Jarvis put off Minnie's singing. We had instead good Italian conversations with Signor Modetti and Monsig're Luciani, private secretary to the Pope. He was very lively and flattering, and promised to come and see us often. Then we went to the Vatican to see the sculpture. One great pleasure of visiting the Vatican is that there is often such a lovely view of the hills from the windows; there was this afternoon in a glowing sunset.
(Note added by Miss W.: With respect to religious ceremonies, the mere facts are stated with careful correctness, but no remarks added about doctrines or the impression made on us, because we were soon made aware that we were watched, and our letters sometimes opened, and as we were on friendly terms with several ecclesiastics of the Roman Church, far more

---

[1] Lt.Gen. Ramsay, a long-time resident in Rome and an active supporter of the English church. He died in 1845.
[2] Joseph Alberghini (1770-1847) made cardinal in 1834.
[3] John Gibson (1790-1866) was one of the best known British sculptors of his day. His younger brother Benjamin lived with him in Rome for many years.

than most staunch protestants, I did not wish to get them or ourselves into trouble.)

I hope my kind friends are very patient with me. I really can write only to you till things are regulated. I only tell you results, but many arrangements cost much time and trouble before they are completed. Our maid is a tall Albano, considerably bigger than I am, sister to Fanny's first maid but, I imagine, very different, not at all a fine lady, but very willing. She does every thing we want except fetch water for which we pay 7d a month as our baths take more than usual. Maria is very gentle in manner, she works tolerably at her needle, is very clean and, as far as I can judge, honest and frugal. We pay her £1-9s a month, giving her no other board than the remains of our dinner after we have taken enough for the next day's lunch. Our dinner sent hot from the Trattoria costs rather more than 1s a head per day. We have soup, two dishes of meat or fish, one of vegetable, and one of pudding. I rejoice in having no man servant who would certainly be a trouble to us. We owe this to the protection Wm.'s presence affords. We have so many advisers and so 'cute ourselves that we do not want the sort of service a valet would render. Our lodgings are £12-15s a month. Coach hire and wood are expensive; we want so much of each, but I expect not to exceed the sum proposed for our maintenance.

29 November. Set off about 9 to hear a funeral service for the late Pope in the Sistine. You would have been amused to see us masquerading which Maria arranged very pretty with long pins, mock pearl for Minnie, sober black for me. Our silk gowns are very handsome and we are quite correct in costume. We got there early and sneaked in to gaze at Michael Angelo's frescoes till the guards turned us out. The Chapel quite disappointed me as to architecture. I looked at the ceiling till my head ached, but can only say that it is most wonderful drawing and that none of the copies I have seen give the spirit of the original, but really one might as well pretend to form an opinion of Dante by reading three cantos, as of that *Last Judgement* in an hour. We had good places. The spectacle was curious and magnificent. The music, or rather the voices, very fine, most rich and affecting tones (there is no instrument). The composition was intricate, and all minor, which made it fatiguing to the ear. Being a lovely day, we determined to keep the carriage and try to get Miss D[ouglasse] to drive with us. She and Mr P[ollock] went with us to the gardens of Mr Mills:[1] roses climbing up the cypresses which grow on the first floor of the palace of the Caesars on the Palatine, very picturesque pieces of ruin, beautiful peeps at the Alban hills, and a thousand storied fragments around. We saw two points where Fanny and Miss C. each took a pretty drawing. We went down into the

---

[1] A property on the Palatine bought in 1816 by Mr Charles Mills and subsequently called the 'Villa Mills'. Charles Mills died in 1846.

rooms excavated, very dismal indeed were they. In one, which must have been a comfortable well-proportioned room, the ivy was hanging like long tresses, dishevelled and forlorn, within the broken dome. We saw through to the flowers flourishing in the sunshine above, for they did not cling to the ruin. Afterwards, we drove about by the walls looking at tombs, aqueducts etc.. Home by the Coliseum and Monte Cavallo, where the Pope now resides and the famous horses which give name to the place. By way of finishing an idle day, we went to drink tea with Miss D[ouglasse] to meet an Italian lady who did not come.

30 November. After our Italian lesson, Minnie and I set off post haste to the Vatican all prepared to begin drawing, but found more vexatious delays which a little civility from the Major Domo would have prevented, so we had a cold drive and a dirty walk for nothing. Genl. Ramsay called the 2nd time. He is a pleasant old man and I think will be an acquisition.

1 December. A quiet Sunday. We had the sacraments, and afternoon sermons began. As we came out of church, a very noble looking lady asked me if 'I was I,' and announced herself to be Mrs John Smith, a friend of Mrs M.'s for whom I had long sought in vain elsewhere. It seems Miss Price had seen me somewhere before, though I do not remember it, and they watched me in Rome till they were sure of my identity.

2 December. Called on Mrs Smith and Miss P[rice]. There is a pleasing daughter also who I hope will be a friend for Minnie. Mr P[ollock] escorted us to the tomb of Cecilia Metella. We walked to the Circus of Romulus and the fountain of Egeria. It was a lovely day. The Alban mount looked beautiful. What with the rich material for imagination and the pleasure of the senses, the excursion was most enjoyable. We finished by seeing in one group the temples of Vesta, of Fortuna virilis, the house of Rienzi, and Ponte rotte. In the evening went again to Miss D[ouglasse], met Sig'ina Petrarca (whom I liked), Miss Fielding, Capt'n Johnson and a french family who seemed well-bred people. It was rather an exercise to keep continually changing about in three languages; indeed speaking at all has not been very easy to me the last few days for I have caught cold in my jaws! at least it seems so.

3 December. Italian lesson and Minnie's 1st singing lesson. I like Sig'ra Jarvis very much; she takes great pains. Then we went to tell Torlonia we had taken the apartments he had recommended. The brother who received us before was very civil, but I do not like him any better than at first. We invited Helen for tomorrow evening, called to thank Mrs Collyer for Burgess's book[1] and shopped a little. Dr Grant spent almost all the evening

---

[1] Rev. Richard Burgess, *The topography and antiquities of Rome*, 1831.

with us. We enjoyed his company very much and flattered ourselves that he seemed comfortable.

4 December. Rainy all day; we do not dislike the rest. As the weather prevented our having other society, we asked Sig'ra Lupienti (our hostess) to come in and talk Italian with us, which she does every now and then. She is as good as a master for she speaks very well, though all she says is great nonsense. We are such gay folks - we receive every evening we can get anyone to talk Italian.

5 December. After a busy morning, set off for the Vatican too late for our permission, but we spent the time most agreeably in the Museum where we met Mrs and Miss Smith. Then we had a troublesome business about getting boots for Minnie; it is an affair of more difficulty than you would guess. We were in late for dinner and, soon after, came Mons're Alberghini who was, as usual, very amiable, and was not frightened away by Sig'na Helen and her sister who arrived afterwards. We had plenty of Italian conversation and a little music, but all our guests left us early. Our large room is not lighted with less than two large table-lamps, two small ones and two candles. Housekeeping begins to be rather amusing now I know the value of things, and the spending of them, in some measure. Our interior government is quite republican, all important matters, such as a change of biscuits or half a libra of Ricotta, being debated in open assembly. N.B. Ricotta is a sort of cream cheese made of goat's milk used instead of the bad butter we get here. It is a great favourite with Minnie. We frequently send into the street for a ha'p'orth of roasted chestnuts to finish our luncheon.

6 December. Sig'r Garofalini and Sig'ra Jervis, then hurried off for the permission to draw, obtained it, but not complete yet! Spent 2 hours in St Peters admiring its beauty, shopped, spent the evening with Mrs and Miss Smith and Miss Price very pleasantly. An agreeable Italian surgeon came in and sat some time.

7 December. Bustled off directly after breakfast to the Vatican. Did actually draw. It is most interesting, but very difficult, to reduce those immense frescoes to the dimensions of our sketchbooks without frames for taking proportions. Minnie begins with great spirit. We were turned out at 11. In fact, we have so many irons in the fire that it is hard to keep all going. I go on with my journal in utter despair of finding time to write a separate letter to anyone worth postage all this way, or I would have told dear Miss Mortons what a friendly reception I met with from Mrs S[mith] and Miss P[rice] for her sake, and with what interest both, but especially the latter, spoke of them. I hope Miss S[mith] will be a valuable acquaintance for Minnie. We have promised to go and see them in the

evening sometimes, as they cannot come to us then, and we all want to be out in the afternoon.

7 December. After posting our letters, we went with Sig'ra Lupienti to the house of her niece, Sig'ra Vanutelli, wife of an advocate whose apartments (part of the splendid Colonna Palace) have a private gallery within the choir of the Church SS Apostoli, where the Pope was to give his benediction today, accompanied by his Cardinals, guards, etc. Sig'ra Vanutelli, mother of 8 children, is a handsome, particularly attractive, young woman with the quiet simple manner of a sensible well-bred Englishwoman. She has charming children. Her husband, some years older than herself, we saw only for a minute. We sat in her very comfortable rooms three quarters of an hour. She played the piano to us splendidly, yet not at all like a person given up to mere ornaments. There is a girl about Minnie's age whose manners are agreeable. I had heard from several quarters that our landlady was well connected, and I think this lady must be a star among Roman matrons. At last the Pope came, and we went into the gallery with the French Ambassador's wife and the Duchessa Torlonia. Neither of them diverted my attention from the splendid pageant, and the perpetual fidgetting about the Pope. There was not much music and that only vocal but very sweet, and the effect of the great crowd in the body of the church chanting as response to a litany *ora pro nobis* was very grand. Wm. counted 104 immense wax candles on the altar alone (it was daylight). On all these feasts, the walls of churches are hung with rich draperies of crimson, gold and white. It is beautiful to look down upon, the Cardinals almost all in scarlet, the purple of the Bishops, the violet satin of some attendants; a profusion of lace, embroidery gold and silver, with graceful forms of dress, made a gay scene gradually becoming more delicate in tint as the eye travels from the assembled multitude through guards and ecclesiastics to the Pope's mantle of white and gold. I am very glad to have seen such a thing, but quite understand how it is that (as an Italian told me last night) the religious among themselves prefer going to their devotions more quietly. Monsig're Luciani called when we were out last night; very polite of him to come again so soon.

8 December. Sunday as usual, only starved with cold, huddling on all our warm things and longing for muffs. There has been ice several mornings on one of the fountains. We growl over our chilblains in this sunny Italy, and Minnie has the most affecting reminiscences of the fat cob who used to circulate her blood so effectually in the riding school.

9 December. Rainy, yet I was bold enough to go in the pelting rain to Miss D[ouglasse], partly for the sake of hearing about Fanny, and partly because Miss D[ouglasse], having been kept in the house several days, I thought she might like the variety, and I enjoyed the visit. It is so disagreeable to

walk in Rome in the rain. The eaves project unequally: sometimes they pour their torrents beyond, sometimes on, the foot pavement. The gutters run in the most sportive meanderings, so that one must be constantly tacking about between these two plagues. For some time, I could not make out why most of the women walking in the streets and in shops had little coarse earthen pots in their hands, till I found out that the vessels contained hot wood ashes which may be bought at a bakers, and this is their very poor expedient for warming their whole bodies. In the evening we chatted with Sig'ra Lupienti.

10 December. Italian and singing. Afterwards we separated, Minnie and I, after shopping, went to the Church Sta Maria Maggiore, just to have a general view. It is magnificent but did not particularly delight me; returned in the rain, very tired. In the evening came Dr Grant who was quite sociable and lively. Fanny's friends have been very attentive to us, pray tell her so with my kind love.

11 December. To the Vatican. Sig'r G[arofalini] had kindly promised for us the last necessary signature and we suppose that, as the secretary is his friend, we owe to him a word or two of notice from the great man himself as we sat drawing. We should have enjoyed our 2 hours drawing extremely, but that our odious Roman boots are very soon wet through and not nearly so soon dry, and our feet were cold and wet all the while. A card of invitation from Principessa Torlonia which we are advised to accept for the sake of seeing a gay scene. Can you fancy us three originals (no one of us being in the smallest degree of the conventional pattern) wandering about among the motley crew. I hear the crowd is far from select. Mr P[ollock] called and Sig'ra L[upienti] came to talk. When shall I have a letter? You must be waiting for my first from Rome - we have been here a whole month. Henceforth I shall only note irregular employments; you will suppose lessons and drawing to go on pretty regularly.

12 December. Drank tea with Miss D[ouglasse], met the Revd. Mr Frith and his wife.

13 December. Went to the Roman Philharmonic Concert; tickets are not to be bought - Sig'r G[arofalini] gave us ours. We were told to go early to secure good places, which we had, but waited an hour and half for our entertainment. There were about 60 voices and 40 instruments. Many of the performers were dilettanti. There was a fine body of voice, and tolerably well trained. The solos were middling. The performance was an opera by Mercadante[1] on the last 7 words of our Saviour. It is difficult for me to judge of a musical composition when all is so new, but I think most of it

---

[1] Saverio Mercadante (1795-1870), composer and musical director.

was very poor. Two ladies played a duet on two harps in a very finished and tasteful style. Plenty of English there. We had been told it would last till 11 and ordered our coach at 10.30. Consequently we waited three quarters of an hour in the cold anteroom in the smell of extinguished candles. True we had company to console us, and that most intolerable great man of Torlonia's patronized us with his most amiable attentions.

15 December (Sunday). Surprised by an evening visit from Monsig're Luciani on his way from a dinner to an evening party. You are not yet acquainted with our Maria; I must introduce her. She is every way bigger than I am, rather handsome, very majestic, has regular features, an olive complexion and a profusion of dark hair. She wears a very full long skirt of *Mousseline de Laine*, or some such thing, a bright scarlet cloth jacket, that is the back, and long tight sleeves. From the back of the waist come narrow ribbons to support a little sort of stomacher about 5 inches wide and 4 deep; the only thing in front outside, a large loose white kerchief which covers the bust. Her hair is always nicely braided, but on Sundays she twines coloured ribbons in it and uses silver or mock pearly pins to fasten it, a pelerine trimmed with broad blond,[1] a large cameo brooch, and, when she goes out, a thick white veil folded square on her head. The Italian ladies often make it a piece of show to take in their carriages a handsome nurse in a very rich peasant's dress. The girls think themselves very fine dressed *à la française*, but I tell Maria, if she comes to England with me, she must bring the Albano jacket etc.

16 December. Were introduced by Miss Smith to a very talented Italian girl Gajotti. We found her in a little room, yclept studio, painting in oil which she does in a very promising way. She sings well, plays the harp and piano, speaks English very well, and, I hear, knows German, french and spanish. She seems also to be well informed as far as I can judge from one conversation. She adds beauty to all this; in short quite a Corinne.[2]

Afterwards the Vatican, and Sigra L[upienti] in the Evening.

17 December. Took Mrs and Miss Smith with our tickets from Monsig're Alberghini to the Vatican gardens, Casino etc. Asked in vain for letters on our return, and called on Miss D[ouglasse]. Guess my delight at seeing on our table your letter of the 30th with every thing to give me pleasure about

---

[1] A type of lace made from silk.

[2] Corinne, the heroine of Mme de Staël's novel of the same name which was based in Italy. The Earl of Malmesbury met Gajotti two years later and described her thus: 'She is very handsome, twenty-three years of age, speaks English and three other languages perfectly, has a very fine voice, is a good musician, playing both harp and piano, and writes poetry for which she was crowned last year at the Capitol. She paints portraits better than a great many artists.' *Memoirs of an Ex-Minister*, London, 1885, p.135.

the immediate home circle and dear Aunt F[anny], for our other friends, a mixture of regret and pleasure. Now you will like to know our dress at this season. It is the fashion of Italian ladies to dress in black, of which we take advantage to have a change. Moreover, the party at Torlonia's is only a *conversazione* - there can be no formal supper because next day's fast begins at midnight. We wear rich black watered silk, Minnie's trimmed with my broad lace and her point, a white rose in her hair which is to be dressed by a person said to perform that office 'divinely', our white gloves prettily ornamented. Sig'ra L[upienti] again in the evening, a great deal of laughing; she says I am very *spiritoso* - it must be the effect of your letter.

18 December. A little drawing at the Vatican, after which we meant to have been studious at home, but Mr P[ollock] came and enticed us to go to the studio of a Miss Chawner, who copies large pictures from the old masters in watercolours with the utmost accuracy and most wonderful effect. We could scarcely believe it was not oil - not merely the bright draperies, but Raffaelle's soft golden light, perfectly imitated. Then we went to Macdonald's, a sculptor,[1] where we saw some excellent busts, among which one interested me extremely, of Lord Lorn, a very intellectual amiable countenance, very young. I hear he is small and red-haired so that his general appearance is very inferior to the bust, but with that charming expression, surely he must be a fit husband for my little favorite Lady Eliz'th.[2] There is an interesting bust of Mrs Somerville who is here; I wish I had an introduction to her.[3]

19 December. Went to Torlonia's. The hair dresser kept us waiting nearly two hours, consequently we were in a terribly long string of carriages, and came to a stop on the bridge of St. Angelo. However, our coachman, by going 2 miles round, contrived to get us in somewhat sooner than if we had stayed for our turn there. The valet is allowed to follow upstairs into an anteroom and there take the shawls. Our names were announced by a row of liveries, and we passed through several rather mean-looking rooms to the concert room. All the seats were already occupied. We stood for some time in a crowd of vulgar slang sort of young men to hear music of which the composition was middling, the soprano solos screeched, and the choruses too loud for the place, otherwise pretty good. Then we wandered

---

[1] Lawrence Macdonald (1799-1878) was resident in Rome from 1832 until his death. In 1847, the American Margaret Ossoli found in his studio 'a complete gallery of the aristocracy of England, for each lord and lady who visits Rome considers it a part of the ceremony to sit to him for a bust.' (*At Home and Abroad*, Boston, 1856, p.221).
[2] The Marquis of Lorne, son of the Duke of Argyll, had married Lady Elizabeth Sutherland-Leveson-Gower, daughter of the Duke of Sutherland, on 31 July 1844.
[3] Mary Somerville (1780-1872) had been living in Rome since 1838. She was well-known as a writer on scientific subjects. She had received widespread recognition for her work entitled *On the Connection of the Physical Sciences*, published in 1834.

about, saw the lovely Principessa (a Colonian)[1] with her magnificent heavy tiara of diamonds. She was loaded with jewels, but the assembly was by no means first rate. It was not till late in the evening that we met Sig'ra Vanutelli and her husband, the only persons there I cared to see. There were refreshments of all sorts. Minnie was disgusted with the manners she saw in the crowd, and did not like the thing at all. Wm. was amused; it was all new to him. There was nothing for me because I had seen much more brilliant affairs before, and the music was not to my taste, so that I was very glad to come away at twelve. We had plague enough to get our carriage with the Valet; I do not know when we could have escaped without him. Our dresses did very well, and put us in our right places, in which particular I shrewdly suspect they differed from the smarter riggings of some of our countrywomen. I forgot to mention what was my evening's real entertainment that evening. A little while before I ought to have dressed came Monsig're Alberghini, and the conversation turning on Italian poetry, he repeated and read with enthusiasm many passages from Dante and Petrarca, which I enjoyed hearing extremely. It was strange to my English notions to see the gentle, rather elderly man warmed with poetic fire, gesticulating and declaiming Petrarch's sonnets. It was ten times more entertaining than the party.

20 December. Notwithstanding our dissipation of the previous evening, we drew at the Vatican, and drank tea with Miss D[ouglasse] leaving Dr Grant, which we much regretted, and meeting only a Mr W.

21 December. Paddled along in the rain to see Mrs Smith, or rather Miss P[rice], who was nervous from having been kept indoors some time and seemed glad of my visit.

22 December. Sunday. Could only go once to church for the rain.

23 December. Called on Sig'ra Vanutelli, and missed Mr Hutchinson, our Pastor, who called on us meanwhile. Made ineffectual attempts to see a palace and a church which were shut. Mr P[ollock] invited Wm. to go with him to a gentleman's party at Mr Macbean's,[2] so I invited ourselves to spend the evening with Miss D[ouglasse], which seemed agreeable to all parties. Mr P[ollock] slipped away from Mr M[acbean]'s to go home with us, as Wm. stayed later.

---

[1] i.e. a member of the Colonna family, a name familiar to readers of Lord Lytton's novel *Rienzi* which had first appeared in 1835 and which Miss W. had been translating in Paris (see 18 April 1844).

[2] Presumably Aeneas Macbean of the firm Macbean & Co., bankers and wine merchants on the Corso.

24 December. Had a most delicious ride to see an interesting ruin, Torre dei Schiavi, in company with Miss D[ouglasse], who has now a small carriage. This was by way of strengthening for tonight's work of which you shall hear in my next. How I wish you from my heart of hearts a merry Christmas and a happy new year, Father, and Josee and all. How very often this Christmas I long to be with you, or that you should be with us, for we are really very merry, considering that I am so far from all dear ones. Clara's letter was a Christmas treat, except that I was sorry to know she had been suffering. The notes Mme Bunsen was kind enough to send are not only delivered, but one person, the Marchesa Lorenzana has called; we were out. Ann's few lines gave me all the pleasure she intended they should, which was a great deal I am sure. Now for Christmas Eve. At 8.30 pm, we went to the Sistine; Wm., afraid of too much fatigue, and Mr P[ollock] went with us. The Pope was not there, the music very dull, the place not half lighted, and the English ladies talked so loud, I was disgusted and ashamed of them - they never seem to have the candour or charity to believe that others may be worshipping though they are not. If I were a Roman Catholic, I should be indignant at such irreverent spectators. We were all tired before it was over, and came away, but were rewarded by an unexpected pleasure. There was the most exquisite moonlight, and the beauty of St Peters and all around was charming. When we came away, the place was still, the carriages lost in the broad shadows, the very fountains seemed to play gently, though one was almost as silvery as in daylight. The scene was worth going all the way to see. We had sent our Maria to bed directly after dinner, so Sig'ra L[upienti]'s Maria waited on us, and our Maria at midnight. We gave up seeing one church to get a few hours sleep, during which time I did not sleep, but felt very ill, still resolving to brave it. At 3 we were aroused, had tea, and went with Wm. and Mr P[ollock] to Sta Maria Maggiore, a large handsome grecian church, lighted brilliantly with cut glass chandeliers, and hung with scarlet and gold. There was music going on all night, and such a crowd! the lowest peasantry, capuchins any thing but fragrant, steaming, and squeezed against some of our English nobles, all sorts in fact. In this press, we fought our way about an hour, and very successfully, though I never was more jammed in and, without the assistance of a friend of Mr P[ollock]'s, should probably have been separated from my party. At last came the procession, tapers and smarteries of all sorts preceding: first, a crucifix carried under a canopy, then the cradle of our Lord (ie the wood of the manger) in a large crystal Vase under a magnificent canopy, Acolyths, priests and a Cardinal Bishop. There is something strange, but not unpleasing, in the manner in which the Pope or officiating Cardinal appears in these ceremonial processions. He walks slowly in his stiff mitre and heavy robes, the train being borne by two priests, and while every body else has something to do, at least to carry a wax light as big as a broom handle, the Pope bends his eyes on the ground and, with joined hands, seems wrapt in meditation. We pushed into

the chapel after the procession, soon had good seats, and listened to sweet music. I was interested and would not but have seen it, yet this ceremony, like all others here, failed to combine pleasure with religion. Whenever any definite idea arose in my mind that this was a commemoration of the birth of our Saviour, there was only sadness - not the cheerful recollection of the Angels' song which makes it so delightful to me to be wakened on Christmas Eve by our vulgar street music. We came out at daybreak, such a beautiful light! Rome is a most attractive place, all the charming accidents of light and shadow touch up some ruin or some column or some church, lovely or historical or both.

Christmas Day. Minnie and I had intended to go to St Peters at 8.30 this morning, but she does not care for these sights at all, and we had all a longing to go quietly to our own church where there was a sacrament. To our great discredit as sightseers, we changed our order for the carriage into one to fetch us from church and take us a refreshing drive by the banks of the Tiber. We drank tea with Miss D[ouglasse], and wished you could have heard us making fun over spiced wine. My address may be considered as fixed till at least a week after Easter.

26 December. La Comtesse Lepel called, a pleasing English woman,[1] who enquired with interest about Anne and especially about Clara. We went to enquire about a new acquaintance, the Revd. Mr Frith, an agreeable man whom we met with his wife at Miss D[ouglasse]'s. They had asked her if she thought it would be agreeable to me that they should call. but the next evening he hurt his foot severely, so that neither he nor his wife have been out since, but he sent me Padre Ventura's[2] sermons of which we had spoken. He is better, so we may hope there will be no serious consequence from his accident. Went to St. Giovanni Laterano to see the Church and hear Vespers. A Cardinal officiated, and there was charming music. We waited more than an hour in a crowd, but had seats. This was on the 27th; I have missed the 26, but must put it in for the sake of a curious sight. We went to the church Ara coelis, itself very ancient and built on the site of a Temple of Jupiter. We had an intelligent barefooted Capuchin to show us about. There were frescoes by Pinturicchio, with that deep and tender expression of devotion, which delights me in many of these stiff old things. You will wonder when I tell you that I was interested, and my sympathy with the Italians called forth by a scene, which seems very silly in words, but to a people who live such an exterior life, who are so made up of the senses and the transient emotions they produce, I doubt if it is silly if

---

1 Frances, Countess de Lepel, was the widow of the German General Friedrich Wilhelm, Graf von Lepel (1774-1840). He had resided in Rome from 1816 until his death. She died in Paris in 1852.

2 Gioacchino Ventura (1792-1861).

employed for truth only. A little chapel was fitted up with pasteboard scenery like a theatre, not badly done, in which were placed images of all the persons and things mentioned with reference to the infancy of our Lord. In a cradle, illuminated from within, was a favorite wooden image of the infant 'saviour', reputed of such virtue that it is constantly carried about to the houses of the sick, and laid on the bed, while prayer is made for their recovery. Opposite, on the other side of the church, was a small raised stage, on which children from 3 to 10 years old were preaching! Yes, indeed, the first was a little girl hardly 4. I could scarcely understand her baby tongue, but she played her part very prettily. There were crowds of peasants and others, and, as the Italians are all (i.e. the best of them) big children, they were delighted. I spoke to several and they mixed up terms of endearment to the children with observations on what they said in the drollest way, praising the beauty and the dress of the little creatures. Then came a clever urchin of 8 or 9 who declaimed and gesticulated with the most capital mimicry of a priest. His small sermon was really very good advice, and I can readily understand these people liking to hear the doctrine of Christ from the lips of a child, when they commemorate His infancy. There were several more small orators, but we came away. Mrs Smith and party were there. Her son has arrived with his feet frost bitten after suffering terribly from weather and his own carelessness. This evening we had a small party: 2 Sig'inas, Mr and Miss Fielding, Sig'ra Jervis, Capt'n Allen and Mr P[ollock]. They were invited to hear Sig'ra Jervis sing. Having unluckily fixed the first night of the Theatre, we had some disappointments, but people seemed amused. Elena recited one of her own sonnets beautifully. We gave them what they call a Christmas cake, something like our twelfth cake[1]; after tea, Argota, a drink something like Argent wine and water, and excellent cakes. I was anxious to show off Sig'ra Jervis by way of compensation for her disappointment in Minnie leaving off singing. Minnie is delighted to escape, and I hope will soon regain her touch on the piano. She is to have lessons of Campana, the fashionable man here. He seems clever and very animated, so I hope he will be able to communicate the style and spirit of Italian music. He is not a pianist such as we hear in London. In fact, we do not hear such good music here as there, and are fastidious and seldom pleased. No doubt the best is at the theatres where we do not go.

28 December. Went for our permission to see the Vatican by torchlight, and walked into St Peters, where the decorations were still up; it looked beautiful. Mr P[ollock] brought Campana to exhibit to us.

29 December (Sunday). I spent an hour or two in quiet talk with Miss Douglass, who has been very poorly lately.

---

[1] i.e. cake for Twelfth Night.

30 December. The brightest thing in the day was your welcome letter. Continue to take care of yourself. I trust the same effectual protecting care will still keep you from sickness and sorrow this coming year. You will have thought, before you receive this, how my earnest wishes have been called forth for you all at the new year. It is useless with so uncertain a post to write for special days. I was most glad to receive a good report from Suffolk, and had been longing for news from Lady B. and her circle. All was delightful except the illness of dear Mr H[egan] for which I am very sorry. I trust Maria Ann will be permitted to keep her new treasure. But I shall never have done if I go over all that interested me, only I must say I am glad you have seen Fanny. She has a letter from me before this and so has Mr H[egan]. I must tell you a Pasquinade. If not very new, it is very applicable just now, when all the best places at ceremonies are filled by foreigners. Pasquin. 'Where are you going, Marforio, so smart with your sword and cocked hat?' Mar.: 'I am going to the ceremonies at the Sistine.' Pas: 'Why you fool! you won't get in.' Mar: 'Why not?' Pas: 'Because you are a Roman.' Mar: 'Oh! but I made myself a heretic three days ago on purpose.' Minnie and I transacted some business, called on the Countess Lepel, and went to the Palazzo Barberini to see that most touching portrait of the Cenci, and other pictures. In the evening, we had Signor Vanutelli, his wife and two daughters, Dr Grant also, who, I am happy to say, agreed with me in opinion about the V.s. It was quite an Italian evening and very pleasant. Dr G[rant] stayed quite late with us.

31 December. Minnie and I went to draw at the Vatican, found it shut (Alas!), called on Mrs Smith, whose son is going on well, though still unable to put his feet to the ground. Went for an hour to the Borghese Palace for just a glance of the treasures therein. After lunch, called on Mr Gibson and, by mistaking our way, saw some beautiful things in Wyatt's studio,[1] saw the cast for the statue of the Queen which Gibson has just taken. It looks an excellent likeness, but is not pleasing. To the Marchesa Lorenzana, then to the gorgeous church of the Gesù, where the Pope assisted at a *Te deum* for the mercies of the past year. The church was brilliantly lighted and decorated, the music was pleasing, and, during an hours waiting, I really enjoyed thinking and hearing the three organs played alternately, but my companions were tired then, and are wary of ecclesiastical ceremonies generally. It gives some idea of the grand scale of the churches here that, very often, several organs of middling size are dispersed about one, and lost among the ornaments. We had but just time to dine and dress and go to Miss D[ouglasse] where we met, among others, Mr Babington and his wife. I told him the good news about Maria Anne which interested him. There was an old Prussian Officer and his wife who

---

[1] Richard James Wyatt (1795-1850) settled in Rome in 1820.

were delighted to find any one who spoke their language, so I blundered on, but it was fatiguing to use 4 languages alternately, especially for me, who do not always find out what language is addressed to me if only I receive the ideas. I could not even send my letter on new year's day. It was such a complete holiday, the post was shut. We had a service at our church, and preferred taking a quiet walk to it over the Pincio, to seeing any more processions. Met Mr Hutchinson and walked a little way with him. Returning, we tried to get a carriage for a drive, but all were engaged. We found our table covered with cards of congratulation on the new year. Minnie and I took a walk for health in the afternoon. In the evening, we went with 2 Sign'inas Montecchi to the Academia Arcadi, where the eldest recited a pretty sonnet with much taste. She looked quite graceful and Muse-like. Many poems were recited, and some prose, on the occasion which was a commemoration of the Nativity, some good and some dull. It was an excellent Italian lesson, but evidently not much to the taste of the English. There were but 3 ladies besides ourselves, and they were Italians. Plenty of priests, monks, and gazetteers, with eyes in fine frenzy rolling, and mustaches, in equal energy, rolled into twists.

3 January. Took Miss Smith to the Villa Ludovisi[1] and hoped to have met Miss Douglass, but the weather became rainy, and she sent a young man named W. There were some very fine frescoes, and a few good statues. From the casino, there would have been a lovely view, if it had been clear. I hope we shall go there again. Sign'ra Lupienti in the evening. I have been purchasing 4 wax torches, each consisting of 4 common sized candles stuck together, and nearly as tall as myself, to light up the statues in the Vatican.

4 January. We had invited to take coffee with us and proceed to the Vatican M., Mme., and Mlle Coulon and Dr Trayer,[2] a pleasing young Irishman friend of Dr Pollock, who came also to bring him. We had met him both at Mr Smith's and Miss D[ouglasse]'s. At the Vatican, we met Mr Harley and their friends, and, after some delay, arrived the Revd. Mr Swinny[3] and his wife, friends of Wm.'s. The wax tapers are cut into lengths of about 2 feet, and put into a huge reflector mounted on a pole, so as to give the light of 16 wicks reflected from one point. You may guess how this, held above a statue while all around is dark, brings out every muscle, and what broad black shadows it casts. Some groups gain amazingly by it, especially the more complicated, for example the Laocoon - the distinct grand effect of the broad shadows disentangles it (so to say). Really it is so very

---

[1] Destroyed later in the century as a result of urban development. The Via Veneto passes through part of the erstwhile park.
[2] James John Trayer, M.B. of the University of Dublin (1839).
[3] Rev. H.H.Swinny, Vicar of St Giles, Cambridge.

expressive, it is quite uncomfortable to look at it. I think the Apollo loses, except that in it, as in all, by moving the light you can appreciate beauties which are lost in daylight. After all, to choose between the two, I had much rather see the statues by the sun, yet the effect of torchlight is so striking and beautiful in its own way, that I would willingly go again, if it were not such an expensive affair, and then I should remember what I forgot last night, that we have to cross a court in the open air, and not catch cold for want of thick shoes.

4 January. Drove to St Pauls without the walls, a church being rebuilt on the ruins of a very magnificent structure lately burnt.[1] The present is very handsome, and the remains curious. It is built, so they say, over the tomb of St Paul. We went on across a most pestilential looking tract, where the dreariness was increased by the want of habitations and the wild look of the goatherds and workmen on the road, which, by the bye, is in a terrible state. It was also rather too late - our coachman had not been punctual. Our next pilgrimage struck my imagination forcibly. It was to three small churches, one of which is built upon the spot where St Paul was beheaded, and within which spring 3 fountains from the places where his head rebounded from the ground. It is quite true! for I tasted the water which is of three different degrees of warmth, and I never thought of questioning the fact on the spot. Went in the evening to Miss D[ouglasse] expecting to have a frolic with children, instead of which there was [a] party of uninteresting people, but I had a little talk with her.

5 January. Sunday. Miss D[ouglasse] joined us at church to partake of the Lord's Supper, a privilege she can rarely enjoy. I was more disturbed than was at all reasonable at the idea how very short must be our christian intercourse here below, even if it is permitted while I am in this country. Her life seems to hang upon a thread, though she is full of animation.

6 January. Went at 8.30 to the church of the Propaganda, where an Epiphany mass is performed in 43 languages. There were 5 going on at once while we were there, of which we heard the Armenian and Maronite, but we soon came away. On the road to our own church, we looked in at the Greek, but as the great ceremony had not begun then, we visited it on our return. The Bishop is a splendid specimen of mankind and, in his rich dress, looked like an eastern monarch. The ceremonies are performed with more gesticulation than the Roman. I believe, however, this was only a grecian branch of the Roman Church. There was good singing by fine sonorous voices in Greek. Besides processions, bowings, incense, elevation of the Host, there was a ceremony of immersing a cross three times in a huge silver vase, from which water was afterwards taken in a smaller

---

[1] Much of the church had been destroyed by a fire on the night of 15 July 1823.

vessel, that the Bishop might dip a branch of Hyssop (Anglica box) in it, and sprinkle the people as he went round. Wm. was tired, but I victimised Minnie by making her work her way with me through a crowd, till we were close to the rails. There was a profusion of various coloured drapery with gold and silver tissue tastefully disposed about the church, and the ecclesiastical dresses were very elegant. Not content with this, in the afternoon, Minnie and I drove to the other end of the town, to see the deposition of the cradle, which has been carried about since Christmas, in the church Ara Coelis. When we arrived at the 124 steps leading to it, we were so afraid of the crowd of peasants and mob, that we went up the Capitol, and in at the east end. There we saw the same grotto we had seen before, differently arranged: the Madonna was nursing the infant Saviour, and the kings of the east were bringing presents. We might also have had good seats to hear a small orator, but finding we might have to wait two hours for the procession, we took fright at the thought of coming out in the dusk in such a throng, not knowing very well our way home, so we came away, to Minnie's delight, for she hates these ceremonies. We sauntered among the ruins, and sat awhile in the Coliseum. On our return, the crowd had so thickened that it was appalling to contemplate getting down the steps. However, we pushed our way through, and, following a carriage, got into a clear space, and safely home. The Coulons and Swinnys had called in my absence; they are both very *comme il faut* people. I have not seen any other quality in them at present.

7 January. After drawing at the Vatican, we spent an hour at the Borghese, then made calls etc. Were sorry to find Mr F[rith] still unable to put his foot to the ground. The evening with Mrs Smith. Her son is going on well towards recovery, but cannot use his feet.

8 January. I am not quite satisfied with Minnie's state of health, and afraid she should relapse into the sluggish constitution she had when she first came to us, now she has not horse exercise to shake her into activity, so I have determined to give up some of our time for good health, and we began this bright frosty morning by an hour's walk on the Pincio soon after breakfast, instead of the Vatican, which we should have preferred. Saw half the Villa Albani, which contains many charming things. We must try and go several times; it is impossible to enjoy fine pictures and statues at a glance. We were so dreadfully cold after two hours, that we almost trotted all the way home. Spent the evening with Miss D[ouglasse]. Dr G[rant] was there, but would not stay. Minnie is, at this moment, delighting her mistress by exhibiting, in accompaniment, a spirit and talent which never appeared in her singing.

9 January. After two lessons we went for our walk. Then, notwithstanding the rain, drove to St Andrea to hear Padre Ventura. We were able to follow

his clear enunciation, which was quite an Italian lesson. He is really eloquent, and argues so cleverly against heretics that we all agree that, in the strength of our own reasoning powers merely, we should be afraid to trust ourselves within his influence, but, having the liberty of prayer and our Bibles, we are not afraid to gather what is good from him, trusting we shall be kept from evil. His application of the types of the new Testament to Christ is very interesting and instructive, and I must say the prominent idea throughout the discourse was to point to Christ as the object of adoration, and to draw us away, not only from the external world, but from ourselves in devotedness to Him, who deigned to appear as an infant for our sakes. He reminded me of the Bishop of Calcutta in his whimsical minuteness of reproof. He scolded the young men for caressing their beards instead of bowing to the altar, and the ladies for their 'balloon' gowns which prevented their kneeling. His argument for a reverential deportment from Christ's having sanctified the body, also to the service of God when he clothed Himself in flesh, was well stated. Some of the typical meanings given by the Fathers to the history of the Magi are sufficiently fanciful, ex gr. that they were 3 to represent all mankind, who descended from the 3 sons of Noah. With abundance of opprobrious epithets, he accused Calvin of denying the divinity of our Saviour, but added that he had been artful enough to conceal his unbelief in his writings - query, where did they learn the fact? When we returned to dinner, I was nearly overwhelmed by a multiplicity of ideas and a cold in my head. There was Fanny's letter awaiting us with mingled tidings. For all that concerns you, I have but to be grateful. I am much concerned to hear of her accident, and feel how far we are because it is of no use to write to amuse her on her sofa, hoping that, by the time we hear of the disaster, she has recovered. We all, but especially W[illiam], long for further accounts of Mr P. I have written a long note to Mons'gre Alberghini in my very civilest Italian. We were quiet last night trying new music and reading Burgess.

10 January. A wet day, but being determined to hear Padre Ventura again, we ordered a close carriage for that and the evening. The sermon was principally upon humility and such as any christian might profit by, more eloquent, less argumentative, than the last. We brought the Revd Mr Swinny home with us. Drank tea with Miss D[ouglasse] to celebrate Mr P[ollock]'s birthday. Cold and indigestion disordered me and made me very sick, but I soon recovered.

11 January. I am as well as before, and have taken Minnie for her walk. Padre Ventura again, Sig'ra Lupienti in the evening.

12 January. Sunday. Being a fine morning, we were taken in like other folks and waited an hour after morning service, before we could get a

chance carriage in the rush etc. The coachman had the assurance to ask a scudo for driving a quarter of a mile.

13 January. First day of our carriage. We called on Mrs S. who is an elegant young woman, then on the Hanoverian Minister, a brisk little man in a picturesque puce velort [velours?] tunic, who came into the room with hop, skip and jump.[1] It seemed I was in imminent danger of a most affectionate salutation till I announced that I was not related to Sir J. Acland. The mention of Mme de B[unsen] (whose note I had sent) revived his courtesy after the disappointment - (he had called). I hope he will present Minnie and me to the Pope, as soon as there are ladies enough desirous of the presentation to make a party. Wm. must find another introducer, for Ambassadors cannot present gentlemen without some uniform. We had a little drive, and then went to get money at Torlonia's, and to hear something about two balls to which we have invitations. One is quite as much as any of us have the best wish to see, and, I believe, even that is more to satisfy our friends in England that we see all sorts of sights, than for any pleasure we expect equivalent to the annoyance in going and coming and risk of severe cold. P. Ventura again. Then your delightful letter with Fanny's addition. We were so concerned about her that we made a great effort and wrote a joint letter to her in the evening. You will perceive I had all your letters, but I fear mine to Fanny was lost. I am so glad you went to her. The weather has been dreadfully severe in the north of Italy. We have a great deal of heavy rain, and I find the sudden change to a warm wind disorders me. Minnie's circulation, instead of being quickened by the warmth, is more languid, and she requires as much care as when she first came to us. We do not, however, any of us, find what people call the depressing influence of Rome, but are in capital spirits, especially when we have such charming letters. I heard of dear Miss Mortons through Mrs Smith. On Saturday, her son can set his feet upon the ground.

14 January. We have been for the last time at present to draw at the Vatican. They are so tiresome about the permission, we are quite disgusted, so we shall begin the Borghese, which is very near. Best love to Father and Josiah. Like Regent Street loungers, we have been driving about for concerts, and caps and shoes and articles of vertù. We have been to the best places in Rome for mosaics and pietra dura, like your little white and green ring, only larger, and fine subjects, the best of them, a small brooch 15£.

---

1 August Kestner (1777-1853), the Hanoverian minister in Rome was a long-time resident of the city. Goethe had been much attracted to his mother, Charlotte Buff, and the relationship between her, her fiancé and husband-to-be J.C. Kestner, and Goethe, was the central inspiration for Goethe's novel *The Sorrows of Young Werther*. The family letters concerning the relationship were only published in the 1850s.

Then we saw cameos of which there is great variety. Portraits are beautifully executed in cameo.

15 January. Drove early to the house of the late Cardinal Grimaldi (or some such name), thinking to see the body lying in state, but it was already removed to the church St. Salvatore, where mass was celebrated for him by a brother cardinal. The church was draped all over with black and gold. In the centre, upon a solid looking structure a little raised towards the altar, but otherwise nearly a cube of 10 feet, was the coffin, covered with gold cloth, armorial emblazonments, and the scarlet hat. All around and about the choir flamed yellow wax torches such as I have before described. The dresses of the principal persons were black and gold. Mournful music from voices only, sweet and solemn. Perhaps the ceremony was the more solemn for the pomp, certainly it was for the strange and awful contrast of the words 'May he sleep in peace thro' Christ our Lord' (of course in Latin). It was a showery day, and we went to the Capitol to see the statues in the museum. There are multitudes of beautiful and interesting things. As to the Gladiator, I hold to Byron's idea before all criticisms.[1] If the sculptor had not the same, the marble grew into such expression in spite of him. It is the only instance in which I have entirely followed the leading of another mind in interpreting these poems in stone. On returning, I went in the carriage and begged lunch of Miss D[ouglasse] that I might have time to see her and also to take a turn with Wm. and Minnie on the Pincio. In honesty, I am obliged to confess that these sudden and extreme changes of temperature give me cold which shows itself principally in pain in my side and difficulty of breathing. This morning (16th) I am rejoicing that we did not go to Torlonia's last night, for I am better, and would certainly have been worse for going. It is the most dangerous place in Rome, a dozen valets could not prevent our having to stand at least a quarter of an hour on the cold stones. Visited the tomb of the Scipios, a number of small chambers or rather passages, with niches and receptacles of various sizes all along, hollowed out of the living rock. We had each a wax candle and followed our guide in the dark cavern, in which a beautiful marble sarcophagus and bust were found (now in the Vatican). Many inscriptions remain. I could have poked about there a long while for my entertainment, but was afraid of being chilled, and therefore came away soon. Then we went to a columbarium, a subterranean chamber about 10 ft. square, lofty, with steep ancient stairs of brick, and the centre filled by a solid mass reaching to the roof in which, as well as round the walls, are rows of small hollows, the entrance this shape ⌂ reminding me in miniature of the prints of the sepulchres in the rocks of Idumaea. These hollows contain each one or more urns of terracotta imbedded in the brickwork, having a cover, and enclosing the ashes remaining from the burnt bodies. Sometimes there are

---

[1] See Byron, *Childe Harold's Pilgrimage*, Canto IV, verse 140.

small marble cippi, prettily sculptured busts, and one large crystal vase, of which a facsimile in glass is placed in the tomb, and the real vase preserved in the Vatican. There is a marble coffin containing the greater part of a skeleton. There is also a piece of mosaic work ornamented with shells. The roof is painted. One lamp remains suspended from it, and there are chains for several. The 2nd Columbarium we saw is twice as big as the first, better preserved, light, and easier to examine, but similar in its contents. It was an afternoon in Ancient Rome. We lingered among the arches returning and I was very much interested. Tell Josiah there was one very impertinent inscription in praise of a buffoon in the court of Augustus who was the first to mock lawyers. Minnie and I went to keep Miss D[ouglasse] company while her cousin went out.

17 January. The blessing of animals at St Antonio. As they came at their master's pleasure all day long, we did not stay to see more than one sorry Rozinante in a peasant's cart who, no doubt, was very glad of the breathing time, while a priest pronounced a prayer over it, and sprinkled its lean ribs with holy water. We then went into the church Sta. Prassede, who is said to have collected the blood of the martyrs slain on this hill in a well, in the middle of the church. The Sacristan told us that formerly the well was open, but so many persons let down into it rings attached to threads, that they might draw them up tinged with the blood of the martyrs, that one of the Popes was afraid all the blood would be used up, and he closed it. The sponge she used is shown as a relic with a pink colouring upon it. There is a fragment of the small column to which our Saviour was tied to be scourged. Wm. only was admitted into the Chapel; we inferior womenkind were content to peep through a grating. There is a picture of the flagellation by Giulio Romano, which does not seem to me to deserve its fame. S. Martino is rich in beautiful marbles and singular fresco landscapes by G. Poussin. The subterranean church beneath it is part of the baths of Trajan, solid brickwork interesting from its antiquity, and as having been the scene of the first general Council after Constantine. Afterwards, we had a short drive into the ever striking campagna, which I enjoyed, though Minnie complains I always come home silent after those drives.

18 January. I believe I must give up seeing all cold churches and subterraneans, for the sudden changes of temperature united to the bilious effect of Rome, disorder me too much, and it seems that neither air nor diet singly are enough. A great many people are complaining. Minnie looks better today. We went to a grand ceremony in St Peter's today. The Pope was carried in procession on a chair supported by 12 bearers, huge fans carried on each side of him, and preceded and followed by all the gay people from Cardinals down to guards. We were very fortunate, entering the west door at the very moment the Pope was placed in his chair there. We followed him up the middle aisle. Unluckily we had not known it was

necessary to wear veils in the reserved seats, so we were repulsed by the Swiss, but Wm and Minnie found a capital place and seats under the shadow of Sta. Veronica close by the enclosure. I, who was not strong enough to bear the risk of standing, retired behind a pillar, took off my bonnet, fastened my black veil round my head and, presenting myself again at the entrance, was admitted to a very comfortable seat. The Pope's chair was there. We had beautiful music. To sit under that dome, magnificent in its proportions, with all around beaming with light and glowing with colour, and add to this the simultaneous movement, all falling on their knees at once, is very fine. Why is it that we cannot unreservedly dedicate to God's service the best of his temporal gifts? Wherever man professes to do so, he does, in fact, seek his own glory in them, or else surely we might call on the silver and the gold and marbles to help us express our gratitude to Him who made our senses the inlets of pleasure from His material creation. We had tried to take Miss Smith with us, but she was out. Afterwards, we walked on the Pincio, then lunched, then drove into the campagna to see the tomb of the Empress Helena. It was like a lovely May day, and we were resolved to employ it for health, so we made the most of our sleek greys and very exquisite coachman with his beard 'a la Charles the 1st'. The campagna, or rather the mountains, were charming. We returned only at five, and were too prudent to accept Miss D[ouglasse]'s invitation to spend the evening with them. My treat awaited me, Anne's letter with good news of you.

19 January. Sunday. 20 January. Today we heard of a ceremony which we were all desirous of witnessing. We ordered the carriage at 11 and went. I will give you an accurate narrative while it is fresh in my mind. There was a commemoration of the miraculous and sudden conversion of Alfonso Ratisbon a year back.[1] In the church in which the vision appeared to him, we had been told there would be a narrative of some subsequent miracles. For the first hour, there was a general communion Mass going on and very sweet music of instruments and voices. Then a preacher began with the 4th verse of the 8th Psalm 'What is man, that thou art mindful of him and the son of Man that thou visited him?', quoted many verses in other Psalms and elsewhere, describing the majesty of God who holdeth the waters in the hollow of his hand. Then his argument ran thus: man must be of importance or such a being would not have become incarnate for his sake. God the Father all Majesty and terror, Christ all tenderness and pity - Christ's exceeding love in saving those who did not seek him. He was not willing that man should perish, snatched them from destruction by sovereign grace - instance, St Stephen, St Paul, St Augustine, the

---

[1] Alphonse Ratisbonne, the ninth child of an eminent Jewish family living in Strasburg. Unforgiving of his elder brother Théodore who had converted to Catholicism in 1827, he himself was converted after a vision of the Virgin Mary in the Church of St Andrea delle Fratte on 20 January 1842.

Magdalene, of sudden and miraculous conversion. 'Why need I go so far for examples - here in our sacred city, under your very eyes, in this Church, as it were at this hour, at that very altar, the same abundant grace was shown. "Where sin did abound, grace did much more abound" - Alfonso Ratisbon, a Jew, docile and amiable in youth, well educated, rich, happy in his family and affianced bride, became immersed in the pleasures of the world, adopted infidel notions, and mocked at religion. He passed through the metropolis of Christianity on his way to Constantinople, not intending to remain, but was persuaded to do so. His mind was uneasy, but he rejected serious thoughts. Some one (I had heard before, one of the society of the immaculate heart of Mary at Paris) entreated him to wear a little copper image of the Virgin round his neck. He consented. Being docile thus to the first inspirations of grace, he was led to enter this Church, and there, at that altar, appeared to him the Mother of God, resplendant in glory. When he recovered from his astonishment, and could raise his dazzled eyes, he went to the high altar, called for a priest, requested baptism, professed himself most happy, and soon after renounced all his worldly prospects for the "melancholy solitude of a cloister," became a Jesuit. By whom was this effected?' - Then followed descriptions of the Virgin in which the Canticles and that part of the revelation to St John, the woman with the moon under her feet, were applied to Mary, and, supposing the application just, the scripture quotations were very beautifully applied. She is 'Omnipotent Virgin', 'source of grace' - then followed a glowing description of her personal beauties and her excellences, and a prayer that the beneficent Goddess would 'hear supplications and deliver sinners from their corruption.' We just returned to lunch, and then drove to the Capitol and spent an hour and half in the museum. We are going to spend the evening with Miss Douglass.

21 January. Set out early in the morning, in the pouring rain again, to see two lambs blessed at St Agnes' shrine from whose wool is made the consecrated Pallium sent by the Pope to the Archbishops.[1] The Church is very ancient and partly underground. There was tolerable music, but very secular - it was a thorough Roman scene. At one time, on the wet marble pavement strewn with box, knelt many of the common people, women with their white cloths on their heads, shaggy looking men with the large Roman cloaks wrapped round them, soldiers with their plumed caps held over one knee, and, in the middle, two large shepherd dogs stretched at their ease among the leaves. There was only a small sprinkling of English fashionables, who, like ourselves, had been ignorant that this year it was

---

[1] Pallia are circular bands made from the wool of the two lambs that are blessed each year in the Church of S. Giovanni in Laterano on the feast of St Agnes. The new pallia are blessed by the Pope in the crypt of St Peter's at vespers on June 28, the vigil of the feast of St Peter and Paul. They are then conferred on the newly appointed metropolitans on the feast day itself.

necessary to have tickets to get into the gallery. I went to sit on the steps of an altar in a side chapel where was a peasant with two young children. I suppose I won her heart by tapping the cheek of one as she made way for me, for she was quite concerned that people of our consequence! should not be in the gallery, and offered to go to her own house in the pouring rain to fetch chairs for us. This is really only one specimen among many of the good nature of the Italians. They are easily won by a smile. We had an opportunity of returning her kindness for she lost her apron and William took the trouble of finding it out for her, at which condescension she was utterly astonished. Presently, there were two snow white lambs, with wreaths of flowers on their heads and little red bows on their fleeces, brought in procession, each on a crimson cushion, placed on the altar where they were incensed and sprinkled and blest. The little animals had been well tutored, for they were very quiet, only raising their meek heads - I remembered Barham Slades and the time when the procession of such a pretty pair would have filled up my notions of happiness. After lunch, we called on Sig'ra Vanutelli and went on to the capitol to see the ancient she-wolf and her nurselings, with other interesting things, and pictures. I must leave the next day to the next letter and dispatch this on the 23rd.

I must go back to the 22nd and the Etruscan Museum where we took Mrs, Miss, and Mr Smith. It was extremely entertaining - not only their early rude sculptures in which their equal and unborrowed excellence were amusing, but the graceful forms of vases, cups etc. and, above all, the many articles illustrating their ordinary life - a chariot, iron dogs for supporting fuels, lamps with pretty extinguishers, innumerable coloured glass bottles, cast iron bedstead or bier, pincers, spoons, a pair of clogs!, metal runs with wood inside, necklaces, jewelry, and yet, now and then, amidst all these indications of a luxurious and elegant people, clumsy or grotesque forms, like savages. Really one sees these things for the 1st time to become sensible how much knowledge and thought is requisite to the full appreciation of them. I thought of Father and how he would have expatiated on these relics of remote ages. We then took our walk on the Pincio. Monsignor Luciani called, offered us a window for the Carnival, and proposed to go in our carriage to Torlonia's. Sig'ra Lupienti in the evening.

23 January. Took Sig'ra Vanutelli to see the pictures at the Capitol, some of which are good, Sta. Petronilla and a Judith by Guido. We returned for some business, and drove to the Borghese Villa. By the bye, we had been put into a wonderful bustle by information that a nun was to take the veil early that morning. We made all our arrangements, and were on the point of starting, when we learnt that it was a mistake.

24 January. Such a day's work for a person forbidden to fatigue herself! It would be too long to tell you all the reasons why it would have been vexatious to have omitted anything, and, in fact, I was very careful. Directly after breakfast, we took Miss Smith and Mr and Mrs Swinny to Villa Albani. It was a delicious morning, and we enjoyed both the sculpture and the mountains. I have already mentioned this Villa. We had but just time to lunch and dress for a morning concert. The music was almost all Choral, well selected, and pretty well performed. There was a charming sacred chorus, without accompaniment, by Bach. The room was crowded to suffocation, and it was so long before we could get out, that we were just in time for dinner, during which came Mons'gre Luciani to propose taking us in the evening to be introduced to the Marchesa Casuti. We were already engaged to Miss Douglass, but promised to take that on our way, so I panted up three stories on the Ill[ustrissi]mo's arm; I cannot tell you how excessively polite he was. The old lady received us very courteously. She had a levy of gentlemen around her, and a Contessa something or other went in [in] the same impromptu way, as we came out. At Miss D[ouglasse]'s we met the Revd. Lawrenson [Hutchinson?], his wife, Dr Trayer, and various other gentlemen and ladies. We were left the last. Miss D[ouglasse], Wm, and Minnie became quite frisky and would have a supper at which Mr P[ollock], Mr Warner, the little dog and I did our best to look grave. Minnie received a letter from Mrs H[egan].

25 January. 1st day of the Carnival. We began by going to the Capitol, to see the senator of Rome receive the humble petition of a deputation from the Jews, to be allowed to live another year in Rome. Formerly, there were humiliating ceremonies and the presentations of a purse to buy themselves off from running in the Corso before the horse race. Now, there is only the semblance of a prostration, and, as far as I could make out, neither request nor answer conveyed anything degrading. Yet I felt indignant at their being thus pointed out as creatures only tolerated among mankind. The senator goes in state along the Corso to begin the Carnival. There are carriages and troops and flags, very much like a Lord Mayor's show, but not such beautiful horses. Now, if you could have peeped at your ancient daughter and grave Wm., by far the most active of the party in the tom-foolery which ensued, how you would have stared! We had Miss Smith with us and her brother on the coach-box. We put on our old cloaks and worst bonnets and had wire masks to protect our faces. We took one basket full of mock comfits made of soft chalk, which powder people all over, and another of good bon-bons, only three nosegays, too few, but we soon had a lap full of those thrown at us. The Corso is a mile long, straight, not wider than for three carriages. Every window was crowded with heads, and many houses decorated. In every vacant space were erected benches, a double row of carriages passing slowly, sometimes stopped, sometimes backing (they take care not to be too near each other), the streets of course thronged

with foot passengers, but not many masks to day. Almost our first salutation, as we arrived on the scene of action, was a shovel full of chalk comfits from a set of great lubberly Englishmen dressed like women. This wholesale way is stupid and disagreeable. We went on returning the bad comfits, and exchanging nosegays with every body we knew, and a good many we did not know except by sight. We each grinned and flung nosegays at each other. A mask ran beside the carriage, gibbering and cutting capers, and snatched a nosegay out of Miss Smith's hand, giving her two in exchange. The one jumped up behind, and, with more pathetic gesticulations, gave Minnie a capital bon-bon, and Miss Smith and I each a nosegay. We had a shrewd guess who both were. We had a capital opportunity of pelting Mr W[arner] while the carriage was stationary. We first whitened him, and then consoled the poor young man by nosegays. Of course, he carefully preserved those from the young ladies. It was all wonderfully great absurdity, but I did not remember to be cynical, which all arises from what Fanny calls my bump of fun and an irresistible sympathy with merriment, which is not vicious or coarse. However, I was glad when we were turned off at the signal of cannon firing, and went to the Marchese's to see the race, which is extremely stupid. The animals, without riders, all bedizened with colours and flapping pieces of tin, run like chased dogs, and the last was so frightened with the shouts to urge him, that he ran from side to side; there were 11. We saw the whole length of the Corso which was a curious scene. As soon as this was over, about 5, we hurried across the Corso home, quite tired and glad of a quiet evening.

26 January. Sunday. 27 January. We have two more windows offered us, so we are glad not to have incurred the expence of hiring one: one by the Rev. Mr F[rith] and another (which we shall accept because it is opposite the starting place for the race) by the Comtesse Lepel. Instead of the Corso, we saw a pleasing Madonna by Sasso Ferrata in Sta. Sabina, a fine view of St Peters and the Tiber from a garden, several ruins among which we attempted to see the ruins of the Temple of Minerva Medica, but no *custode* is to be found this carnival time. Returning, we stopped a little while to look at the Masks. It was a very gay day, a carriageful threw confetti to us, but we did not recognize anyone. Sig'ra Vanutelli came with her son and daughters, one of whom looked very pretty in the costume of Palestrina. They sat with us while we dined, to see the Corso from our windows. About the time we usually conclude our day, we dressed to go to Torlonia's. Sig'ra Lupienti came in to admire us. Perhaps you may choose to have a peep too. Minnie's dress was a very clear white Organdi with two rows of delicate crewel work, orange and red, with ribbons to match, over a glossy white petticoat, a garland of flowers, white shoes and gloves. I could not so far depart from myself as to adopt a turban, bare neck, or short sleeves, but by a light cap, scarf and white gloves kept near enough to the rest of the old folks not to be remarkable. My gown was purplish brownish

greenish. We all think it very rich - I hope you will see. Wm. always looks himself without any pretension to elegance; he is unaffected and always a gentleman. He was a most attentive and useful beau to us. Monsig're Luciani overwhelmed us with politeness. He wished to have found partners for Minnie, but she was determined not to dance, and I did not urge it, because her nose had bled just before, and I feared renewing that trouble. The Polka was a familiar romp. I wonder that any man of delicacy can like a woman dear to him to engage in it. I believe there was nothing remarkable to those accustomed to the dance, but to my eyes it was strange to see one lady measure her length on the floor, another just able to save herself from falling on her partner's neck by considerably deranging the set of his shirt. I heard of two tall men who knocked noses! over the heads of their respective short ladies. There were splendid dresses and jewels, which amused Wm. and Minnie. For me, having no taste for these, my only gain was talking a good deal of Italian. Supper was brought in to several rooms, ready placed on many tables. There was then a general scramble. Ices and various refreshments had been handed about all the evening, but, among 1500 people, you may suppose there was no great abundance. While the supper tables were removed, there was a little music; gambling was going on in a separate room. We arrived at home about 4.30, but the dance was kept up till day break. You may guess it was nearly midday when we breakfasted on the 28th, and rainy, so we had the close carriage and made calls, and, as it cleared up afterwards and masks began to appear, we went through a part of the Corso to the Comtesse Lepel to see the horses start. It was a capital place. I cannot account for the little animals' eagerness to start. One leaped the rope flinging his groom to some distance, and they were obliged to let the rest go before the signal. The first day, a poor woman who lives on our ground floor, and has a very fine cat which we admired, brought Tom out in her arms to meet us as the first Mask in a scarlet baby's hood and petticoat. There was a very good monkey led by a smart footman who played diverting antics, and a lame beggar with orange peel eyes who was wonderfully agile in hopping about on the carriages. All the residents in Rome say that the carnival has gone down greatly since foreigners have brought in the custom of throwing disagreeable things. The Romans like to dress smartly and do not like to have their smart things spoiled. We spent the evening with Miss D[ouglasse] who was alone.

29 January. We were to have gone to the Catacombs of Sta. Agnese but Fra Marchi sent word that the weather was too uncertain and my gay young folks were bent upon the carnival again. We took one of the Vanutelli with us. It was much gayer than before. We were three quarters of an hour going an eighth of a mile before we entered the Corso, and in two hours had not time to go quite up and down. However, we kept up a brisk fire of comfits and nosegays. I am somewhat tired of the amusement to tell you the truth, but Minnie likes it better than at first. There were several advocates, very

comical, who made orations in costume, a brigand presented a musket at us for which we pelted him with nosegays, harlequins, clowns, sailors, men in women's dress driving ladies with fine black moustaches - in short, all manner of extravagances. Minnie and I went to see the race more that we might not undervalue the Marchesa's civility than for any other reason. Wm. took a seat in the street to see the arrival of the horses.

30 January. After taking our leave of Sig'r Garafalino, we went out and were advised by Miss D[ouglasse] to see a picture by an Englishman Latilla[1] which is going tomorrow to be exhibited at the British Artists in London. It is Abraham sending away Hagar and Ishmael. Miss D[ouglasse] talks of going in the Corso to take some children. We have bought some fresh flowers to throw to her. Elena is going with us masked. There was an immense concourse of carriages. The soldiers compelled them to make a very long circuit, so that some never got into the Corso at all. We went up once, had the satisfaction of pelting Gen'l Ramsay, Lady Belcher, Mrs Hayward and Capt. Allen, but were too far off our other friends. P[ollock] came across the Piazza de Spagna during a stoppage and exchanged gifts for Miss D[ouglasse]. To show you what a saturnalia it is and how capable the Italians are of enjoying such a thing without abusing it, a chimney sweep, i.e. so dressed but one of the lower class, came upon our carriage opening his mouth for a comfit which I threw into it. He was not at all rude, but went away good humoured when we told him that was enough. A punchinello, also one of the poor, begged a nosegay etc. When he had it, put it to his heart with the accustomed airs and graces. They frolic among one another with the utmost good nature. Whatever evils there may be concealed, there is nothing worse than childishness on the surface. On our return, we had a room full and the windows open while we dined, and Elena with us, after which Wm. took her home, and we had just time to take off our boots before the carriage returned to take us to Mrs Smiths. Wm. went to Mr Pollock and with him to a place where the Masks meet. It is a theatre and ladies go into the boxes to see them. I have no doubt it is amusing as a national custom.

31 January. A wet day. We could only go to the concert which was very pleasant, but I think an audience in London would have thought it great impertinence to have several of the things repeated from the last concert. The excuse was that it was impossible to persuade the singers to practice in Carnival time. The Contessa Lepel sat next to us and during the concert told me that a very pleasing looking woman who spoke french had asked her if I was I. She was Mme Vollard with whom I had exchanged sundry cards without once seeing her. In the evening I felt the effects of the bustle

---

[1] Eugenio Latilla (c.1800-c.1859) was a member of the Society of British Artists from 1838 to 1851. He had an Italian father and an English mother.

and the bad air, but all our very unwholesome engagements are over now, so I hope to be better in a few days. In the concert, we had another of Bach's fugues, voices only, a very interesting novelty to me. Sig'ra Montecchia is coming to read with us once a week.

1 February. Went to see Canova's monuments in the Church Sti. Apostoli, then to S. Gio. Laterano where, among other things, we saw a sculpture of the dead Christ and Mary, very interesting, though by Bernini whom I generally dislike, two Giottos with their quaint pathos, and a beautiful cloister. Then to Sta. Bibiana to see her statue which is pleasing, but I did not stay long to admire it for the little neglected Church is cold.

2 February. Sunday being the day of the sacrament and I not very strong, I only went once to church. Wm. and Minnie left me with Miss D[ouglasse]. As they came out, a lady and gentleman asked her if it was not Miss W. who was with them in the morning. They were the Revd Mr Connor[1] and his wife whom I should like extremely to see, but neither party had the wits to give an address so I must hunt them out.

3 February. Felt very poorly with a strong suspicion that it arose from too much medicine and the Sirocco - in which I was glad to be justified by feeling better for my lunch and for a drive in the Corso in a cold tramontana. The Carnival was dullish. There were more of the common people, but few good costumes, and the carriages were too much dispersed. Miss Smith went with us. In the evening Monsig'r Luciani. Minnie has a letter from Mrs H[egan] including one for Sir Wm. Ross which we left with a card. I hope Mrs H[egan] has one from me by this time. I am pining for a letter, but, remembering my own counsels to you, I wait without forebodings. Very likely the roads are blocked up or, during the Carnival, the letters are not regularly delivered. Tell Fanny the new Papal treasurer is Monsig'r Antonelli. I hope she will have written before this to tell me she has recovered. We have tried in vain to find Vittorio Durante. Our Maria has just introduced her brother, a fine boy of 13. I constantly mention Miss D[ouglasse] but I have left you to guess that she is a very charming person and we have all become quite fond of her.

4 February. We conclude the Carnival by the Moccoli[2] tonight - right glad am I to have done. Mr S[mith] goes with us. I do hope I shall not proceed far in this sheet without having to acknowledge a letter from you. Went to the Church Sta. Maria degli Angeli but, in the form of a Greek cross, the grandeur of its proportions and its general appearance pleased me

---

1 Rev. James Connor, c.1792-1864, Rector of Knossington, Leics.
2 Lighted tapers - the fun consisted in everyone trying to extinguish the tapers of others.

extremely. We were turned out at noon before we had time to see the pictures, so we wandered round the ruins of the baths of Dioclesian on part of which this Church is built, basked in the sun, and ate the lunch we had brought with us. Then went to the curious ancient Basilica St Lorenzo. After a long examination of it by Minnie and Wm., we returned to Sta. Maria and saw the remainder. I was rather afraid of the bustle of the evening and therefore proposed that Mr P[ollock] should take my place and go with Minnie and Wm. and Mr Smith while I stayed with Miss D[ouglasse]. They had much difficulty in getting at all into the Corso to see the fun, which consisted in its being illuminated, not only from windows, but by almost every person in the Carriages carrying a wax taper, and the further amusement that people endeavour to snatch away or put out each other's tapers and then yell at them for being without Moccoli. They were soon glad to be out of the fray, looked at it for a little while from the Marchesa's, and came to fetch me who meanwhile had had a very interesting conversation with Miss D[ouglasse]. Mrs Craigie and her two daughters came in, a specimen of what delicate people can do on a journey. They had left Naples 5 days before to be here at the Carnival, were detained on the road in their carriage 6 hours of one night, arrived at noon, could not get lodging, jumped into a hack carriage, drove about the Corso, saw the race, and the Moccoli, then engaged beds and a dinner, and came with battered bonnets and merry faces to call on Miss D[ouglasse]. We stayed to tea with her alone.

5 February. Ash Wednesday. Went to the service of our own church. Drove to the baths [of] Caracalla. We had just read about this fine ruin in Burgess. The size alone of these majestic ancient buildings is a new idea to me. I feel that my eye becoming accustomed to it, my enjoyment is increased, and fear that most of our public buildings will seem like pretty toys to me. Moreover, I have now a great respect for mosaics, which, in a small specimen, I always despised. Restoring in imagination the pavement, of which large pieces remain, and the vaulted rooms, I fully believe no other materials could be at once so grand and so durable. I sat upon a wheelbarrow in the sun musing, while Wm. mounted the walls and Minnie gathered sweet violets. It was very enjoyable - the worst was that I could not be in such good company as in the Coliseum or the Forum. I was obliged to take refuge among the Roman populace from the shades of the detestable Caracalla and his satellites. It was an Italian day. I not only wished for you but indulged myself in saying so which I only do now and then for fear of exacting too much from the sympathy of my young friends. We found cards from Sir Wm. Ross, Mr and Mrs Connor (on whom we had called) and the Marchesa Caucci. Read again a very interesting letter received yesterday from Lady B. which brought me back to a far different world in which my concern is far deeper and in this instance full of pleasure only. I forgot to mention that Fanny Nince [?] has been here on

her wedding trip and paid us a visit; she seems far less prepossessing in manner than our Maria.

6 February. Oh! that charming letter just received from you. I was going to write my journal steadily but now it is quite impossible. There is nothing but the dregs of me left in Rome at this moment, so for fear I should give you back your own news I will leave off. Well, each and every particular interested me. I am much gratified by Mrs H[egan]'s kindness to Josiah and it was very attentive of Theresa and Fanny to send you news. At St John Lateran, we saw a painting representing the Saviour appearing in answer to the Empress Helena's prayer that he would bestow peace on the Church, and in this church they omit the sentence 'dona nobis pacem' considering it unnecessary to pray for what has been already granted. We went at 10 to fetch Monsig're Luciani to go with us to the Sistine where the service was in commemoration of the Pope's coronation. There were very few English present. Mrs Swinny, who is quiet and well-bred, sat by us, so that I listened without interruption to Palestrina's majestic music. There were fine strains and striking harmonies, but I still find my ear longs for an occasional relief from the full choir. Nevertheless, I enjoy it so much that, to follow my own inclination only, I should never miss the Sistine. We returned with Monsig're to see a huge wax taper weighing 30 lbs gaily painted and adorned, presented to him by the Pope, and which he meant to present to a convent. We then went to the Borghese, chose pictures, and obtained permission to draw there. After sitting a long while with a book in my hand reading in reality the letter in my pocket, we went to a party at Miss D[ouglasse]'s but she was disappointed of most of the ladies. Our favourite Dr Grant was there and Mrs and the Misses C[raigie] with whom I do not expect any great intimacy.

7 February. Our first lesson from Sig'ra Montecchi whom we like extremely; she has so much life and spirit in her manner. Then we took Mrs Smith to the Barberini Library where a most courteous Abbate showed us, among other things, an illuminated Ms. french Bible of the 14 cent., Ms. of Dante's *Comedie* also illuminated, with copious notes, sepia pen drawings of the ruins in Rome made in the 18th cent., containing cornices and capitals etc. of a richness and gracefulness proportioned to the grandeur of the remains of external walls and pavements, autograph of Tasso's minor poems, most of them written in letters to his friends and patrons, and, what pleased me most, Galileo's handwriting of criticisms on Tasso's *Jerusalem* which he greatly underrated from his partiality to Ariosto. The Abbate told us that Galileo lost this little note book and had been anxious to recover it in the latter part of his life that he might make additional remarks in it. Whereupon I immediately conjecture that, on further examination, his prejudice wore away, and he who so delighted in the exuberant fancy of Ariosto found the charm also of the noble and gentle muse of Tasso. When

you hear that Minnie and I drank tea again with Miss D[ouglasse], perhaps you may fancy we make her room a sort of coffee house, but in fact this time it was more for her sake than our own. Mr P[ollock] had invited a party of artists and, not liking a riotous men's party, asked his cousin to receive them. We went to support her. Minnie and I had had a drive in the bitter cold Tramontana by way of tonic and it certainly did us both good. The weather is now like one of our March frosts, but it agrees with me. Minnie looks and feels well so long as I am very particular about air, exercise and diet, but the moment we take any liberty in that way, she begins to be languid. Therefore I give up much time to the important matter of strengthening her constitution. Wm. is a most valuable assistant for they take two turns of the Pincio while I take one, so we each have the sort of exercise which suits our state. I feel quite brisk today. I forgot to mention that Mr Connor came. I should not have known him but there was all his former kindness and lively interest about Mr C.'s family. Mrs Connor and I always miss each other and she is afraid to come out in the evening till the weather is warmer.

8 February. Went out early to hear a lent sermon at the Gesù, but there was none, so we contented ourselves with seeing more of the church. At St Pietro in Vincoli, I was a long time while occupied with M. Angelo's Moses. At first, the countenance displeased me - two small horns, an immense beard, and great prominence of the lower part of the face, make it remind me of one of those odious satyrs, but this impression wore off on studying it. The lips are all but alive. Of the figure, I had but one idea, that it is noble and animated, and all criticisms of that seemed to me contemptible. There were some good pictures, and the nave of the church pleased me. Then we went to eat our lunch in the Coliseum. All cold and grey today. Father would have laughed to see us caressing a pretty new horse of which our coachman is as proud as if it were his first-born. He begged Wm. to stand up in the carriage to watch its action. We find something new to observe every time we pass the ruins. I have quite a personal friendship for some of them. At the Academia St Luca, we saw some excellent landscapes and other pictures, a bust of Thorwaldsen (of which the mouth is very like Father's), and several original casts of his works. Only think of my having the delight of reading Dr Arnold's life from the Church library;[1] I have devoured the first volume in spite of my continual engagement. In the evening, we spent an hour with the Marchesa Caucci; there were 3 Italian gentlemen and a french lady whom we had met before at Mrs Smith's, so we had a good lesson in languages.

---

[1] Arthur Penrhyn Stanley's *Life and Correspondence of Thomas Arnold* had been recently published.

9 February. Sunday. Had the pleasure of walking home from church with Mrs Connor.

10 February. Sig'r Campana gave his first lesson. He seems very animated and likely to be useful. In the afternoon, joined a party conducted by P[adre] Marchi to the catacombs of St Agnese. Mr Erskine, the author of the evidences of Christianity,[1] was in my party instead of Dr Trayer whom I had invited, but he has left Rome. Mr Erskine is a very pleasing unaffected old gentleman; his sister Mrs Stirling and Capt'n Paterson also went. We were altogether about 16 in number. The Padre, who is a Jesuit, would not condescend to go in the same carriage with us womankind, but he was very communicative and answered even my questions most good-humouredly. One hour and a half, we groped about in the bowels of the earth, yet I not only forgot my extreme dislike to anything like being buried, but also all fear of freshly excavated places falling in upon us, and fatigue, and bad air from our multitude of tapers. In short, I was quite happy in remembrance of the noble army of martyrs, and thought more of their heroism and its glorious result than of the sufferings of which there were such evident traces. The catacombs are subterranean cities of the dead with now and then a small chapel or place for catechumens where the living took refuge beside their hallowed graves. The passages would not admit any one with arms a kimbo and often required that the gentlemen should stoop. In the upright walls were hollowed out horizontally graves of various sizes only just large enough to contain their inmates without coffins, sometimes two together. We saw one where the mouldering bones were still perfect enough to show that they had been placed head to feet. There was often hardly 10 inches between them vertically. They were carefully closed with slabs of stone or marble fixed with mortar, inscriptions remaining on many, on some the place for the bottle or glass plate of blood, and on others the palm branch indicating that the martyr died a bloodless death. There are only a small proportion of martyrs. The chapels (into some of which we could scarcely squeeze all our party) are decorated with frescoes, some of them, though rough, in a very good style of art, a little sculpture. The good padre was very anxious to persuade us that the early Christians were careful to separate men and women in worship and in teaching. There exist still their narrow stairs, and their contrivances for obtaining air, and for ingress and egress when, in times of persecution, they lived underground. P[adre] Marchi has written at great length to prove that the Xtians were the original fabricators of the sepulchres and did not adapt pagan excavations. Granting his premises (of which I cannot judge), I think his reasoning good, but to my mind that question is not important. My interest is fixed on what is universally

---

[1] Thomas Erskine (1788-1870) had published his *Remarks on the Internal Evidence for the Truth of Revealed Religion* in 1820.

acknowledged, that these were the hiding places of the living and the dead who were counted worthy to suffer for Christ's sake. We were late home and found letters from Clara to me and from Fanny to Wm., which put me in a whirl by suddenly and strongly turning my thoughts in another direction, most pleasantly however. Tell Clara I am very much obliged by her friends' thoughtfulness. To complete the day, we went, according to promise, to drink tea with Mr and Mrs Connor and Mrs Clarkson, her sister. You may guess how exciting this was and how we talked about Mr C[onnor]'s family. We all enjoyed the visit but I was quite over-tired.

11 February. Went early to see a school founded by Cardinal Tosti[1] for orphan boys not of the lowest class. We saw their studies in the fine arts, heard their music, saw various branches of manufacture, and met several of our friends, but were not shown what would have most attracted my attention, anything of the daily routine of their life. There were indications of talent for music and painting in some boys. We then saw two churches, St Francesco and Sta. Maria in Trastevere, the latter ancient, and it contains a beautiful fresco of the assumption by Domenichino; the worst is it breaks one's neck to look at paintings in a ceiling. We then had a drive and I a chat with Miss D[ouglasse] before we came home.

12 February. First drawing in the Borghese which is much more convenient for us than the Vatican. Then took a beautiful drive by the ancient aqueducts in the campagna and stopped at Trinità, a convent which Dr Grant had promised to show us. It is the place of education for many girls of the first Roman families. The arrangements seemed all very good and the children of all ages looked happy. The nuns we saw were agreeable women, their cells exquisitely clean though bare, and nothing terrifying to me in the life they indicated except the breaking up of social ties, in short nothing to contradict my old idea at 16 years that if I had no family to love and could but think it right, it would suit me very well to be a nun. Mrs Stirling went with us. I quite forgot to mention our soirée. It was stupidish because we were disappointed of so many, among others of Sir Wm. Ross who has left Rome. We had Misses Price and Fielding, Sig'rina Petrarca, Monsig're Luciani, Messrs P[ollock] and Smith. We talked and we talked till I almost gasped.

13 February. Drawing again, saw the subterranean of St Peters. Then Minnie and I had a starvation drive, and shopped a little. Sig'ra Lupienti in the evening. We had agreed to keep our carriage for the remainder of our stay.

---

[1] Antonio Tosti (b.1776), made cardinal in 1838.

14 February. Italian lesson. Then to hear a sermon, rather eloquent, in the style of Mr Melville. You shall have one idea, though it suffers from being translated from his beautiful language: 'Those who deny the immortality of the soul destroy the strong chain which links earth to heaven and leaves man trembling, suspended by the slender thread of life over the unknown abyss of annihilation'. We are now going to take Elena with us to the Palazzo Corsini. We are all shivering and chilblained, longing for spring, but we none of us take severe colds. I think you are very wise not to encounter the cold more than you can help. I am quite well today, but whether the excitement or the air of Rome occasioned my indisposition is not yet ascertained to my mind.

15 February. We are so industrious now in sightseeing that I cannot pass over a day. A nice long letter from Fanny containing a good report of you. It required an early answer so I have written with Wm., but, as you will probably hear, without deciding for next winter (that is about staying). We went to an ordination at St John Lateran. We saw Acolyths, subdeacons, deacons, and priests ordained, about 20 of each. We were not in time for the tonsure. The ceremonies indicating their respective duties and the prostration during a solemn litany were impressive. I saw but little expression of devotion in most countenances, and to me it was a mournful sight. I spent an hour with Miss D[ouglasse] and, in the afternoon, we went to the Palazzo Sciarra where there are many good pictures besides Guido's most lovely Magdalene. Dr Grant spent the evening with us. We have unluckily missed him several times, so he declares we are very gay and continually with Miss D[ouglasse], which latter accusation has some foundation, but then she cannot come to us.

16 February. Sunday. Monsig're Luciani came in for a few minutes in the evening and explained some of the ceremonies we had witnessed in the Lateran as, for instance, that the Chalice and Patten were presented to the sub-deacons who have the charge of them, and passing over the Deacons, then to the priests who administer the sacraments, then the care to anoint every part of the hands which comes in contact with the sacramental elements.

17 February. Again two hours at the Corsini looking at many beautiful pictures. One particularly interested me, not only for the merit of expressive drawing and colouring, but because it was painted by a young woman Sirani[1] who died at 25 as was supposed poisoned by her jealous competitors; it is a Madonna and Child. There are beautiful landscapes by G. Poussin and Rosa and Canaletto, and two beautiful different heads of 'Ecce Homo' by Guido and Guercino. Being nearly starved, we drove back

---

[1] Elisabetta Sirani 1638-1665.

to sun ourselves on the Pincio. In the evening Minnie and I drank tea with Mrs Connor and Mrs Clarkson. Mr C[onnor] had gone to the Vatican.

18 February. Went to the Castle St Angelo or Hadrian's tomb. While Wm. mounted and descended the interior, Minnie and I stood among the cannon overlooking Cincinatius' farm and the sluggish Tiber towards beautiful Soracte and the snow-covered mountains interrupted by a fine grove of pines. On another side, the great mass of St Peters and the Vatican. Then, to complete the view of Rome present, on the ragged banks of the circumvallation, stood a slatternly sentinel contemplating an old cow, the busiest thing in the neighbourhood, for she was grazing. Presently there came an old soldier to the battlements where we were and emptied a pocket handkerchief and a small bag full of earth upon the sloping part. He had the innocent Italian face so I addressed him and found that this was his garden and he was preparing for his spring flowers. Then we had a beautiful drive up the Monte Mario where we overtook Mr P[ollock] and Mr Adams. Minnie had a nice walk up with the three young men while I followed them in the carriage. The view was charming, the Tiber absolutely blue. I could not persuade the lazy youngsters to go out this evening, so here we are engaging our own society which they declare is the best possible.

19th February. Your welcome letter which reminds me to tell you that I have felt better for several days past (this is 21st). This bitter cold weather agrees very [much] with us all except as to chilblains which are deplorable. I have left off medicine and drive every day in the open carriage which strengthens my digestion without quickening the action of the heart. In short, there is so good a result from the measures I have been lately pursuing that the prescription of a week at Frascati, which Fanny suggested and Mr P[ollock] had already advised, is by no means necessary as an interruption to our plans. Today the fountains are covered with icicles. On the 19th, we went [to] the baths of Titus on the foundation of the Villa of Mecenas and the house of Nero, therefore rich in threefold memories. On the lofty roofs of the corridors are very elegant Arabesques in fresco from which Raphael took hints for his beautiful ornaments at the Vatican, a fresh proof among the many, which continually meet one where so many monuments of earlier ages remain, that most of those who leave beautiful things to delight their successors do not create them from nothing, but have, in their turn, received some light from those who went before. We spent the evening with Miss D[ouglasse] and met Mr and Mrs Latilla. He is an English artist with whom we have had some artistical talk.

20 February. To the Pope's gardens which are all stiffness without magnificence, and his palace Monte Cavallo, where there are some pretty good pictures, but nothing of much interest. Minnie and I had a beautiful drive but the mountains are too snowy now.

21 February. I being forbidden to ascend the dome of St Peters had asked Mrs Smith to let Minnie and Wm. join their party. They fixed today, so I stayed to receive the Italian lesson, then went to St Peters where I heard part of a sermon on the love of God, too theatrical and violent for my taste, yet in some degree eloquent, and then I enjoyed walking slowly up and down the middle aisle till my party came. We adjourned to the Sistine and had a leisurely and favourable study of M. Angelo's last Judgment (it was a brilliant day). This is a wonderful picture for the immense number and variety of figures, but it is principally a technical beauty to my mind. The images of horror and disgust which leave an impression of grandeur and solemnity in poetry are too loathsome in painting, and then the wrath of the Lamb is too terrible an idea to enter through the medium of the senses. The richness of imagination and beauty of drawing in some of the compartments is wonderful. I should like to go several times and study them. We took Miss Smith a drive with us. For once I must tell you of two projects which I think you will like, first to go with Mr and Mrs Connor to Naples, next to go with Miss D[ouglasse] and Mr P[ollock] to Venice. I do not think we should have much difficulty in finding companions further, but, unless they are something especial, we are very much disposed to prefer our own society. Indeed I am forced to lecture my young friends on their excessive partiality for the trio.

22 February. For the second time, a miserably cold rain prevented our taking Monsig'r Luciani to Torlonia's Villa. He had called the evening before to hear about it, so we went to the Farnese Palace where there was little to see, to Palazzo Spado where there was a splendid Guercino (Dido dying) and several other fine pictures, the Chiesa Nova which was not interesting, and the Church St Louis where were fine frescoes by Domenichino. I must tell you another scheme for Minnie's birthday, the 28th, or, if that is not a fine day, the first after it - we hope to go for the whole day to Veii taking a cold dinner as there is no inn near the Roman ruins; our party to be Miss and Mr Smith and Mr P[ollock]. It would be too fatiguing for Miss D[ouglasse].

23 February. Sunday. I have so extremely enjoyed Dr Arnold's life. Minnie would tell you she is excessively glad it is done, for it made me silent. Perhaps it did. I could not always talk to them about it, nor could I easily think of anything else.

24 February. A wretched day, however we saw the beautiful staircase at the Palazzo Braschi, which I did not ascend, and went the 3rd time to the Corsini. In the evening to Miss D[ouglasse] where we met Dr Grant and exchanged condolences with him on the subject of chilblains.

25 February. A call from Monsig're Prospero in consequence of Mr H[egan]'s letter which we had left the day before as soon as we received it. He was very polite in his offer of services. He is a very spruce young man and in Rome goes by the name of little Monsig're 'bright eyes'. We then went and sunned ourselves among the gigantic fragments of marble and the orange trees of the Colonna gardens, thence to the Aldobrandini where there was very little, then to the ruin of the temple of Minerva Medica, very picturesque, the charming drive by Posta Maggiore, the campagna all painted purple and rose by the partial clouds. In the evening, an agreeable party at Mr Swinny's, Italian and English chat which entertained me till I was too tired. There was a young lady from Durham who knows dear A. and of course admires her. I have forgotten her name; she is travelling with her father for his health. She has two brothers educated by Dr Arnold whom she venerated. Heard afterwards it was Miss Fox.[1]

26 February. Saw Guido's Aurora, a fine fresco, at the Palazzo Ruspighiosi with other things. We had before been in Trastevere to fetch Wm. from a monastery. We lunched in the carriage between the Coliseum and Constantine's arch. Miss D[ouglasse] had agreed to go with us for a second drive in the campagna. She read us part of a letter from Fanny. Drank tea with Mr and Mrs Frith. Minnie accompanied Mrs F[rith] and the gentlemen who sang. The English are so scandalously gay this Lent, in defiance of their own church and the Roman government, that, so we say, the Pope must interfere to prevent their corrupting the morals of his flock. I am afraid you will suppose we are of the number when you learn that, besides several quiet visits, next week we are engaged on Monday to the Countess Lepel.

27 February. Palazzo Doria, where are a multitude of pictures - some good. Then we had to provide eatables for tomorrow, and, after leaving Wm. at the Vatican, Minnie and I went to see again the lovely view from Monte Mario, the young folks having determined on doing their best to keep me in good order for tomorrow. We have such specimens here of the utter shamelessness with which all tradesmen here attempt to cheat, that I am quite disgusted with having so many battles to fight. Indeed, considering my antipathy to bargaining, it is rather wonderful I have not been in more scrapes. My letter having come to you unsealed is by no means a proof that it was sent so. Some of yours have shared that fate. I do not know whether you can send by the French steamer, you must ask in London. Letters by Uringa[?] are sometimes 15 days. What a treat - yours and Aunt Kedington's letters, just arrived on the very eve of Minnie's birthday. Her heart is quite full at the thought that you remembered it and wrote to her.

---

[1] The daughter of George Townshend Fox. Three of her brothers were educated at Rugby.

The post too was so lucky this evening; tomorrow we hope to be off before it arrives. My last contained our projects of engagements. This is to give an account of how we have been permitted to fulfil them. It was a very doubtful morning. However, the weather soon improved. We had a famous store of provisions, and off we went, bells jingling. Mr P[ollock] was on horseback almost all the way, only exchanging with Wm. for a little while. Isola, the ancient fortress commanding Veii, is extremely picturesque, a desolate ruinous village just above a ravine richly wooded with a stream at the bottom. Mine host, the *custode* of the Etruscan tombs, looked just what one might expect from his character, a ferocious cunning giant. We desired to have three asses for us ladies immediately, so, after half an hour's delay, they came fresh! from carrying wood. They had all men's saddles, but we contrived to sit lady fashion. There is very little visible of the ancient city, but it was pleasant to feel some connexions with distant ages and go wandering up and down romantic hills and dales, passing waterfalls, and woods, and torrents, and the most savage looking shepherds dressed in sheepskins with the wool outside as shaggy as Esquimaux. We were accompanied by a Capuchin Friar, two men, and a boy with the donkeys, the Ogre *custode*, and were joined by four of the wild shepherds. Can you fancy what a curious group we were. Our three young men were the only persons too civilized to look picturesque. We ladies in our cloaks were excellent figures. Minnie turned her cape over her head, and the purple cloak fell over the ass's tail, so she looked like a small dragoon. Presently, we came to a second torrent; the first we passed easily on foot by planks, the next we bipeds managed also dry-shod by the help of the Capuchin, but the donkeys (sensible fellows) knew the danger and would not budge at first. However one was beaten in, down he went but scrambled up again and came out dripping the other side. Another was taken to a different place. He would not leap so stepped into water too deep to stand and too narrow to move in, where he would probably have been drowned but that all hands were set to work, and they 'pulled him out by the tail' frightened out of his asinine senses, poor brute. The third was a hopeless case and we sent him round. Indeed, it was only I who rode all the way; the young ones preferred walking often. The open tombs are small caves cut in the rock. It struck me as extraordinary that the roof of one was cut into the semblance of rectangular beams such as we see in old houses. We saw many vases, an altar, one stand for a vase, the lip with very good small *basso relievo* in terra cotta, an iron helmet through which a lance had gone so as to come out on the other side, the lance etc. The story goes, that the first man who looked in at the hole accidentally, saw on the iron bedstead, now in the Vatican, the perfect figure of a man, even his features. As he looked, the air entered, it all trembled and shook into dust, and the armour clattered down. Leaving the tombs, we ladies rode up a very steep path through a wood, all tangled with briars and underwood and knee deep in mud, attended by Mr P[ollock] and the donkey man. The threatening rain still kept off. We sat down to dinner at a decent table in the *Custode*'s house, having invited the Capuchin to join us. He, however, would only have a glass of Marsala and a lent bun, while we heretics worked away at pigeon pie, chicken, ham, etc. and our coachman seemed also to have had a dispensation. The ogre played the guitar and sang tender ditties to us. As usual upon such occasions, we were rather later than we had intended, but we came so fast that we were in by six, and had scarcely any rain. We did not stop to dress, but went on to drink tea with Miss D[ouglasse] and met Miss Macartney, sister to a Dr M[acartney] at Naples, for whom I have a letter and of whom I have heard a very high character. We came home early, and I confess to being tired and feverish, but hope in the course of my letter to tell you I am no worse.

1 March. Mr H[egan]'s letter. I hope my friends will have laid aside their anxiety for me before this arrives. I do think I over worked myself without being aware of it, for this air gives me a continual tendency to feverishness which disguises one's sensation of fatigue, and I also think that the sirocco always disorders me and the best remedy is driving in the open country. I am quite sure I could not get on in Rome if I frequently went into crowded places. I do not at all plead guilty to thin shoes, for we both find the stone stairs of Rome so terribly cold that we go everywhere in cork boots! Took Monsig're Luciani to Torlonia's Villa where there are a multitude of rooms, some or them very prettily ornamented, everything very magnificent, but some odious make-believe ruins disgusted me. Afterwards we found the Marchesa Lorenzana at home for the first time. She is a pretty, elegant young woman.

2 March. Sunday. You will see perhaps in the papers the death of Mr Codington, rector of Warre, of whose disputes with his parishioners so much was said last year.[1] It is a melancholy circumstance which has excited much sympathy. Though an ailing man, he was seriously ill but one week, and has left a young widow with 7 very young children.

3 March. Employed all our time in going from shop to shop to execute commissions: statues and cameos, bronzes and prints, and, as you may guess, found the selection most difficult. There are a few excellent things one would covet, but they are a price for princes. Then there are multitudes of manufactures to suit the full purses and empty heads of foreigners, and here and there a few things good of their kind, and cheaper because their

---

[1] Henry Coddington had been rector of Ware in Hertfordshire since 1832. He died early in March in Rome. His dispute with the parishioners concerned the form of service he had introduced. After his death, parishioners planned to present a petition to Trinity College, Cambridge, seeking the appointment of a clergyman who would adhere to the old plan of performing divine service and discontinue the innovations which, according to Coddington's obituary in the Times, had 'already been productive of incalculable mischief.'

value is not technical, but either consists in beauty or association. I am pleased with my purchases. I hope my friends will be pleased, also especially dear Aunt Kedington, but we must have several days more before we decide, notwithstanding our previous observation ever since we have been in Rome. Minnie is to begin to sit on Wednesday for a cameo likeness. I hope it will turn out well - some are extremely pretty. We saw an exquisite miniature copy of Guido's Magdalene and went to enquire its price of the artist but unluckily it was 20 instead of 10£.

4 March. A multitude of business people teasing all the morning. Drove to Monte Mario and walked in the grounds of the villa to see the Mediterranean glittering in the sun, but it was bitterly cold, were disappointed of seeing the Borghese, and went to an exhibition of modern pictures tolerably creditable. In the evening, at the Countess Lepel's with about 50 people, about equal proportions English, French, Italian, and German. It was somewhat dull. People seemed strangers to each other and we as well acquainted as almost any: there were 4 or 5 we knew.

5 March. Minnie sat for the sketch of her cameo; it promises well. (I forgot that we had a pleasant chat with Dr Grant on Monday evening). Saw several studios of painters and the Villa Borghese which did not equal my expectations; there are many respectable things but nothing of great interest. Monsig're Luciani for a few minutes after dinner. Drank tea with Mrs Connor concocting plans. Miss D[ouglasse] is very poorly. We have been hoping to take her out with us but obliged to defer it from day to day.

6 March. Wm. went with two friends to a monastery and we to draw. Then we tried a little walk but, as I was somewhat disordered, my two young ones insisted upon my giving up sightseeing today. Therefore leaving Wm. among the ruins, we two drove quietly into the campagna which has done me good. Italian shopping. Wm. wanted to buy him a ball of string. He was asked about 4 times its value, so he required 2 for the same money which was immediately acceded to, but the woman said to her husband in Italian, he does not understand, and proceeded to give only two thirds of the change. When Wm. demanded the rest, it was given with the utmost effrontery and most amiable civility. We have met with several such incidents, though they were too long to tell. There is a church close to the forum with this inscription cut in the marble 'Sancta Maria libera nos a penis infernis'.

7 March. Nothing done today but a little of the commissions and a drive cut short by the rain. The sirocco and perhaps a little too much bustle have rather demolished me again.

8 March. The Palazzo Farnesina where are some very beautiful frescoes by Raphael and his scholars; the church St Onofrio, paintings by Pinturicchio very graceful, and good frescoes by Domenichino; Tasso's grave and the stump of an old oak, his favourite haunt; a fine view of Rome where I stood while Wm. looked at a cast of the poet in the monastery and thought of the unhappy man gazing on it with all the morbid sensibility which Goethe has described so well and Clara so ably translated. It is very odd that I should relish Tasso or Ariosto, but so it is, that to this day I have not lost my youthful love of chivalry and fairy land. I leave this anomaly in my mind to be explained by phrenologists by the existence of some bump to me unknown and certainly what Fanny calls my bump of fun. We found her letter of the 25th and one from dear Anne to delight us. Both give a tolerable report of you, for I consider that we must all expect some little indisposition in the spring. We are never entirely free from such at that time. Miss D[ouglasse] has been ill for several days. I sat half an hour with her this morning. She has been too feverish in the evening lately to see us. I had just written to Mrs C[onnor]. Our idea is to leave this place for Naples on the 8th of April and return to it for (perhaps) only one night about the 8th of May, starting immediately for Venice which we may reach in ten days. Let me have a letter here before we go (it is at least 12 days post) and one from you Poste restante Naples. Other letters may be addressed before the 8th of May to me at Miss D[ouglasse], Via Gregoriana; afterwards, Poste restante, Venice.

9 March. Sunday, a summer day all on a sudden, pleasant, but so very relaxing, that I did not attempt going twice to church, and spent the afternoon in quiet Sunday talk with Miss D[ouglasse] who was a little better. The changes of weather give her fresh colds continually. In the evening, there was a procession in this parish of the Madonna addolorata, i.e. 6 sorts of glass chandeliers carried on long poles, boys and men carrying the long wax tapers, their liveries are extremely smart, always covered with gold and worsted lace, acolyths and priests, a huge banner representing on each side the Virgin and others at the foot of the Cross. A wooden cross 26 feet high with gold ornaments. I forgot to say the procession was preceded by drummers who beat all the while it was stationary, about 5 m[inutes] in each street; a band of wind instruments, and priests chaunting in splendid golden garments, other priests surrounding a painted wooden statue of the Virgin with 7 daggers sticking in her breast on a fabric 30 feet high, embellished with gilded cherubs etc., and carried on poles by a great number of men. As this passed, many knelt, a poor sick woman opposite to us who [h]as been long bed-ridden was dragged to the window to see it; abundance of tapers accompanied the whole line about a quarter of a mile long, and soldiers brought up the rear followed by a crowd.

10 March. Took a farewell look at the most charming statues and paintings in the Vatican which, however pleasant, was very fatiguing, so that I was not sorry to hear our intended visit to Sig'ra Vanutelli was set aside by her going to the Austrian Ambassador's. We had also to go to Mme Clarisse to provide ourselves with spring dresses, and indeed with summer ones, for unless we go to Vienna, we are not likely to be in any place so convenient for furnishing apparel, and I begin in time to make my preparations for departure that I may not be in a bustle at last. We shall not be able to return to our lodgings from Naples for they are let immediately on our departure, but if we are only one night here that will be no inconvenience as we leave our heavy luggage with Miss D[ouglasse]. Tomorrow Minnie and I are to be introduced to the Pope by the Hanoverian Minister Kestner. We must go in black and veiled. I hope Sua Santità will be pleased to speak to me and that I shall not make such a blunder as a countryman of ours did. He was asked by the Pope if he had seen many of the ecclesiastical ceremonies of Rome and replied that he had seen everything he particularly wished to see except a conclave: the Conclave is only summoned upon the death of the Pope. Was not he a blundering fellow! The bad weather sadly discomposes our excursion plans. I am afraid all we English rushing together as soon as it is fine to places in the neighbourhood of Rome, we shall make each other very uncomfortable. It is such a jumble of society here. People's divers oddities stand out in strong relief from their forming such small groups. Society in Rome would be a fine subject for a satirist and, by the by, I hear Dickens is here, so there's 'a child among us taking notes'.[1] Do give me some idea of what Father thinks about Mrs Ward and such things. I could not resist reading a letter in the papers, though half information is rather irritating. Just fresh from his Holiness the Pope, can you imagine the thing. It seems to me quite comical when I connect it with my ultra-protestant friends, but it was no such wonderful matter, as you shall hear. 14 carriages met in the Piazza di Spagna, from which peeped bright faces of English girls disguised in black veils. After half an hour waiting, the Commendatore arrived and we were rattled off to the Vatican. There we assembled in an anteroom, 30 ladies and 5 gentlemen. We two came late up stairs and without a moment's delay followed in the train to the audience chamber: a handsome room beautifully adorned with copies of Raphael's Arabesques etc. At the upper end was a table covered with scarlet and, on it, a scarlet hat ornamented with gold and a silver bell. Before it stood the Pope, a brisk looking old man with as few signs of infirmity as I ever saw in one past 80 years.[2] He was dressed in white woollen made like a scanty double breasted dressing gown down to the feet, with a small cape, scarlet

---

[1] Dickens had been in Rome for a few days at the beginning of February, had then gone on to Naples, and had subsequently returned to Rome, arriving on 2 March. He stayed until 25 March. For the quotation, see Robert Burns, *On the late Captain Grose's Peregrinations*, verse 1.

[2] Pope Gregory XVI had been born in 1765. He died in 1846.

slippers embroidered with gold, and a small white scull-cap. He was very affable and conversed all the time with the gentlemen, speaking also to one or two ladies related to the minister, only generally to the rest of us. I am sorry to say many of our party were most uncourtly, neglecting to curtsy when introduced, and turning their backs upon the Pope in going out. One German not only did that but, when especially presented, took upon her to speak first. I did not hear if she said 'How do you do Mr Pope, I hope your family is well' but it seemed nearly as free. Before this [by] way of preparation, I had taken a quiet drive, and we had leave to take Miss D[ouglasse] with us. It came on rainy and windy which rather frightened me for her, but she was no worse. We spent the evening with her, meeting Mr Horne and his two simple pleasing girls, and Mr Adams.

12 March. Spent the day in hunting statues, prints, and cameos for commissions, and viewing carriages for our journey, troublesome and not refreshing, but good enough for a wet day. Dr Grant in the evening.

13 March. Saw the galleries of the Chigi and Colonna Palaces. Of the first, but half is exhibited now. There was a fine St Francis by Guercino, but nothing of first rate interest. The latter remark applies also to the Colonna: in the magnificent apartments, there are many good things, but nothing exquisite. We called on the Vanutelli who inhabit part of the Palace, and then drove about in the rain to execute a commission for Miss D[ouglasse]. Then came your nice letter with Josiah's postscript. One also for Minnie from Mrs Hegan [deleted]. I cannot understand her complaining now of Minnie's silence; she has certainly written frequently of late. I often write after I have sent her to bed and now I never touch the piano. It is not easy to find much time.

14 March. Saw the Pantheon, i.e. the interior. We had often passed it, a very noble building in its proportions, and capable of being made beautiful, but now it is a mixture of ancient magnificence decayed, and modern rubbish. I had quite a longing to restore it. The Doria palace for the second time and found that we had seen almost all the good pictures at first so we enjoyed them once again. Then we left Wm. to grub among the ruins, in which I should have enjoyed joining him, but it was a very warm, enervating day, and a quiet drive was better for us two. We took a little outline in the Campagna for the first time. In the evening with Miss D[ouglasse]. There is a story afloat that while the Pope was going to the different altars in St Peters as is usual on this day, an Italian lady threw herself at his feet having broken through the guards, and presented a petition which he handed to an attendant. She was then dragged away by the guards. If I learn that there is anything in the incident interesting to Fanny, I shall ask you to let her know it. I do not expect to see much more in Rome. We must still spend a great deal of time to do our very best about

commissions which, by the bye, I do very cheerfully only wishing we could be sure of pleasing. Then there is sitting for the cameos and as much as I can go through of the Holy week; afterwards Frascati etc. and packing. The weather promises well for Tivoli on Monday. Mr Connor has just been here for a final decision, subject only to the skies. I think the excursion will do me good. I am obliged to leave my letter here in Rome or it would be too late to reach you on the 28th. The incident I mentioned had no interest for Fanny.

15 March. Went upon a permission which we boldly begged of himself to see the Etruscan Museum of Signor Campana,[1] who obligingly showed it himself to us and three English gentlemen. There are some things more beautiful and curious than in the Vatican, a vase like this unique in its workmanship, statues, great and small, elegant as the Grecian, together with rude and monstrous forms, implements of war, household utensils, and in sculpture or terra cotta representations of religious and civil ceremonies such as mark a high degree of civilization. These remains are quite a history. Father would have liked to hear Signor Campana point out how their early efforts, resembling the Egyptian, showed a common origin. There are many things confirming his favourite theory. I feel quite provoked that the savage Romans would have destroyed such a nation, whose genius led them so far towards all forms of beauty. When they were enslaved, they became mere imitators. The gold ornaments are beautifully worked, necklaces 1 and a half feet long and 3 inches broad interspersed with pearls, precious stones, sometimes with intaglios or gems set in the gold, elegant gold wreaths for the hair, but nothing struck me as a greater evidence of civilized stationary life than an iron fire place, a sort of shallow tray perhaps 2 and a half feet square for hearth, and an open cradle for fuel suspended on bars for air to pass under (as I suppose), tongs and shovel. There were also some ancient Roman frescoes, mere modern things compared with the Etruscans. I thought myself obliged to come away because signor C[ampanari] looked tired. He was just recovering from illness, but I was loath to leave these curious things without a hundred questions. There was a very pretty sonnet also written upon one of the cabinets which I found was his own. Altogether our successful impudence procured us much gratification. After a little drive to refresh us, we went about the cameo. The third sitting and two more at least are to come. We have agreed to take a balcony with Mr and Mrs Swinny for seeing the Girandola.[2] Spring seems to be coming at last and our chilblains going. Minnie's hands have been worse than at any time last winter, notwithstanding warm gloves and muffetees, and Wm.'s are quite ridiculous, but yesterday, for the first time, I saw the leaf buds opening on

---

[1] Campanari, one of the first to excavate and write about Etruscan art.

[2] Firework display at Castel St. Angelo sponsored by the Popes from the 15th century.

the forest trees, and there is a tolerable prospect for our trip to Tivoli on Monday. Is it not a pleasant thing to see the sun shining on a morning anxiously looked for on account of a party of pleasure? Merry we were all, six precious souls besides the coachman's (if he has one), and the horses jogged merrily on and their bells rang merrily out. The first part of the road to Tivoli is through the dreary campagna, but then there is Rome on one side with St Peters and, on the other, the beautiful mountains, and ruins scattered all around, and, by way of foreground, the wine carts, long narrow drays drawn by one horse. In front of them is a shelter something like the fabrics the apple women set up in the corners of the London streets. It is made of sheepskins stretched out between sticks and is placed according to the wind, therefore very often askew and in all manner of picturesque ways. Coming up to a long string of these, the coachman either shouts till he is hoarse and then turns off the pavé into 2 feet deep of mud, or till the horses hear him and they politely turn out of the way in the midst of their meal, for each has a bundle of hay tied to his shaft and eats as he goes all day long. The men are sound asleep with their limbs in all the varieties of free attitudes Michael Angelo drew. There are also carts drawn by Bufaloes, less shaggy and fierce than those of N. America. We crossed the Anio into the Sabine territory and soon came to the petrifying lake where the gentlemen walked to see it and procure specimens. Before long our noses told us we were approaching a milky stream of sulphur, a perfect abomination. Through a grove of fine old olive trees by a steep ascent, we came to Tivoli which is perched upon the rocks from which the Anio precipitates itself, and consists of a confused mass of ancient Roman buildings, those of the middle ages, and the squalidness of the present town. We ordered beds and a dinner, and finding the place perfectly inundated by multitudes who like ourselves had taken the first fine day, we went down to the Grotto of Neptune on foot upon the promise that donkeys should be sent as soon as any were at liberty. Mrs Cl[arkson] is lame, Mrs Co[nnor] and I have bad hearts and she has bad lungs besides. We crept on very amiably knowing we had plenty of time - it was not one [o'clock] - enjoying ourselves extremely. The trees are budding, the whole atmosphere perfumed with violets, the banks gay with flowers, and, above them, the grey rocks and cascades tumbling in every direction. It is not equal to our favourite Switzerland, but it is very charming. We had a good deal more walking than we bargained for before the steeds arrived, but were no worse. At the great cascade, the whole river bounds over 80 feet and is lost in a cloud of spray on which, when we first looked from the inn, there was a beautiful rainbow. Further on, there are two clusters of smaller cascades among projections clothed [in] the most brilliant green. Through olive groves and over an ancient Roman bridge back to dinner at 5.30. Minnie was here able to solve (by analogy) a difficulty which has long perplexed her. She said that if those very free and loosely draped statues could walk, they would certainly leave their garments behind. Now our young grooms

157

were as loosely draped, but then they clutched their clothes and the halter in one hand, and thrashed the donkey with the other, that is the boys did so, the men were fully employed in keeping the saddles on to Mrs Clarkson's donkey and Minnie's, and the latter (brute) upon his legs. Minnie declared she was going through his back bone once. Mrs C[onnor] assured her it did not signify, she would sit very well on his stomach. I must record for the benefit of the 'Sybilla'[1] that we had good fare, clean though very homely beds, and moderate charges. After dinner, the two gentlemen and two others (young germans) joined to have the Grotto of Neptune lighted up. We ladies were to ride, but as I had just turned a corner of the zigzag precipitous path, I heard Minnie scream and saw her lying above me, on a soft mossy bank it is true, but close to the next descent of about 10 feet. Before I could get to her, the gentlemen had lifted her up and the Germans swore at the donkeymen in most of the modern languages. She was more frightened than hurt, and I was scared too, so we walked down the rest of the way. The water rushes under a fine cavern of travertine down a dark abyss. They throw lighted hay upon the stream and it floats down illuminating the depths and the vaulted roof. As we came up, there was a flame made within the temple of the sybil, and the delicate, well-proportioned pillars looked very pretty by the glare of the fire. Next morning by 8.30 we were on donkey-back, saw the delapidated Villas d'Este and Maecenas and the cascades again, then had a good lunch, and set off for the Villa Hadriana on our way home. Here we rode all over the extensive ruins - extremely picturesque, beautiful pines and cypress among the ivy-covered ruins, and blue mountains behind. There was a very little rain which did not much interfere with us. We returned to a late dinner very tired but much satisfied with our trip.

19 March. Here begins the dreadful holy week. Through the kindness of Monsig're Alberghini and the civility of the Hanoverian minister and Torlonia, we had many more tickets than we wanted, and were able to oblige several of our acquaintances. We went very early to hear the *Miserere* in St Peters expecting there would be little crowd and plenty of air. First we mistook the place and when Wm. discovered our mistake, we found that there was not a seat to be had in Chapel and scarcely standing room, the King of Naples being there. I applied in vain to Monsig're Prosperi who is one of the subordinates at St Peters; he could do nothing for us. Therefore we stood, hustled about in a most unsavoury crowd, heated, and devoured by fleas. However, we heard the *Miserere* perfectly, that is Mrs C[onnor] and I did; the rest would not stand so long. Afterwards in the twilight, relics were exposed in a balcony lighted up near the high altar, hundreds, perhaps I might say thousands, kneeling before them. The

---

[1] La Sibilla, an inn near the Temple of the Sybil.

partial light gave a most sublime effect which so delighted us that we went in three days to see the scene repeated.

20 March. The morning was cold and a little rainy or we should of [i.e. have] taken Miss D[ouglasse] with us to see the benediction. I had not thought it possible to see more than one thing that morning, but Mr P[ollock] insisted that he would fight my way into St Peters, where there was no going up stairs to see the feetwashing, so he went with us. We waited about an hour in the Piazza before St Peters in the carriage among a crowd of others. Cavalry was ranged between the fountains and the steps and, on the latter, enclosed by a dense throng of infantry and a band. On a balcony which looks but a small part of the front of St Peters but which contains 20 persons abreast, there were splendid trappings. The bells began to ring, and we saw approaching the balcony the Pope carried on men's shoulders on a high chair surrounded by all manner of splendour, the large Oriental fans carried on each side. It was just like watching the movements of a puppet. He rose slowly, outspread his arms to heaven, and then extended them to give the benediction. The action was graceful, the scene around was very striking. In a moment every knee was bent and every head uncovered. The silence in that immense multitude was such that we heard the old man's voice distinctly, with the accompaniment of trickling fountains. He threw down two paper indulgences for which there was a rush as they slowly fluttered down. The moment the Pope retired, we jumped out of the carriage. Mr P[ollock] and I went as fast as we could to the Lavanda, Wm. and Minnie among other friends to the Tavola.[1] We had a thorough crushing, but by hard fighting, Mr P[ollock] brought me to the benches where most of the ladies had been sitting three hours. A civil guard let me in and some kind Italian ladies allowed me to pass to Mrs C[onnor] and Clarkson and soon after I found a seat. Thirteen pilgrims sit upon a high bench. They are dressed in white with white caps like Fig drums. The Pope approached, attended by dignitaries who carried the basin, towels etc. Each man slipped the shoe from one foot, which is always clean, before the Pope bestows a small washing, a kiss, a nosegay and two medals on each. There are 13 from the tradition that when Gregory the 1st used to feed twelve pilgrims, an angel joined himself to the party. After this, we three went to the carriage where our friends were very glad to share the lunch we had brought instead of going home. Wm. and Minnie had had a worse squeeze than we had, besides the rush up stairs, to see the Tavola, i.e. the Pope serving 13 pilgrims at table. There were ladies fainting and gentlemen screaming. At 2.30, we went up to the Sistine to hear *Miserere* which began a quarter before 6!! One additional cause of the throng was the presence of that great lumbering blockhead, the King of

---

[1] The acts of humility performed by the Pope on Holy Thursday involving washing of feet and serving at table.

Naples, his wife and his infamous mother. We stood nearly an hour in a crowd and then were crushed in, so as to be taken off our feet. I am sorry to say our countrywomen and some others behaved shamefully. I heard this remarked by three different parties, and I was much annoyed by the loud talking and climbing over benches of those near me. Once in, there was no more fatigue and not much heat. The *Miserere* lasted only about 20 minutes. It is the 51st Psalm in Latin, the verses alternately chanted by the bass voices in a plain chant and sung by the higher ones in the most singular strains I ever heard, exquisitely touching, but such a complication of harmonies that I could hardly enjoy for wondering, felt the sort of eagerness to arrive at the close of the modulation that one does to see the end of a forest path. All the way is pleasant and one does not doubt being satisfied at the end, but it is so tangled that one is in a state of the utmost curiosity. It was said that the composition was by Allegri. On coming from the Sistine, we went into St Peters for the fine sight, and then came home tired enough. On St Joseph's day,[1] the custom is to eat fritters upon the tradition that the St. was a cook as well as a carpenter. Our Maria brought us some very nice light ones of her own making. All Easter week, the cheesemongers' shops are very smart, decked out like ours at Xmas. There are churches of butter and other excentricities. Minnie nearly sent our coachman into hysterics, insisting (by a slight mistake in the word) upon bringing me home a cheesemonger in the pocket of the carriage.[2] The fritters are sold all over Rome in temporary booths adorned with boughs.

Good Friday. Went to our own church in the morning and took the Misses H-s [Horne?] for a drive. By the by, you know nothing about them; they are two pleasing scotch girls, a little older than Minnie, whom we met one evening with their Father full of spirit and plans for the future. In two days, he was senseless and in imminent danger from apoplexy. On this day, he was somewhat better, out of danger, and I thought might go with us - they could not. I now remember the drive was another day when they were very glad to have an airing. In the evening, Mrs Cl[arkson] and Mr C[onnor] and I went to the Sistine for another *Miserere*, but not so early. We had no crowd, but some difficulty in obtaining seats. However, we were among a polite, obliging set of ladies. Minnie, Mrs C[onnor] and Wm. went to a convent and hospital where the nobility of Rome go at this time to wash really dirty feet and feed the hungry, gentlemen and ladies separately. Among others, the Queen of Naples was high busy and Lord Fingal's daughter. There was such a chattering that a cardinal in vain attempted to obtain silence to say grace. Again to St Peter's.

---

[1] 19th March.

[2] Presumably by extending the word *formaggio*, cheese, into *formaggiaio*, cheesemonger

Easter Eve. Early in the morning at the Sistine. Had a capital study of Michael Angelo's frescoes before the service began. There were very few spectators. The ceremonies were curious and some interesting as symbols. A procession went through the chapel and returned with 4 large pine cones silvered and one gilt stuck in the form of a cross on a huge Easter taper. There was also a taper of three branches carried on a long pole; on passing the first door it was lowered and one lighted. Then a hymn *Lumen Die* was chanted; this was repeated on entering the Choir, and on approaching the altar. Then the huge taper was lighted and afterwards all the others. The plain vestments of cardinals and other officiating priests were changed for richer ones. Before this, however, there had been a total silence of 5 minutes, emblematic of the period of our Lord's stay in the grave. Then the coverings which concealed the ornaments of the Pope's throne were taken off and, as the veil fell from a picture above the altar representing the resurrection, the *Gloria in Excelsis* was sung, of which the music somewhat disappointed me. In the afternoon, commissions. I must send this before I write up to the present time. You may guess I have not been able to write much. This is the 29th. I am no worse for the fatigues. A letter from you dated March 11th, and one from Mrs W. I think I told you we spent the morning of the 22nd at the Sistine and the afternoon upon commissions. Sunday, we went to our own church and thought with unspeakable happiness of the many dear ones whom I knew to be rejoicing in a hope full of immortality. What a choice blessing to have such a circle; yet I would that it were larger. Wm. did not like to go in the evening to see St Peters from the Piazza. I respected his scruples but, not sharing them, had intended to go and ordered the carriage, but finding Miss D[ouglasse] and Mr P]ollock] had both colds so that they could not amuse one another, I volunteered to go and read Dr Arnold's life to them, and I think they liked it. St Peters is seen admirably for a distant view from their windows. The first illumination was the most graceful aerial object of the kind I ever beheld. The yellow light of sunset had not faded when the lighting began. It was as if the building gradually became transparent. If bricks and mortar had a soul, I should say it was the spirit of the edifice rising into the sky. In about an hour, the cross at the summit suddenly started into bright light and, in two minutes, as if one gigantic hand passed over it, every point was kindled into star-like flames far more splendid, but to my taste less lovely, than the first.

24 March. My companions being quite tired of ecclesiastical ceremonies, I gave up my idea of going to those of this day and the next, and went hunting statues and bronzes. In the evening, we drove through an immense crowd to a house opposite the castle St Angelo where we had taken a balcony with the Swinnys and Connors to see the Girandola. It was a small place, hardly big enough to give standing room to all ten of us, close on the very brink of the Tiber and very near the bridge. Consequently we saw the

fireworks excellently and heard the noise terribly. I bore it as long as I could and then retired within the room with Mrs S[winny] who is no more born for a soldier's wife than I. The fireworks were splendid; such a blazing, whizzing, spluttering brilliantly, I never saw, and of all colours. One of the prettiest was a gentle stream of fiery particles to imitate waterfalls.

25 March. Had a great treat seeing Overber's studio; he is the first painter of these parts (or any parts I should say) in the expression of deep religious feeling.[1] I had a little distrusted the good Dr Grant's enthusiasm in his favour and resolutely refused to go and see them on Sunday, but took advantage of a festival. They are only drawings and small but full of expression and meaning down to the smallest detail. The scourging of our Saviour and the murder of the Innocents are among the most touching things I ever beheld. The drawing is also quite Raphaelish in grace. The prints of these two are not yet engraved but I have some others for Aunt K[edington]. Overber himself is an extremely pleasing man such as one might suppose Pascal to have been, ascetic to himself, gentle to others. Our old *Vetturino* Divoto found us out. We were mutually sorry that our respective plans could not be made to agree that we might take him again. Another very respectable looking man with capital recommendation came, but when you hear that his name is Amico Cupido!!! you will not wonder that at my years I could not trust myself to his guidance. To be sure, there was the trifling circumstance that he could not come back from Florence at the time we wish to start, but that spoils the story and must be kept in the background. This evening was our levée. We were disappointed of ten persons so the muster ran thus: Countesses: Lepel; Monsig'res: Alberghini, Prosperi; Drs: Grant; Revds: Frith and Connor; Poetesses: Montecchia; Musicians: Montecchia and Campana; Mrs Frith, Misses Price and Fielding, Messrs Smith, Exquisite, Raphael the Valet. The people chatted and did not seem more than usually dull, but we missed some of our brightest. Maria was the star of the evening. Minnie persuaded her to put on her holiday costume: the scarlet jacket with gold lace, full white skirt, silver pins and quilled ribbons in her hair; she looked magnificent.

27 March. Set off with the C[onnor]s for Frascati; they are most contented fellow-travellers; he is as enthusiastic as a boy, and the ladies enjoy everything and complain of nothing. The weather was delicious. We had a charming drive to Frascati where we immediately mounted donkeys to explore Cicero's Tusculum.[2] The scene recalled to me a translation of

---

[1] The artist Friedrich Overbeck (1789-1869) had been born in Lübeck. He moved to Rome during the Napoleonic period and remained there for the rest of his life.

[2] An ancient Etruscan site where subsequently many rich Romans, including Cicero, had villas.

Cicero's letters which I read many years ago. I could fancy his domestic and literary life among those beautiful woody hills, but I rather think his mind was too much fettered by the world to emancipate itself enough to feel all the soothing effects of the country. I wandered on foot a good way up to the summit where a wooden cross was placed, but upon the gentlemen's remonstrating I returned. We visited the Villa Aldobrandini on our return, and set out directly for Grotta Ferrata, eating our lunch as we went. At the latter place, we saw some good frescoes by Domenichino. Then we passed Marina and Castel Gandolfo, passing along the lip of the crater which constitutes the Albano Lake, and having a glorious sea view on the other side; we could see the white sails far out. While the dinner was preparing, we walked in search of Maria's mother who afterwards came to the inn. There was a glowing sunset. We went early to bed, but mine was of unrest from being eaten up with fleas and ticks burying themselves in my skin, a foretaste of the miseries I may expect in my summer travels.

28 March. Set out early in the carriage for Gensano and Nemi. The united charms of the scenery, the flowers, birds, and sunshine, kept us Oh!ing all the way till I, being tired of that part of speech, seated myself on a stone above the Lake Nemi at an unsocial distance. Some of our party prefered this lake to Albano; I did not. It is beautiful and tranquil, but has the gloom of a Swiss lake without the grandeur. The earth is gay with blossoms, a most lovely sort of hyacinth, deep reddish cyclamens, a yellow bell lungwort, snow drops etc. The view towards Naples was beautiful; we saw the Island St Felice distinctly, but the atmosphere was not quite clear enough to see Ischia. After a second breakfast about 11 at Albano, we mounted donkeys to ascend Monte Cavi - seven miles of steep and very rugged pathway, but well worth the fatigue. High above the Lake, but on the lip of the crater, we wound our way sometimes through a wood where the very light spring buds scarcely intercepted our view of the lake or the very picturesque villages and convents which crowned the hills around, sometimes over the bare rock, slippery enough ascending and rather too much descending. We were however well mounted. My steed was capital except an occasional bray accompanied by an attempt to flourish his heels and set off in a canter. In the midst of an extremely dirty village, Rocca del Papa, a lane too narrow for any carriage, too steep and badly paved for anything but a donkey, too filthy for any but Italian noses to tolerate, I, as advanced guard, shouted here come more beasts down upon us. The stupid men did not stop the other donkeys till we were all huddled together in the very worst place, where, with the additional charm of hearing the shouts and curses of all the drivers, we waited till forty! heavily laden asses, a horse. and a ram, were squeezed past us one by one. We held our noses and laughed. At the summit, we were kindly received by a monk who brought us excellent bread, wine, and apples, under the shade of a fine old olive, where there was a glorious view of snow-capped Appenines. The snow had

only disappeared from Monte Cavi 20 days, yet everything was bursting into leaf and flower. The monk spoke like a religious man. On our return, we stopped at another monastery where there are remains of an Etruscan tomb. An Irish monk was very civil to us ladies, while the gentlemen were admitted within. It was altogether a delightful expedition, but we were two hours too late and did not start from Albano for Rome till 6.30. A fine sunset was succeeded by bright starlight and I enjoyed the quiet close of our day, though I caught a little stiff neck.

29 March. Instead of indulging in a longer nap for which we all felt the greatest inclination, we were off by 8.30 under Dr Grant's guidance for the Catacombs of Monte Verde, Mr C[onnor] and Mrs and Miss S[mith] accompanying us. There was the same deep interest as in the others but there is less to be seen in their structure. Then in St Agnese we drank of the spring which supplied the Baptistry. I spent a few minutes alone while the others mounted a steep piece which, as I was rather oppressed with weariness and the hot day, I declined. When the party turned the corner and the lights and voices disappeared, my little taper alone lighted the roof which there was lofty and I heard the slow dropping of water at a little distance. Altogether the scene impressed me, and seemed to bring me so near the dead of past ages that future time grew short also. I felt it a small interval before I should join them and as if I must be in hurry to do some little service to them who gave me all my hopes, lest the night should overtake me too soon, even at the close of the longest life.

30 March. Sunday. 31 March - 4 April. During these days almost all our time has been spent about dress, commissions, visits, Vetturini, in fact the multitudes of little cares which must attend the change of place and of season. To refresh ourselves, we have had one sight each day: Church of the Cappuchini, the St Michael of Guido is fine, but did not interest me so much as the countenance of the St Francis in extasy by Domenichino. Villa Albani for the 3rd time - I did not however see much more for we took a party, and while the young people walked about, Miss D[ouglasse] and I sat in the sun. Villa Pamfili Doria, fine grounds, beautiful view, and lovely wild flowers. English burying ground, close by the old wall surrounded by remains of pagan grandeur and, on a little eminence commanding a pleasing prospect, I found the tombs of Hester Barrett and of Mrs D., the only ones of much interest and of happy thoughts for me. 1

5 April. Calls - people were most inconveniently at home. However, we got through in time to see St Clemente, very ancient and interesting, said to be

---

1 Hester Barrett had died in Rome in January 1833, aged 21. Mrs D. is possibly Mrs Frances Dowglass, widow of George Dowglass and daughter of Joseph Pollock. She had died in 1843 aged 57.

built on the site of the house of Clement, the fellow labourer of St Paul. There are not only fine pulpits of marble in excellent preservation, but the enclosed choir, and separation between men and women. There are curious mosaics in Sta Croce di Gerusalemme - did not amuse me much.

6 April. Sunday. The Communion, our last in Rome, where we have had much enjoyment and very many mercies. One great privilege has been that church, not that I think the instructions given there at all efficient (humanely speaking) to my mind. Mr P[ollock] walked home with us on his way to dine at a Trattoria, but, as it began to rain and he had not yet recovered from a severe attack of feverish cold, we insisted upon his dining with us. He went to a patient directly after and we had our usual quiet evening. On saturday evening, we had Miss Price, Mrs Smith and Signori Garofalini and Campana at tea.

7 April. Monday. Bills and bronzes and endless people coming three times each for matter they might just as well have done at once. All our arrangements are satisfactorily made (except being cheated out of 8 scudi) for starting in a roomy Berlin with a *coupé* with 4 horses on Wednesday at 7.30, the Connors going with us, and Mrs Volpy's family and friends of the C[onno]rs following in two carriages, so we shall be a large party. Today we had a last look at the Campagna out of Porta Pia. Minnie's Cameo is done and very pretty. There I must finish, for our Italian friends think it necessary to take leave twice, and the tradesmen require scolding three times. We had an agreeable evening with Monsig're Luciani first for a little while, then Monsig're Alberghini who will, I hope, drive with us today (the 8th). Dr Grant and the Signori Montecchi, ever so many more self-invited this evening, letters from Mrs C. and E.H.C. At last the continual succession of visits of various sorts ended by our escaping. I must tell you I called on Monsig're Alberghini hoping he would accompany us on our last drive in Rome. He could not, but he received us most courteously and took me through his handsome rooms to his library. I saw his brother the Cardinal. We then went to take a last look at Ponte Molle and St Peter's and returned to finish packing and see more people. We have been most fortunate about our apartments: not a murmur, nothing lost and very little broken. We parted on the best terms, and our Maria received a handsome present from our landlady for her care and good conduct. She is an excellent creature and I believe was really fond of us, besides being content with her wages and service. We had quite a levée of dwellers around to give us good wishes as we departed. We find our carriage comfortable. The *coupé* would be fatiguing for a whole day, but, for part, it is an agreeable change, and that arrangement leaves plenty of room for the four inside. We have a very pleasant looking *Vetturino* and tolerable horses, though one would not think them big enough for the quantity of luggage. The Campagna as far as Albano we had passed by starlight before. It is a

mournful looking plain. A line of tombs marks out the Appian Way, and ruined acqueducts etc. are scattered all around. The lovely country from Albano to Gensano I have already described when seen under a brighter sky. All the way to this place we could guess it to be lovely by occasional glimpses of the mountains on the one side and the sea on the other, but alas it rained almost all the way. We are but poorly accommodated here. We have agreed to dine with Mr and Miss Volpy and their family and are now very hungry. We sat down 15 to a dinner barely enough for six. Luckily several had very poor appetites and I for one was satisfied, but it was shameful treatment. The Volpys are a good-natured interesting family who rather remind of the C.s. We had only three rooms miserably furnished, five beds and a sofa between us, but our friends are so much disposed to be accommodating that the inconvenience is lessened as much as possible.

10 April. After a deluge of rain all night, we had another rainy day. Having risen at 6 and hastened our breakfast, when we saw 3 horses harnessed to the carriage, we thought we could take our places. Having sat some time expecting the other horse, we had the satisfaction of seeing the shoe brought with which he was to be shod before we went further. All the beautiful mountains obscured by rain, a straight level road bordered with a double row of beech and elm, not fine trees but pretty in their spring foliage, a canal on one side and a ditch on the other, for many miles a stagnant marsh looking like an inundation. We had a vicious leader who kicked about every quarter of an hour and entangled himself in the long rope traces. The *Vetturino* generally flogged him till he kicked himself out again, but often was obliged to get down and release him. The halfway house was so miserable that we consented to come on without stopping to Terracina having provisions with us. This place would be beautiful in fine weather with the sea and the rocks. Minnie and I went out for five minutes but were driven back by the rain. Mr Volpy coming before us had secured the utmost he could by taking two bedrooms and a sitting room for his large family, and two rooms with four beds for us. However, he insisted that Mrs Co[nnor] and Mrs Cl[arkson] should take one of his rooms and all his girls sleep on the floor in their sitting room. In spite of my protestations, it is so decided, and we have our two beds. We thought Mr and Mrs and Miss Fl[etcher] were behind us and sent down my card to Miss Fl. with an offer to share with them, but they had arrived early and were well accommodated. Ours is evidently the Hostler's room, for there is a bell at the window with a rope outside down to the street. There is not a woman to be seen. Our chamber *man* came in before dinner to look under our beds for knives and forks. In about two hours, we had a tolerable dinner and we are going very early to bed to prepare for a very hard day tomorrow. Oh, luckless wight, not one wink of sleep had I, and Minnie very little. Every quarter of an hour I was driven to desperation by the attacks of the enemy, lighted a candle, and killed from 6 to 10 fleas, and

tried to sleep, but fresh legions came on and rendered that impossible. Then was a violent storm, the sea roared, the windows clattered, doors banged, and the unfortunate grooms who were obliged to sit up among the over-crowded horses to keep them from hurting each other, shouted and swore. Glad we were to get up at 3.30 and, after all, had the mortification to see the carriages drive off before us, for our tardy *Vetturino* was not ready.

11 April. The road to Mola is close upon the sea and picturesque. We noticed the tomb of Cicero said to be raised on the spot where he was killed. Mola de Gaeta is a charming spot. Mrs C[onnor] and I took a little walk but were driven in by rain. There is a new suspension bridge over the Garigliano; it looks so un-Italian. Hereabouts comes the plague of custom houses. We were turned out while the carriage was completely unloaded and searched. Mr C[onnor] was obliged to leave his box of books behind. Nothing was forfeited and they were civil. We had been particularly anxious to get on this day because we heard that at the small inn at Sta. Agatha, there could not be nearly room for the number of travellers upon the road. Here again Mr V[olpy] stood our friend. He secured two small rooms for us. We four ladies took one and the gentlemen the other. We were not so badly off, however. We all slept and, considering the circumstances, we were well fed, and attended much better than in Parete's inn (the man of whom we hired our carriage) against whom I hereby warn my friends.

12 April. The road to Capua is very pleasing, continually varying outlines of the mountains on the left, and, on the right, the bright sea with the Islands of Ischia and Procida. At Capua, we saw a Cathedral and church which were not worth seeing. There we observed a difference in the appearance of the populace from that of Rome; they are as lively as their fleas. Such strings of maccaroni hanging up to dry like paper at a paper mill. The road to Naples, dull and flat, between vineyards where the vines are trained from tree to tree. There was a flat-leaved cactus as big as a full grown apple tree, many beautiful flowering shrubs and the Judas tree in full blossoms. More plague at the custom house on entering Naples from the circumstance of coming up with the diligence - which might have been avoided. On arriving, we drove to four hotels before we could get a night's lodging. I forgot to mention the great additional interest of remembering that it was along the very road we were travelling that St Paul passed to bear witness of the truth. There is so much dispute about the locality of the 3 taverns that one's imagination cannot attach itself to any particular spot, but this never disturbs my enjoyment in memories of all that is noblest and best. I could not fully give my mind to this pleasant train of thought because Mrs C[onnor] is very fond of chat and she is so willing to oblige that I was ashamed to wrap myself up selfishly in my own meditations. We all profess ourselves entirely satisfied with each other as companions, and

indeed I think we did contribute to each other's comfort. You will be amused to hear that the coolness and resolution of the party belonged to our trio and a thousand good qualities to the other trio. At the Bellevue, we were comfortable enough, and very merry over a good dinner, but my day's work was not done. We had seen some snug little rooms at the Hotel de Rome which would be vacant next day and wanted to know if we might take them, and spare ourselves the trouble which belongs to lodging, without being extravagant. I had previously dispatched a note to Mrs F[letcher] asking if I might call so late in the evening and Wm and I set off with a valet to see her; we were most kindly received by Mr and Mrs F[letcher] and Miss. An accurate calculation was made, and the result was that we could save but little by lodgings and might probably lose much by being more exposed to knavery.

13 April. Sunday, welcome rest. The church here is very convenient in its arrangement. The sittings are clear, the service well performed, a good sermon from a Mr King whom we had often seen at Rome. We met several acquaintances, and Minnie and I walked along the Chiaga (i.e. quay) to secure our favourite rooms. Poor Wm. had a head ache, partly bilious and partly fatigue - he exerted himself very much for the benefit of the whole party on the journey. Mrs C[onnor] also was knocked up; I stayed with her in the afternoon while Mrs C[larkson] went to church. Mr and Mrs F[letcher] gave much useful information to us all. Now of Naples; it is lovely.

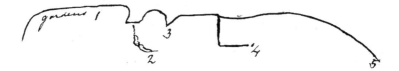

The Bellevue is at 1 looking over a very long public promenade (the Bay has this form just where the town is) - promenade with trees and the charming outline of Capri, but one cannot see over the trees except on the 3rd floor. 2 is a massive castle in the sea, 3 our present abode, 4 a lighthouse connected with the land by a low mole over which we look towards 5 where is Vesuvius. It is delightfully varied and pretty, quite answering my expectations.

14 April. In our new apartments, which are comfortable, and we are well attended. We dine at a restaurant attached to the hotel, going down stairs to a room built close upon the sea, so that it seems like being in a cabin. There are many other people and, though we have a separate table, we should rather prefer our own room, but we think 4 shillings a day too much for the difference. We soon settled ourselves and determined upon half a day's

sight-seeing. We drove by the gardens along the bay, then turned to the lake Agnano which is as like the Crater of an extinct volcano as anything can be. It is surrounded by conical hills. There are ancient baths of warm sulphurious vapour in small chambers. In the first is a bath like our modern warm baths in size and shape, and from two holes, into which the hands may be put, issue streams of warm vapour. Everywhere the ground sounds hollow under one's feet. In the second, much smoky vapour is continually issuing. It is said to be connected with Vesuvius on the other side of the bay. When the least spark of fire is kindled, even at the distance of 6 feet from the mouth of the hole, the smoke is instantly doubled, and increased still farther by more flame or a nearer approach. I am longing to know why, and hoping for many many days of delightful occupation in trying to understand the causes of some of the strange things I see. On our way to the grotto del Cane, we plucked some field flowers (it was a perfectly wild place). Up came a great fellow, armed at all points, who declared that the flowers belonged to the King of Naples and that he was *custode*. This was meant to extract money from us, but as we only laughed, he proceeded to inform us that the lake and the mountains were also the king's. Here our mirth became so great that he did not venture to assert that the sun too was the King's and he *custode*. At the grotto were two poor dogs waiting to be thrown into convulsions by carbonic acid gas for our entertainment, but I protested against the cruelty and we had two torches, a long and a short one which showed the effect of the gas, and the precise height to which the cave is filled with it, quite as satisfactorily. We went in with impunity, and putting up a handful of this heavy gas to our noses as if it had been water, it felt like the effervescence of champagne. We returned by a tunnel called the grotto of Posilippo, a third of a mile long, about as wide but more lofty than our railway tunnels, badly lighted in the middle by oil lamps, filled with bad air, and resounding from one end to the other with the accustomed shouting and screaming of Neapolitan drivers. The original passage is very ancient. Our coachman told us gravely the Devil made it. The contrast of lights and the rocky entrances are picturesque. Then we went a steep ascent (being told it was nothing) to Virgil's tomb, of which the remains would not identify his grave, but I believe writers do. It is but a vaulted chamber with a modern inscription. Certainly Pompey, Cicero, etc. whose names belong to this hill chose their places well - the scene is so beautiful all around.

15 April. A deluge of rain almost all day and a violent thunder storm at night. However, we were not idle. In the morning, M. Henri, pasteur of the french church, called and offered to introduce us to a private concert given by M. de Seivers. We then went to the cathedral which is a hodge podge of all styles and ages; St Filippo Neri rather a curious old church, pictures, including Guido's St Francis, but middling. There was preaching to which I listened for a while. The subject was the shortness of life. The orator

wound up his exordium by praying that his hearers might obtain the grace of our Saviour and the Virgin by the intercession of St Philippo Neri. At S. Severo (a curious old place, most barbarously suffered to go to ruin) there is a figure called modesty with a thin veil all over sculptured in marble. The transparent effect of the veil is extremely well given. Another statue is allegorical, an angel helping a man to free himself from the snare of the world. He is half enclosed in a fish net wrought out of the solid marble extremely [delicate ?] and light - but the third is full of beautiful expression as well as fine execution. It is a dead Christ wrapped in a winding sheet. The body is entirely covered, but the expression of past suffering and resignation is very touching. At 8.30 came M. Henri to accompany us to the concert. The singing was some of it very good and none bad, only piano and a small organ as accompaniments. The wife of the former Austrian Ambassador here and her daughter were among the best performers. There were about 150 smart people present, 3 officers of the royal guard in their uniform. I was so terribly sleepy, I could scarcely keep up, and it was not over till nearly one o'clock.

16 April. The pleasure of your letters and Fanny's, and I think both would find answers to their questions in mine already sent. I trust real spring weather has ere this sent away all coughs and colds. We have had many callers, Mr Temple, the Principe D. Dentice, Miss Cracrofts, while we were out. Dr and Mrs Macartney very pleasing young people, Mr and Mrs Fox pleasant elderlies. The Contessa Caradini, a lively Italian, M. Henri again, visits to and from the Connors and Fletchers do not count, the latter are most kind to us. They all enquire with much interest about Fanny - you will suppose we have had these calls to return, and to go to the bank etc. We drove with the Connors to the Campo Santo, a public cemetery in a beautiful situation overlooking the Bay and all its gems. Its little hills are covered with flowers and flowering shrubs. The place is still unfinished, but there seems a good arrangement and the precautions necessary in a hot climate. Then to the King's palace, Capo di monte, a large handsome house rather tastily furnished and having tolerable copies of fine pictures.

17 April. Set out with Mrs C[onnor] for Caserta, were too late for the railway which I thought very lucky, though I did not fail to scold about it. The weather was showery. We went to see part of the museum, some curious Egyptian antiquities found in a museum at Pompeii so doubly valuable, capital specimens of papyrus. The celebrated group of the bull and the Hercules both fine, but I think the Bull is the most gentlemanly. There is a little sentimentality in the attitude of Hercules which strikes me as ridiculous. Went shopping for coral and gloves.

18 April. Had the most exquisite drive and walk you can imagine to see some ruins above Poselippo said to be Virgil's house. The path down to the

road on the other side is on the face of the cliff, following all the indentations of the little coves with their still transparent waves, and there were the Isles of Ischia, Provida, Nisida varying their position continually like graceful dancers, and each new attitude the prettiest, and such colouring! so soft, so bright, so clear, and such wild flowers - nonsense, I cannot make you enjoy it. But I was not content with wishing only for you, my dear Mother, I wished for every one who is likely to read this. My sheet begins with a great day for which there was not room in the last.

19 April. Went by the 9 o'clock train on the railway to Pompeii. It is the oddest thing to see the hissing machines rattling along the very edge of these shores, Vesuvius frowning above, and the lovely mountains and islands on the other side of the sparkling sea, which is all studded with little boats, everything having as much the air of pleasure and as little of business as you can conceive. The very embankments of the road are covered, often more than 20 feet in length and for a great part of the way, by a large Mesembrianthemum, a bright pink blossom with yellow stamens, 4 inches in diameter. In an hour, we arrived, and within a quarter of a mile, I placed myself in a sort of Guy Fawke's chair, in which I was conveyed almost all the time we spent among the ruins. It is very strange to wander about the streets of this city. The pavement is perfect, even to stepping stones for foot passengers to cross the road. Then you trace long rows of small shops, and, in the dwelling houses, much of the details of their lives, their small sleeping rooms, the little garden, the tank for rainwater, the kitchen stove, the oven, the cellar, the mill stones. Of course, the objects of most value have been removed, sometimes copies are placed instead, and, if not, the guides point out where the most interesting discoveries were made, such as the threshold of a large house where one skeleton was found with keys and jewels, and another, following, with gold and silver vases, the cellar where the impression in the ashes of the bust of a woman was found. The circumstances you may read in many books, for the earliest excavations were the most fruitful. They are going on slowly. We saw pillars, opened about two months ago, from which the ashes had not crumbled away. In magnificence, the public buildings are not to be compared with those of Rome. They are principally brick with stucco, and far inferior in magnitude. The interest is that you see here the whole life of the people as if it were of yesterday. The very tombs unfinished, death came before they were ready, and their possessors were buried in ashes instead of marble. Everything was still, but bright. The little green lizards were darting about in all directions, and the view all around is charming, but Vesuvius was just overhead, smoking and looking treacherous. I should not like to stay here; the contrast is too oppressive. We stayed till 3.30, and returned by rail. We had wine and music there, both native produce and good in their way. The mountain flageolet has rich tones. A comical fellow with a big stick contrived to give what, till I saw him, I took for a song with

guitar and castanet accompaniment, but he had no other instrument than voice and thumbs. I could write such a glowing description of the view from our windows, with the silver moon bright, and the torches of the fishing boats wandering about the bay as if the stars had mistaken the blue sea for the blue sky, and Vesuvius flaming so as to send a long streak of red reflected on the water to us, and the prettiest shipping by way of foreground, but I spare you the fruitless attempt to convey any lively idea of the scene.

20 April. Sunday. A quiet day which I much needed.

21 April. Determined to nurse myself for Vesuvius. We did very little beyond a quiet drive with the Connors to Pozzuoli. Wm. slipped into a gutter and grazed the skin on his leg, so he was glad to be quiet at home. In the evening, we met a party at Dr Macartney's. He and his wife are very pleasing people. We were almost all English, and passed the evening in concocting plans for excursions together. I had a letter from Miss D[ouglasse] giving Mr B.'s opinion decidedly against her attempting to go to England or even cross the Alps. She longs to set out for Venice with us.

22 April. After a stormy night, a rainy day. Our schemes sadly defeated, we spent two hours at the Museum seeing a few good statues and some very entertaining collections of household utensils etc. found in Pompeii, magnificent candelabra and other things found in those baths of Caracalla at Rome where size struck me so much; these articles are, in proportion, grand. Found out the use of a vessel like a frying pan which has often puzzled me in painted or sculptured representations of ancient sacrifices. It served the priest carry about part of the victim. In the evening, we made calls and finished by drinking tea with the Connors.

23 April. Vesuvius wore his nightcap, but there was a freshness in the air with a bright sun which promised fair. Therefore, at two o'clock p.m., we with Mrs Clarkson, Mrs Connor and M. Henri in one carriage, Mr V[olpy], three daughters, a son, a niece and a courier in the other, arrived at Resina. The crowd of men, boys, horses, donkeys, mules, kicking, screaming, fighting, shouting, made a most ridiculous scene. Never in England, in any crowd, have I heard anything to equal an ordinary Neapolitan tumult. At last, we were mounted, the gentlemen and myself upon spirited young horses. Mine began operations by biting the others and jumping on all fours, Wm.'s ran away with him and 2 men holding at the tail, Minnie's mule set off at a canter on an independant trip to the vineyards, and, on our return, M. Henri's charger thought fit to dance a *pas seul* on his hind legs which unseated his rider. However, they were all surefooted. Such a helter-skelter procession it was, you would have thought it impossible we should go safely up a most steep and rugged road. However, we never hear of

serious accidents. At the Hermitage, we rested awhile, every body full of courage and fun. The young V[olpy]s are very spirited. Half an hour's riding and then the climbing, a most fatiguing scramble for an hour among loose rugged lava. Mrs C[onnor] and I were hoisted up à la Guy Fawkes, the poles of our chair being placed on 6 or 8 men's shoulders. Every now and then, they stopped to fight about who should carry us, so that we were in danger - and no very tranquil position for those carried. We were carried through the clouds, which were welcome shades for the sun though they intercepted our view, giving us, however, little peeps upon the sunlit plains below, as if we were looking down upon another world. Arriving at the outer edge of the crater, where every crevice sent forth sulphurous smoke, I expected to be set down, but over the lip they went to the sea of lava between it and the inner cone. I do not know how to describe the place, gigantic waves of blackish lava with great fissures, masses of green and yellow sulphur like mossy stones. We were close under the cone. First, I heard a hollow rumbling (thick smoke was always issuing) every few minutes. Then was a rushing sound like steam, and a volley of red hot lava was shot up, and fell down the cone. Notwithstanding this, all the party went up the inner cone except Mrs C[onnor] and myself. To me it was quite frightful to see the red lumps flung up as if the sport of demons. There was not so much feeling a personal danger as in the glaciers, but it was so treacherous, such a living acting power, that I longed to escape to a little distance. With a guide and a stick, I walked round to where the stream of red lava was flowing, tumbling heavily over in thick waves, where I stopped. The crevices under my feet were red hot, the guides poked out some in a liquid state. I have a piece with the impression of a coin in it, which I saw vomited from the crater. The girls' boots were burnt and torn and their gowns singed. My intentions had been to remain after sunset till the moon rose, but the clouds were gathering again, so I did not like to oppose Mrs V[olpy]'s wish to make the first part of the descent before it was quite dark. We went down a different way as far as the Hermitage. I imagine about two feet depth of black stuff as loose as sand with blocks of lava in it so perpendicular that the wonder was how it could possibly be piled up. In this, the walkers slid at a pace which made them giddy and we were carried backwards fast enough for running, but the long steps made it smooth except when my men fell. Anything more hideously desolate than this scene, with the sea of grey clouds beneath into which we were plunging, I cannot fancy. At last, we remounted, and by the time we reached the Hermitage, it was dark. We proceeded by torchlight, and a picturesque party we were, defiling through the rocks. There is such a childish recklessness among these Italians, and such a tremendous clamour, that it is impossible to make them act upon any plan, so that we were too much scattered, and I, being last but one, was sometimes left in the dark, but my sagacious horse performed admirably, and the ride was really amusing. The carriages were ready at Resina and, after seeing our friends home, we arrived ten minutes before eleven, glad to have seen such a wonderful phenomenon, and thankful for our safe return. I do not feel disposed to go again.

24 April. The weather was not promising enough to induce us poor tired mortals to leave our beds and go by steamer to Capri, which we had half intended, but we joined the C[onnor]s bestowing a cold rainy afternoon on Herculaneum, corals and calls. This city is very curious from the solidity of the lava which buried it, but nothing in beauty after the antiquities of Rome and Pompeii. There is little more than a large theatre excavated.

25 April. Shopping about commissions all the morning, two evening parties at night, but I think one will content us. We meant to have had a boat this afternoon, but it rains. Drank tea with Mrs F[letcher], met several people.

26 April. Set out early to Baia in a carriage and 3, looked again at the volcanic Lake Agnano, then to the Solfateria, an extinct crater from which immense quantities of sulphur have been extracted and which is now all over sulphurious and smells horribly. The ground sends forth a very hollow sound when a stone is let fall upon it. Everything tells of active operations below, but a sweet scented broom and a beautiful cistus blossom tranquilly above. A great earthquake has done much of the work of time here and changed the face of the country. Where there was a plain, there is a high hill produced in one night; there is a salt lake where were fertile fields. At Pozzuoli Putroli, we saw the ancient pier where probably St Paul landed and probably never thought of the pretty islands around, for his mind was set upon bearing witness for Christ at Rome. At the temple of Serapis, 3 fine columns remain, and above the marble pavement, fish are swimming, for the sea comes there though there are houses between it and the shore. The bridge of Caligula and the Amphitheatre. Then we went to a fine point of view close upon Misennum where we sat awhile to admire, and to drink the celebrated wine of the country. As to dinner, we took that in divisions as we went on in the carriage. All around Baia are remains of villas in the most charming sites, Marius, Caesar, Pompey, a theatre, a piscina, a circular temple to Mercury, where echo repeated whole sentences distinctly, the 100 chambers of Nero's prison. We went by torchlight into long narrow dark passages, so low in the entrance to the small rooms that we had to stoop - the most dismal places you can imagine, nothing grand, stupefied despair. There, we were close upon the Elysian fields and Acheron, the Lakes Lucrine and Avernus, the former nearly filled up by an earthquake. It is the strangest medley of thought here. There are all these evidences of volcanic agency which I quite detest; they give me a shudder. I look upon them with a mixture of terror and disgust which no other material phenomena ever excited in my mind. Then there is the smiling

beauty of the present state of things, the memorials of paganism and of Christianity and the actual superstition; quite too many and too various things to see and enjoy at once. At the hot baths, more long dark narrow galleries. A poor old man, nearly stript, proceeded to parboil himself in getting a little pailful of water from the natural spring to boil an egg. On the lake Avernus is the grotto of the Sybil. Another long dark gallery leads to several small chambers with low entrances where the water is above a man's knees. In these Wm. went astride a man's shoulders and crouching over his neck. We were much persuaded to do the same, and the example of all manner of princesses adduced, but we declined and did not lose anything worth seeing. It is not very certain that this was the haunt of the Cumaean Sybil. I had been on a donkey whenever we were obliged to leave the carriage and enjoyed the day without much fatigue.

27 April. Went to church where we had the sacrament, enjoyed the lovely view from our window. Mr and Mrs C[onnor] called to take leave before we set out on our week's tour. They have contributed much to our pleasure in Naples so thoroughly kind and sociable. We had plenty of friends around us, more than we had time to see. This letter is to be taken as news of my having returned to Naples, though it does not contain the journal to that time. I think we shall not return alone to Rome, and shall probably have one of the Divotos for our *vetturino*. I get on very well. We are none of us equal to much exertion, but we spare ourselves. We English ladies almost always over-work ourselves. Thank Father for his epitome of church affairs. I am by no means forgetful either of church or state in our dear old Isle.

Hotel Luna, Amalfi, 29 April. On the 28th, by dint of a grand bustle, we were in the railway by 8 a.m. for Castellamare, with only cloaks and carpet bags in true wanderer style. It was amusing that Wm., entering into conversation with an Italian gentleman, who gave us some information about our proceedings and recommended us to an inn, this person turned out to be the Duca S. Teodoro to whom we had a letter but who had never noticed it. We had a very pleasant drive in an open carriage to Sorrento on the edge of the cliff. Such narrow streets, it is wonderful how *one* carriage can get on in them. I must be sparing in my commendation or you will be quite tired of the beauties of this bay. We found perfect cleanliness and comfort but not cheapness at 'La Sirene'. The whole town is perfumed with orange blossoms. After a first drive, we went in a good boat with six rowers to Capri. The wind allowed us to sail only a little way, but it was calm and most delightful to all but Minnie who was sick. She soon recovered. We went direct to the blue grotto in about 3 hours. There, a little boat awaited us, in which Minnie and I squatted at the bottom, yet were obliged to stoop as we entered, most curious it is. The water is the most lovely bright blue reflected on the fantastic arched roof. The lesser caverns

175

look like so many little chapels around the large one where 8 boats might be together. Wm. had been landed first on a little spot within and looked like a ghost. The water is inconceivably bright. A child brought by the boatman plunged in to show the silver sparkles of the splash; the fish looked as if they were on the surface. We had been charmed by the transparent blue sea as we came. The rocks rise perpendicularly from the water in most parts of the island. It is very fine to look up at them and the fringe of light at the top. We returned to the town of Capri, mounted donkeys, and rode up to a height whence we had a glorious view of the two gulfs of Naples and Salerno. Indeed, all along the road was lovely. Here our guides and others proposed dancing the Tarantella for our amusement. An old woman beat the tambourine and two couples danced in very graceful movements, notwithstanding their bare legs and ragged dress. An old hermit received us very civilly, query, does he live there for the benefit of 'forestieri'.[1] We just tasted the nice wine and gave the bottle to our attendants. Into the boat we jumped to return to Sorrento as it was very calm and we were afraid to trust to the morrow. The evening was delicious. There is no telling how pleasant it is to float on the Bay of Naples while the sun sets gloriously. A specimen of Neapolitan manners: our six men began to sing 'Oh Pescoto' all together. At the end of every verse, they made the most ridiculous screech, all of a sudden pulled the boat violently with irregular strokes, splashing the water over us and rocking us, shouting out 'Macaroni Macaroni, we shall eat Macaroni tonight', then 'coraggio' and, as one of them had been to London, 'pull away'. We had several other songs and all sorts of nonsense. The men have all their mahogany-coloured legs and feet bare, and, as they grew warm, they invariably dispensed with jackets and trowsers, leaving only shirt and white drawers and very smart ear rings. We landed at 8.30, having had a delightful excursion. The perfume of orange blossom was wafted to us a quarter of an hour before we landed.

29 April. At 8, we mounted fine mules very smartly caparisoned with bells and fur and cock's tails on their bridles. It rained a little only, the dispersion of the mountain mist. We were told we had an hour and half across the mountain, and then would find a boat to take us to Amalfi. Instead of which, at the top of an excessively rugged descent which took us three quarters of an hour, we were told to dismount, because there was no practicable mule track further. The boatmen declared they would not stir except for an exorbitant price, and the muleteers said they must leave us there before we knew so much as whether there was a boat at any price. However, by refusing to pay the first before we were sure of the second, we brought them all to reason. The fatiguing descent repaid us by its beauty. Thence, i.e. from Scaricatoje, the coast scenery is lovely. The sea

---

[1] i.e. foreigners.

was perfectly calm. At the rough but clean little inn 'La Luna', we were most cheerfully served from the mention of Mr P[ollock]'s name; he is a great favorite there. After an early dinner, we set off upon donkies to see the beauties of Amalfi, though from the terrace of the inn, there is beauty enough to make the fortune of an English watering-place. If I could pack up one of their asses in my carpet bag, it would be a valuable acquisition, for they walk up and down stairs 'like any christian'. The *roads* all over the town and for miles round are (with short intervals) stone stairs; there is no wheel carriage nor even horse to be seen. We went, on asses, through several houses to a narrow rocky ravine, where a stream with a succession of cascades turns several mills, some for the manufacture of paper which is sent to Naples. This path is exquisitely picturesque. The finest summits are crowned with towers of the middle ages, or of the Saracens, or convents. We went to that of the Capuchins, and then went a little way on the road to Castellamare. The loveliness of this neighbourhood exceeds all I ever saw. We much regretted we had not time to stay a week or more.

30 April. At 9, we set out with an old chattering cicerone, two donkies and their leaders, a big arm chair tied upon poles in which I was carried by six men, poor fellows. It was desperate work for them and no joke for me, though they were very steady. My utmost efforts were required to keep my seat in going down; several times I walked. The charming scenery up to Ravello and down to Minore was a full compensation. At the summit are very curious Saracenic remains, and, in the vestry of the church, very pleasing pictures which have not yet been be-named and be-praised, a handsome pulpit of Byzantine work, and some Greek pictures. Here, to our great surprise, we found Mr S[winn]y enjoying the place as much as we did. There was a good boat waiting, and four stout rowers waiting for us with our luggage. We escaped with some difficulty from the importunate crowd. On our way, we went into a beautiful cave, penetrating 8 times the boat's length and it was large and had an awning. At last, we were nearly separated by a wall of rock from the sea and the reflected light sank into darkness a little way beyond us, very striking and making me feel a slight shiver. The cave was rugged and wild, hung with stalactites. Just below the water's edge were bright scarlet shells like holly berries, so hard and firmly attached to the rock that the sailors could not break them off. They looked beautiful in the clear water. As we proceeded, the wind rose and little white breakers began to appear, whereupon Minnie and Wm. disappeared from the benches and sat in the bottom of the boat. We bounded from wave to wave, the wind in our favour. I liked it extremely and the others were no worse. We were speedily in the bay of Salerno which, though beautiful, will not bear comparison with that of Naples. Minnie and I contented ourselves with lounging luxuriously in the balcony watching the mahogany legs draw in their immense nets. The men came home from work singing and playing on their sort of bagpipe very harmoniously. The impudence of

beggars in Italy is astonishing. The urchins pull a long face and make the most lamentable story; then if you say anything funny to them, they burst out laughing and the next minute resume the whine. They beg when they are so far off they look like dolls and you can just hear the scream 'Signore, Signore, da me qual cosa'. In order to be very insinuating they almost always tell us we are very handsome; once they tried that flattery on Wm. The country people are excessively curious. They would like to know our birth, parentage and education, and are equally willing to tell their own. Mr S[winny] was informed before he met us that there was an English milord with his two daughters! Women come down the mountains with immense burdens on their heads, helped by stout sticks and by no means encumbered by the length of their petticoats. We saw some beautiful knitting among them. In my bedroom at Amalfi, I had a curious representation of the Nativity in painted wooden figures, the Angels having gilt-edged wings and the Virgin being very smart. Painted wood seems their favorite way of representing sacred subjects. Looking once more on the sea before I went to bed, I saw little stars of light dancing to and fro on the shore which at first appeared to be Will o' the wisp, but when they went over the houses and over the sea, I could not tell what to call them, so we summoned the waiter, and he told us they were Fireflies and brought half a dozen of the pretty creatures into the room where they crawled and flew about to our great entertainment, showing everything distinctly 2 or 3 feet around them as they flew. We watched them flitting about among the myrtles, which, by the bye, were blossoming among the mountains. It was quite romantic and filled my head with poetry and song, which I spare you my dear Mother; if you want it however, ask Josiah to supply you.

1 May. Being a lovely morning and the sea very calm, Minnie and Wm. determined to risk sickness, partly to save me fatigue, and, according to what we were told, there appeared to be nothing to fear. We were to be on the water 4 hours each way to Paestum, and the waiter wished to prepare dinner at 5. By 8 a.m. we were in the boat with six men and a boy. After rowing about 2 and a half hours, they put up a huge sail, nearly square, which, with a side wind, carried us along famously, but alas! my poor companions could not enjoy it. They tucked themselves up in the bottom of the boat and looked very mawkish. The men, meanwhile, stretched themselves along all manner of ways, eating onions with bread and cheese, then took their pipes. They were very lively and remarkably well behaved. On landing, a donkey was procured for me whose equipments were a halter and a sack. I can assure the inexperienced that the play of an asses lungs in a hearty bray, with so little between oneself and his ribs, is a very comical sensation. Paestum exceeded my expectations. The plain is somewhat dreary - to me it looks like repose, not desolation. There is a profusion of wild flowers, with the blue sea on one side and fine mountains on the other, some snow-topped. The massive noble ruins are very striking on such a

site. Some cork models convey a most accurate idea of their proportion, colour and rough surface, but the real size is essential to their full appreciation. We could stay but 2 and a half hours, having employed 5 and a half in the voyage. The sailors rowed out some distance to catch the side wind and then hoisted sail. The yardarm broke and, in the midst of the confusion, one of the men stripped himself almost naked, screamed, stamped, tore his hair like a madman. I could not understand the patois in the tumult, but connecting this with the breaking of the yard (our only means of going 36 miles quickly being the sail), with the sailors having hurried us on board, with the threatening appearance of the sky, and with what I had heard of the frantic proceedings of Italians when in danger, I was heartily frightened till I succeeded in getting an answer and found the despair arose from the anchor having been thrown overboard in the scuffle. You cannot imagine anything more dramatic than the scene. For a long while, there were but two men cool enough to do any thing. The master threatened one man with an iron which made him sulk and refuse to work for more than two hours. They spliced the yard but the sail served only to keep the boat from going back while the men rested, and, as they could not or would not furl it, gave us a most disagreeable rocking. By degrees, the poor master recovered his senses and his shirt, which latter he caught up, sobbed upon it, wiped his eyes and put it on, then began to row, but often stopped, with all sorts of adjurations, to wring his hands. The whole scene was worth witnessing at some expence of fright and sickness. Happily there was but little wind for it became contrary. The clouds discharged themselves on the mountains. After a fine sunset, the stars came out so bright that they cast little streams of light on the waters. We crept close under the coast of Calabria, flat and desolate, relieved only by a few bushes, and the fires kindled on the beach by the fishermen who had drawn up their boats and were supping there. The evening star (Venus) was brilliant enough to cast a shadow, though I could distinctly see she was only a crescent of light. This part I really enjoyed, though certainly it seemed a long time before the fireflies welcomed us to Salerno. We arrived at 10.20. Our friends the boatmen were content with the present we gave to compensate the loss of the anchor. They were really fine fellows notwithstanding their passionate Italian ways so unmanly to our English notions. Very satisfactory was a good dinner and comfortable bed at the Hotel d'Europe.

2 May. As might be expected, we were not very active this morning, but we had a beautiful hour's drive among the mountains to La Cava where we sat enjoying the air, the quiet, and the view. In the afternoon, we mounted asses and went up the mountain to a picturesque spot where is the monastery St Trinità. - the scenery very Swiss, rocky defiles among wooded mountains with little cascades; the wood is different: it is the bright, yellow green of Spring on beeches and elms instead of the dark fir.

At the grotto, water is perpetually dripping through a large mass of rock forming stalactites which look like so many natural props. Then we went to the Boccatella. You cannot imagine anything more picturesque than this ride: the villages and churches are so well placed on the mountains, and, at every turn, there is a little glen and a stream.

3 May. We allowed ourselves time on our way to the railroad to see the ancient Baptistry of Noiera, which well repaid the trouble. It bears all the marks of having been a heathen temple. It is circular. The inner circle, about 10 ft. dia. with small columns, contained water. The next circle is of a double row of pillars set in radial lines. The arch connecting each two is more than half a circle. Arches at rt. angles to these last connect each pair of pillars with the outer wall. There are vestiges of the middle ages in the altar and some sepulchres, and there are frescoes. We were in Naples by 10.30, went directly to Mr C[onnor] who gave me your letter and dear Anne's. It made me very homesick to know that you and dear Father had been [ill] though the conclusion gave me reason to hope you are quite well by this time ...... We hear there is no certainty of a steamer from Ancona before the 26th; therefore we are glad to take advantage of remaining here till the 12th, when we are to have a *vetturino* we particularly wish for. At present, I am not sure we shall have companions. We shall be 10 days later in our arrival at Venice and you may reckon upon our being there at least a fortnight in June. We were making a round of farewell calls when at Mrs F[letcher]'s we found the note altering our plans. We therefore laid aside that business and had a drive along that beautiful Strada Nuova with the Connors.

4 May. Sunday. Went twice to church and walked in the Villa Reale afterwards, more than I have done before, and all the better for it.

5 May. After changing to other apartments to have the view of Vesuvius, we went to the gallery again, and Pompeii. The custom of decorating the walls of rooms with illustrations of the occupations carried on in them makes these frescoes (or rather distempers) very amusing. There is the kitchen, the schoolroom, the bath, the garden house, the fishery, etc. The bronze utensils are curious, just such a thing as a tea urn, only for charcoal instead of an iron, a portable kitchen range. I wonder how they could have parties in their small rooms if each dinner guest was stretched upon beds such as I saw; bells, the clapper to be struck against a flat circular piece of metal, very sonorous. In the evening called on Mrs M[acartne]y and returned to dress for a party at Mr F[letcher]'s. I had a long and very interesting conversation with Mr E-e. Miss F[letcher] is extremely agreeable, clever, unaffected and well bred, as far as I can judge.

6 May, To the gallery to see the cork models. That of Nocèra does not do it justice. The Neapolitan paintings with others, very few good. Directly after our early dinner, at which by the bye we met M. and Mme de Hässler, came Mr C[onnor] to entice us to go to the Camaldoli, a monastery on a neighbouring hill whence there is a fine view. We were sanguine about the weather and consented. We had a pleasant drive and a merry ride of donkies up to the top, but when we arrived, it became excessively cold and stormy, and the inhospitable monks would not take us in. We came down in a drenching rain and were rewarded by beautiful colouring. I believe the worse result was the destruction of our gloves and the consumption of an immoderate quantity of macaroni for supper. In the evening, M. Henri.

7 May. To the gallery to see more pictures, ancient jewellry, bread, eggs, pastry, fruit of various sorts, grains, vegetables, pigments of all colours found in Pompeii. A splendid agate vase. The sky was too cloudy for us to take a ride we had projected with M. Henri. Therefore Minnie and I had a walk in the cold but pleasant air of the Villa Reale. It is quite winter again. We stopped at Mr C[onnor]'s having promised to drink tea with them, but, after waiting there nearly an hour, the party arrived from Pompeii very hungry and tired, so we thought we had better come home to devour macaroni. Novel mode of conveyance, a boy seated on an aloe leaf which being split towards the top served for shafts as well as carriage, another boy dragging him.

8 May. Museum again, after which, as the sea rose and the dust made driving unpleasant, Minnie and I sat drawing or reading at our bedroom window, enjoying the rare treat of not being in a bustle. Mrs C[onnor] was again too poorly to allow us to drink tea with the C[onnor]s.

9 May. Very rainy day. As it cleared up in the evening, Minnie and I went out to make calls during which time Mr and Mrs Close called, not the Mr Close to whom our letter of introduction was addressed (he has been dead two years) but the brother and his young bride. We drank tea with the C[onnor]s.

10 May. Minnie and I took Mrs F[letcher] and Miss O. to the Campo Santo which we enjoyed and to the palace Capo de Monte where we were overtaken by violent rain which prevents Wm. going to Vesuvius, and our going to St Elmo with M. Henri. We called on Mrs Close, her mother and sister; they seem good-natured people. Amico Cupido! has made his appearance and we have agreed to let him convey us to Rome and to Ancona. Do not be alarmed - he is an honest *vetturino*; we were anxious to have him.

11 May. Sunday. We took leave of several acquaintances returning from church, particularly Mr E-e and Mr F. and his family, hoping to meet again. The C[onnor]s and F[letcher]s called in the evening, the former I believe regretted, as we did, to part company, but I hope we shall meet in England.

12 May. Professing to start at 6, we were off soon after 7. Wm. left us that he might go by rail to Caserta. Our carriage is very airy and comfortable, and Cupido seems a fine fellow. The avenue all the way to Capua, I have already noticed. Today the road is excessively heavy from the quantity of rain which has fallen lately, but the sun shines now upon the multitude of holiday folks pouring in from the villages to the festival of the Madonna del Orto at Naples, and to a fair at Capua. We might have been tempted to stay a day more at Naples to see the procession if we had not been informed it was on Sunday only. It is pleasant to think, as we set out on our travels, that a welcome awaits us at Rome. My companions quiz me for finding pleasure in the idea that we are every step nearer England. From Capua to Pietra Storta, the road approaches the Appenines, some of them snow-topped. It is pleasing like the Vosges from Strasbourg to Basle - it is not very much frequented. Cupido does not approve our coming this way. We suspecting him of being rather slow told him one reason why we were badly served on the other road was that our *vetturino* was always in last. 'Oh!', said he, 'we shall always be the cream (*à fior di latte*) for we shall be quite alone.' Mine hostess was making our beds in a place like a hay-loft. When I objected to the sheets because there were brown marks upon them, she assured me it was only the birds when they were hung out to dry and they were quite clean. To our astonishment, we all slept comfortably, and were not starved. Wm. accomplished making tea by pouring boiling water from a saucepan into a coffee pot without a lid. We had 3 dogs, a lamb, and cat for company.

13 May. A beautiful drive among the mountains to S.Germano, where we arrived about 10 (less than four hours). Minnie and I on donkies, Wm., on foot, set off immediately for Monte Casino, a Benedictine monastery on the mountain above the town. The ascent is lovely: snow-topped mountains and lower ones of varied and most graceful outline, a fine old ruined castle, an old Roman amphitheatre, a river in the rich plain below, wild grey rocks, among them young oaks and other trees of brilliant foliage, then, on the summit, an imposing building capable of containing many more than the 200 who inhabit it. There is a large seminary in the monastery. The church is splendid with marble and paintings in the style of St Peters, and pleasing also in its proportions. While we waited for Wm. who was allowed to go into the monastery to see the Mss., etc., Mass was sung to a very skilful organ accompaniment. The *Incarnatus* was extremely harmonious. It was long since I had heard music; I was delighted to listen. Minnie no doubt greatly edified the monks by her air of profound

meditation for she took a quiet doze. The vestments of the priests etc. were rich. There was the most picturesque contrast: on the handsome marble pavement, urchins nearly naked with women barelegged, having a sort of horse cloth striped in gay colours literally only wrapped round them, and white veils worn square upon their heads. We then sat awhile under a tree, and, when Wm. came, went down again, right hungry, having spent 3 and a half hours on the expedition. By one of the odd turns to which I am becoming accustomed, this rough ride did me good - I had been rather poorly the day before. The amphitheatre is the largest piece of reticulated brickwork I have seen. The effect is rich; little is visible beyond the outward walls. The road was still among fine hills and fertile vallies. For a little while it rained. The scenery became tame as we approached the frontier of the papal states. Five times in 2 days, our passports have been examined. We are at Cepeano, a wretched place.

14 May. In our bare rooms, we had notwithstanding good rest. We managed to make tea in 3 gruel cups from a huge vessel without a spout. There was neither tea nor coffee pot, but we had a good breakfast by the contrivance of Cupido who had brought butter from Naples and bread from St. Germano. The *Lascia passare* did good service at the custom house - we were not troubled. The country rather wild and dreary, mountains distant, the roads very heavy and hilly. A long ascent, for which we had oxen, brought us to Frosinone, perched in a picturesque way on the summit of a hill, thence past a sulphur stream to Ferentino, also on a hill top. We are in a rough little inn. Just now we were attracted to the window by harmonious voices singing a Litany, *Ora pro nobis*, etc., about 15 women and 4 men. They had each a large bundle on the head and a long staff in their hands, and a very pretty group they made, kneeling and singing on the steps of the little chapel. They had a small doll representing the Virgin which they wrapped in a shawl as carefully as if it had been a baby. They come from Loreto and were passing on to other churches. After the Litany, they sat down to rest and eat. For our part, we have eaten the pigeons which were fluttering about as we drove up, and by way of fruit were offered sweet fennel which we declined, and then raw peas in the pod were served as an accustomed desert. A thorough rainy afternoon in which we passed a little tract of dreary country and came into rich woodlands which reminded me so much of Suffolk that I dreamt of being received with my dear Aunts' kindly welcome and longed for the cheerful fireside. The little town Valmontane perched upon a hill and surmounted by a palace of the Doria family, to whom all the neighbourhood belongs, clipped the wings of my fancy, brought me back to Italy and the probability of beds full of fleas and unwholesome food. On arriving, we are agreeably surprised. New people have just taken the inn which is large. They are very anxious to please, and the place is clean, though not yet in thorough repair. Peasants in the district through which we have passed have a very simple method of

stacking their wood: they pack it into branches of a spreading tree. I think they cut away a little to make room for it. The women carry immense burdens on their heads. They are a savage looking race, so very little clothed except on their heads; their begging gesticulations are inimitable. What different notions they have from ours about ornamenting their houses. Our hostess explained to us that they were expecting their Landlord (the Dorias) to share the expense of painting the walls so as not to leave the shabby white. No doubt there will soon be pretty arabesques, but the brick floors will remain; they suit the climate. I always dread carpets: they are such nests for vermin.

15 May. Through beautiful hills and the mournful Campagna to this strange city, Rome, where the memory reigns with such despotism that she has banished Hope. It looked beautiful in the distance, but the old fate awaited our approach, i.e. a torrent of rain. By virtue of our *Lascia passare*, we were not stopped at the gate, but accompanied to the hotel by a dragoon who turned carts out of the way with a wonderful air and by a soldier on the box. Our Neapolitan treasures were not molested. We found Miss D[ouglasse] still poorly, Mr P[ollock] better. We settled ourselves at the Hotel d'Allemagne and drank tea with Miss D[ouglasse].

16 May. A pouring day, but we had too much business to stay in. I will not detail all our work about commissions etc. We went to see Mr Smith but, to our great disappointment, found that Miss S[mith] has the chicken pox so slightly as not to occasion any anxiety, but we could not put ourselves in the way of infection. By way of treat, we went to see Raphael's Sybils in Sta. Maria della Pace; they are very graceful. Then to St Peters. The galleries leading to it are already adorned with fine tapestry etc. for the festival Corpus Christi, which I regret not seeing. It was the third time I had wandered about that magnificent building to take leave of it. Dr Grant and Mr Frith came in the evening.

16 May [wrongly dated - presumably written on morning of 17 May]. Mrs and Mr Smith called. They fully expect to be in Rome next winter and hope to meet us, Mr Frith also. We are going to drink tea with Miss D[ouglasse] and, if fine, with Messrs Smith and Frith and Dr Grant to see the Coliseum by moonlight. This afternoon to the Sciarra Palace[1] and anything else for which we can find time. We start on Monday for Ancona expecting to go on the 26th to Trieste and on the 27th to Venice where we hope to find letters.

17 May. When I concluded my last, I thought there could be nothing more to say about Rome, but I had too great a treat to be forgotten. We went to

---

[1] Contained many paintings formerly in the Barberini collection.

Miss D[ouglasse] finding her overwhelmed with leave takers. Minnie and I had a quiet drive round the Pincio looking on Rome, then returned to tea, and at 9.30, with our party, drove to the Coliseum. The moon was bright, the place was not crowded with visitors, the owls flitted about with a melancholy musical wailing cry quite different from the 'tu whit tu whoo' of our owls, though we heard also the scream as of a child in pain which I have heard in England. There was the Cross in the centre of the amphitheatre as we looked in from the surrounding passages. Looking outwards, there were the ruined palaces of the Caesars, all as it were bound into one whole by the indistinct moonlight, and they seemed to me more than ever present realities linking me with past ages. It is impossible to describe the scene, but the enjoyment is not to be forgotten.

18 May. Sunday. Miss Price and Mr Smith called and brought us a beautiful cameo of Mrs S[mith], a good likeness of her fine face, but not equal in workmanship to Minnie's.

19 May. We are fairly under weigh with our new companions and Maria. It is her first journey, poor girl. It remains to be seen how she will get on. Every thing promises well at present. Miss D[ouglasse] arrived at our dining place without much fatigue. We jogged on very comfortably to Civita Castellana. Nothing very striking on the way but the view of Soracte which stands alone beside the road. We are in quite early, Miss D[ouglasse] very bonnie.

20 May. Off early that we might have time to see the fall of the Velino (see Byron).[1] A fog hid the beautiful descent from Castellana, but the latter part of the road to Narni is lovely, fine wooded hills and rocks, the river Nar in the valley, and several picturesque buildings on the heights. Increasingly beautiful all the way to Terni, where, as soon as we arrived, we had another carriage with post horses to go to the celebrated falls five miles distant. Minnie and I went through the valley on donkies, Wm. and Mr P[ollock] on foot. Miss D[ouglasse], I am sorry to say, is not equal to such expeditions. The valley has all the beauties you could desire united, picturesque mountains, woods, towns, and a rushing river. There is no conveying any impression to you. It is most lovely, and the cascade more beautiful than any other I have seen. There is not only the water itself in all manner of graceful and magnificent forms, but also, on one side, a splendid landscape. There was a beautiful rainbow continually changing its place. One peculiarity was that, from the spray which rose from the very top as we looked into the sky, there was the most graceful rainbow, like a delicate drooping coloured feather, while, from below, rose another nearly meeting it and completing the circle. The obstinate postillion would not drive fast,

---

[1] *Childe Harold's Pilgrimage*, Fourth Canto, verses 69-72.

though we were anxious not to keep Miss D[ouglasse] waiting for dinner. However, she seemed none the worse, and we all went to bed, as usual, very soon after this meal.

21 May. Through a lovely mountain defile the whole way to Spoleto. We got on capitally. Miss D[ouglasse] grows better daily, and we are very happy together, Maria and the little dog included. The afternoon drive, less striking but still pleasing. We got out of the carriage to drink of the clear stream Clitumnus and visit a small temple on its banks. I wish you could peep at our party. We must look very snug: the *coupé* has such low windows that it by no means cuts off communication between its inhabitants and those of the inside. It is in such request that I have not attempted to sit there yet. Sometimes Wm. sits beside Cupido, Mr P[ollock] sometimes on the luggage at the back. Sometimes we listen to Lord Byron or Shakespeare, sometimes to Murray or Punch! Miss D[ouglasse] reads St Catherine of Sienna, I, Niccolò de' Lapi, Minnie Thierry's *Norman Conquest*.

22 May. Seven hours crossing the ridge of the Appenines to Muccia, a beautiful mountain road made doubly enjoyable by pleasant weather. You will be tired out with descriptions, so I will only tell you that just at the very top, there was a lake. The trees up so high were not yet in leaf though there was only one little patch of snow. There was my great favorite, a bright dancing mountain stream accompanying us most of the way.

(Omitted from yesterday). Arrived at Foligno, Minnie, Wm. and I went to the cathedral which had very little to reward us except an ancient Lombard gateway.

We have had a long journey today, so much of it foot pace - we had four oxen for a long way. We travelled beside the river Chienti which twists itself into all manner of fantastic meanderings. The valley is rich in trees and corn, altogether a very pleasing landscape. Tolentino is on a cliff immediately above the river. I had expected something special in the way of accommodation but am disappointed. Minnie has found a little boy to play with to her great delight. So ends our 4th day and I begin to feel, as usual after a few days, a sort of acquiescence in my fate of being boxed up and jumbled along all day, almost hopeless of the relief of arriving at the end of my journey. What a pity so much shaking should be wasted on me. However, the beautiful scenery is by no means wasted.

23 May. Macerata, where we lunched. An agreeable but not striking road, very fertile. Macerata is a very respectable looking town. We had a sprinkling of rain on arriving, but afterwards went to see the cathedral where there was nothing of interest. The same scenery continued till we

approached Loreto when we came within view of the Adriatic. This is a clean little town, but it is quite ludicrous to see the traffic carried on in rosaries, crosses etc. which the multitudes of pilgrims to our Lady of Loreto buy and have them blessed at the sacred house. We were quite beset in passing through the street. There is a depot in the hotel at which we heretics have been purchasing. Before dinner, we went to see some pictures in the Pope's palace. The only one worth looking at was a sketch of the Nativity by Gherardo della Notte. We should have seen the coast of Greece if the sky had been clear; I was quite vexed to miss the sight.

24 May. All very merry this morning. Miss Douglas even able to accompany us to see our Lady of Loreto. The church is ugly outside but has three fine bronze doors. Within is a small room of which you see, on entering, the bricks and mortar and dilapidated plaster, but it is almost covered with silver and gilt lamps. It was crowded with worshippers. The altar is brilliant with gold and gems, a black image of the Virgin (the work of St Luke!) is quite a blaze of diamonds and other precious stones. There are two modern house bells, and a brass window grating said to belong to this original house in which the Virgin was born, to which she returned from Egypt, and which, after many wanderings, she caused to be set down here. This room is enclosed in handsome marble walls, of which some of the bas reliefs and statues are very good. Outside, on the pavement around it, are two grooves worn by the knees of the pilgrims who go round it kneeling. Maria went with us and seemed to value the privilege very highly. Poor girl, she seems faithful to her measure of light. We then went to a dispensary to see 380 galley pots! they are ugly things, painted terra cotta done after the designs of Raphael and G. Romano in a manner said to be unknown now, but as the colours are burnt in and varnished, I do not see any advantage over our present porcelain. Six hours brought us to Ancona where the best inn was too full of English to admit us. Therefore, instead of a beautiful view of the Adriatic, we have very suspicious looking apartments in a back street. So ends our carriage journey together. I hope we have contributed mutually to each other's comfort. Miss D[ouglasse] has borne the fatigue extremely well. The country today was like the Sussex coast, except that once a fine range of snow mountains came in view.

25 May. Sunday. Found we had nothing to complain of in our quarters. After some indispensible business and a little walk, we read the service together. When I enquired about English, French or German public workship, and the waiter answered in the negative, he endeavoured to console me by saying there was a Jew's synagogue. We had some discussion about proceeding on our journey by land, seeing that we have to wait here at least two days, and at Trieste nearly two more. Miss D[ouglasse] was so appalled at the prospect that she would have gone in a

sailing vessel if there had been anything tolerable. Happily there was not, for it would have been imprudent for her. After dinner, we had another walk and more reading.

26 May. Miss D[ouglasse] much better for a quiet day. Mr P[ollock] and I had a tedious attendance at the bank and the unwelcome news that the steamer is not yet in sight; it is one of the Levant vessels. We should have had 7 and a half days more land travelling, two of them on bad roads and much more expence, so we determined on the sea, and I believe we none of us reckon the voyage any great treat. Maria never saw the sea till she came here and is afraid of being sick. I have been a good sailor lately but am afraid of seeing the others ill. I would not have you here for a good deal. At six, we were to be on board. It was raining but soon after held up. After waiting awhile in a nasty office, we were put into a large boat with about 20 more and all our luggage and thought we should reach the steamer in a quarter of an hour. No such thing: we were taken by the surliest of a charon who ever rowed in this upper world to the Sanità, or quarantine house, where we sat in the boat on our boxes during a most ridiculous scene of calling over our names. In spite of the annoyance, we laughed at the caricature of slowness and stupidity exhibited. A good tempered friar helped as well as he could through the Italian and french, but the English he declared impossible. At quarter to nine, we were on board and moving. The vessel came from Athens and was nearly full before 50 were added. You may think what a scuffle there was for beds. I secured one for Miss D[ouglasse] and a sofa for Minnie. We were 27 ladies, a nurse and a baby in a cabin about 14 ft. by 10. Happily there was no rain, therefore five ladies and several gentlemen passed the night on deck wrapped in blankets. Miss D[ouglasse] was comfortably tucked up and slept. Minnie was very sick. I lay on the floor beside her, for if we had not helped one another, there would have been terrible catastrophes. The steward was so very seldom to be found, though very civil when he did come. The floor was completely covered with ladies, some of whom had mattrasses, and they were almost all particularly good-humoured, well-bred people. Every one was ready at little kindnesses. A wind very nearly contrary sprang up, and we had such a rocking with all its consequences on which I shall not enlarge further than to mention that none of the droppings of the oil lamp swinging over us lighted on my nose - by good luck. The heavily laden steamer creaked as if it must go to pieces at every roll. At four, Minnie was quite asleep, so I dragged myself on deck. You may guess what a set of miserable objects I found there. A fine sunrise, and a very chatty french lady amused me. I was not sick but very uncomfortable with head ache and side ache.

27 May. In the course of the morning, the wind lulled and the air revived me so that I could go and visit the captives below. Mr Pollock and the little

dog made their appearance, and a sorry figure it was; they had both been ill all night. Wm. escaped, having been well dosed beforehand and keeping himself quite still. In the course of the day, a mattrass and deck [blanket?] were brought on deck for me and that was comparative luxury. At 2.30 p.m., we arrived in the harbour of Trieste, and here we had the greatest vexation of all. The wind rose again and we were kept rolling about till 7.30. Not only the ship's papers were examined, but everything (even the carriages) was taken out of the vessel before we were permitted to land. You may guess how we English stormed, and how we vowed never to come again, and to tell all our friends. I hear we are 150 persons at the Hotel Prince Metternich, but everything so clean and orderly it is delicious.

28 May. We had a vehement desire to go to the Cave at Adelsberg,[1] but we must have had a day of 15 hours travelling and much fatigue to arrive again at Trieste for tonight's steamer, or have waited till friday. It is also a very expensive trip, and we did not wish to part company with our friends, so the plan was given up. I wished Minnie to have a walk to make her sleep tonight. Not liking to send her alone with the gentlemen, and not daring to mount the hill myself on foot, I asked for some sort of quadruped. The only thing to be had was a fine tall horse upon which I was perched in my cloak. I am surprised to see such a very bright flourishing place, good streets, shops etc.; in the suburbs and neighbourhood, pleasant looking country houses. The eastern costumes and merchandise we see here are novelties. There was a Turk squatting on his heels just before our window, such a picturesque figure as hitherto I have associated only with painting. The women have a very graceful white head dress and are often pretty. We had two Greeks on board in their white petticoats and handsome jackets trimmed with fur. When I came on deck at sunrise, there was nothing to be seen but the interminable sea, not even a sail within the horizon. The first land which came in view was Istria, so I have looked upon Greece not without wishing to see it nearer. I have no taste for more sea, nor for the rough travelling there, but some how or other, the ancient Greeks always interested me more than the Romans, and my historical recollections of them are the most lively. Trieste is surrounded by hills which look like chalk, and the shore approaching it from the south is flat and ugly. At a delicious table d'hôte where we met almost all our quondam companions, many expressed their fear about going in the evening boat which they said, if there was the least wind, would wait at the lighthouse all night - but the sky promised a perfect calm, and at ten we were under weigh, Minnie and Miss D[ouglasse] comfortably tucked up in their berths, I with some other ladies on deck. The night was warm, and lovely starlight, moonlight, and early dawn succeeding each other within a few hours, I enjoyed it

---

[1] An enormous complex of underground caverns lying between Trieste and Laibach (Ljubljana).

extremely. In such scenes, one gains glimpses of the true proportion of things climbing 'creation's golden steps'.[1] I visited the captives below and found them comfortable, so I took my coffee on deck at daybreak and felt no chill. The boat rolled abominably notwithstanding the calm. At last Venice 'rose like an exhalation'.[2] It is indescribably pretty, and, as the boat skirts the long low island which shuts in the entrance, the beautiful forms seem animate, and glide swan-like in the waters. In spite of all past miseries and impatience for land, I no longer wished to arrive, but only to continue seeing that charming succession of pictures. I knew them all before through Canaletti; he is inferior only to the reality. As soon as we stopped, I was told a gentleman asked for me; it was Mr C. who most kindly came in his gondola to help us. Minnie and I stepped into his boat, the rest followed in another, to find rooms at some hotel. We could get none to our mind, the town is so full for the approaching regatta. By this time, we were terribly hungry: we landed at 7 on the 29th. Mr C. most hospitably insisted upon taking us all six to his house to breakfast. I have not room to tell of half his kindness, or of Mrs C., but never were people more thoroughly hospitable.

You will not wonder that there is a gap in my journal after I heard of dear Father's illness. I neither observed or remembered any thing, but I will begin from the time of having my mind set at rest by two favorable reports.

June 3. Saw part of the Doge's Palace; the exterior pleases me extremely. If I were to describe it, you would probably form an idea of a motley tawdry building, yet the effect is rich and pleasing. The rooms have the remains of magnificence in the walls and ceilings painted by Tintoretto, P. Veronese, Titian etc. Very few of these are interesting simply as pictures, but many as records of Venetian history and manners. We saw the original of Fanny's picture: Religion appearing with a cross to a Doge arming for a crusade.[3] Her's is a very faithful copy, only in the countenance of the Doge there is less manliness and more of what Italians would call *accoramento* than in her Doge. The chambers of the council of ten, and of three, and the prisons are divested of all the terrible legends belonging to them by the zeal of the old *custode*. For the honour of the extinct Republic, he will not allow the tenth of deeds of treachery and cruelty in its days of vigour, but says they are fables told to foreigners. The prisons are gloomy and secure, but not even underground, still less under water. They are small closets boarded all round with no other furniture than a raised plank for a bed and a shelf, and having only so much light and air as comes through a hole, half a foot in diameter, in the thick wall, from a passage. We have not seen the

---

1 Edward Young, Night Thoughts, Book IX.

2 John Milton, Paradise Lost, Book 1, l.710.

3 Doge Antonio Grimani before the Faith, by Titian.

'Piombi'.[1] The hall built for the Library collected by Bessarion and Petrarch[2] is handsomely ornamented, having in the ceiling three very fine paintings by P. Veronese. Certainly I had no notion these Venetian painters were so good, seeing their works only in other places. The palace of the Viceri is nothing remarkable; some of the pictures are good, but none very interesting except a 'Christ brought out by Pilate' by Albert Durer. This is the strangest place! a water city. We make walks for ourselves with some difficulty. Otherwise we need only glide about in our gondola in a thing covered with black cloth, like a big chest with windows, a door, two comfortable back seats, and two uncomfortable side ones, enough to rest our feet, sometimes with a canopy on poles over us, or, if there is neither sun nor rain, without either. I cannot do justice to the attitude of our gondolier. He stands like the Flying Mercury with the most graceful lightness just perched on one side of his boat. In the afternoon, we went to the cemetery which possesses no great beauty or interest, but half the pleasure of any sight here is the going there, whether through the small canals or the open lagoons. We returned by the railway to Padua, i.e. seeing that part which is built four miles on the sea. The young men exercise themselves by taking a second oar in each boat. They find the manner of handling it different to their English practice. The little dog has become so accustomed to this way of moving that he amuses himself with jumping from one gondola to the other when we go along side. It is really the most luxurious method of conveyance imaginable. The Gondoliers turn a corner or pass other boats (without touching) so close that I should be sorry to leave a finger between them. On turning a corner as they approach, they call out in their barcarolle language 'me first'. If another is coming up, he answers, and the first says 'right' or 'left' generally in a quiet tone. The stillness ....

---

[1] The Piombi, the prison cells below the roof (*sotto i piombi*) of the Doge's Palace, had been made famous by Casanova's description of them and of his escape from them in 1775. They were destroyed in 1797 and subsequently converted into living and store rooms. Some cells in the storeys below, the so-called *Pozzi* were still open to visitors.
[2] Petrarch had donated his collection of manuscripts and books to St Mark's in the 1360s, and the library had been further enriched in 1468 by the collection of Cardinal Bessarion, patriarch of Constantinople. The library had been moved to this location in 1817.

Postscript

So far, this journal has been presented as one which is interesting and entertaining from its intimate and often humorous style, from the circumstances of two women travelling alone, at least for part of the journey, at a time when this was still uncommon, from the light it casts on the lifestyle of British travellers on the Continent just before railways fundamentally altered the habits and speed of travel, from the way the character of the two women emerge, and from the memorable way in which people and events are described. But there is another dimension to the journal, for it describes, without any explicit allusion to it, part of a most remarkable personal history: how the illegitimate daughter of a Liverpool merchant born in Peru came to marry a doctor whose brothers included a clergyman and a judge, and who, himself, became a private consultant to Queen Victoria. This aspect of the journal can only be appreciated when more is learnt of the identity of the two women who feature in it and thereby some access gained both to the reasons behind their tour and to the consequences of it. To uncover this information proved no easy task.

Having been bought rather than inherited, the journal came with no anecdotal background - the starting point of any investigation had, therefore, to be the text itself. In the most obvious ways, this proved unhelpful. In particular, there was no indication of the writer's name on the flyleaf or at the start or end of the journal, and, because the first entry was written in Boulogne and the last in Venice, no indication either of where, in Britain, the travellers resided. The first clue as to the writer's name emerged from the account of Minnie leaving behind at the inn at Empoli the watch given to her by the writer's mother, Mrs W. On the assumption that the writer was not a widow, she must have been Miss W., an inference further supported by the entry for 2 February1845 where an acquaintance believes they have recognized her at church and asks Minnie and William for confirmation.

Final ratification came from the following up of what proved to be the single most productive clue in the journal. On 24 April 1844, when the ladies were in Paris, Miss W. received a letter from her mother mentioning a mutual acquaintance named Mary. Miss W. responded with the request to 'give my kind regards to her and tell her Miss Malvars does not forget the kind care she took of her and desires to be remembered.' As this sentence is phrased, Miss Malvars could have been either the writer - impossible if she was indeed Miss W. - or Minnie, or a third party. It just so happened that while I was speculating on this, I was engaged in research on British Passport registers and therefore took the opportunity of examining applications for the period prior to 8 April 1844, the date the two ladies arrived in Boulogne. Here, by good fortune - and it was good fortune because at the time only a very small proportion of British travellers went to the expense of purchasing a British Foreign Office passport, when a passport from the French Embassy could be obtained free of charge - there was a register entry on 23 March for a Miss Marianne Wilkinson and a Miss Marianne Malvars. This combinationn of a Miss W. with not merely a Miss Malvars but a Miss Minnie Malvars left little doubt that these must be our two travellers.

All family historians know that the more common a surname, the harder it becomes to identify individuals with certainty - and the names of these two ladies make the point forcefully: while in 1844 there were many British women named Marianne Wilkinson, there was, almost certainly, only one Marianne Malvars. The unusual name led immediately to the record of a marriage which took place on 2 September 1846 between Marianne Malvars and James Edward Pollock. If the latter name did not immediately ring a bell, a glance at the profession and residence columns on the marriage certificate identified the groom as a doctor of medicine resident in Rome. Clearly the encounters between Minnie and Mr P. as described in the journal began a relationship of which the writer, if conscious of it at the time, gives no hint.

The marriage certificate, while helping to reveal what happened to Minnie after the tour, also posed more questions. The wedding took place in West Derby, a suburb of Liverpool, where the officiating clergyman was a Reverend William Pollock. This turned out to be the brother of the groom - but was his presence sufficient to explain the choice of venue? The certificate gave Edward Malvars, merchant, as the father of the bride, but neither he, nor any one else by the name of Malvars, signed the certificate as witnesses; nor, for that matter, did any Wilkinsons. The names that did appear were those of a Joseph Hegan and a Frances Douglasse. Remembering from the journal that Dr Pollock's cousin was called Douglasse, it was assumed that the latter was a relation of the groom; the name Hegan at the time meant nothing.

The next advance came from the discovery that James Pollock had featured in *Who's Who*. This not only gave the dates of his birth and death, but also indicated that he had returned from Rome to England around 1850 and thenceforth worked in London. Post Office Directories provided his address in Upper Brook Street, from which it was easy to move to census returns. These showed that Minnie had given birth to at least eight children during the course of her marriage. At the same time, they threw up one extraordinary fact about her - although a British subject, she had been born in Lima, Peru. While explaining perhaps why it had been impossible to find the name of Malvars in English registers, it added mystery to her background.

Short of taking a perhaps fruitless visit to Lima, I decided that a descendant of Minnie's, if one could be traced, might be able to recount something of her background. With this in mind, I obtained a copy of the will of James Pollock in order to identify which of his children were still alive at his death in 1910. In fact, the contents of the will opened up another line of investigation, for it gave the full name of Minnie's second son as Joseph Hegan Pollock, suggesting that the Joseph Hegan who had been a witness at the wedding had some close link with the Pollocks or possibly with Minnie herself. Liverpool directories identified a Joseph Hegan, merchant, with a Liverpool business address, and Cheshire directories had an entry for Joseph Hegan at Dawpool, Thurstaston, near Birkenhead. That Minnie was acquainted with Dawpool was proved by the inclusion in James Pollock's will of a picture of Dawpool Common painted by her.

While pursuing the Hegan connection, it was also important to find out more about Miss Wilkinson. Here there was no simple key for unlocking the problem of her identity. However, the journal did contain a host of clues as its writer let drop the names of people and places she knew. The name of Josiah occurred frequently in contexts which suggested he was probably her brother and, by profession, a lawyer. Aunts too were mentioned: an Aunt Fanny, an Aunt Kedington and an Aunt Kirby. While, in June 1844, the two ladies were in Bern, they received news of the death of Aunt Kirby and recollected the days they had spent with her at Barham the previous summer. Because there are several Barhams in Britain, this lead was not easy to follow up. However, other place-names featured. In particular, when trying to describe to her mother the house and garden of Monsieur Saintine in Marly, the writer reckoned his house held the same rank as Babergh, but that both Baylham and the Parsonage were much superior, as was Aunt Fanny's garden. Initially these clues also proved frustrating. There was a village in Suffolk called Baylham, but there were no Wilkinsons resident there. Babergh was not the name of a village but of an administrative district, also in Suffolk, but neither there, nor in the house within the district called Babergh Hall, was there a trace of any Wilkinsons. The clues seemed to be leading nowhere, until, almost by chance, the Parsonage was brought into play when, some time later, I was consulting Crockford's Directory over another matter. An impulse led me to look up Barham and Baylham and there, leaping out from the page in the entry for Barham in Suffolk was the name of the Rector, the Reverend William Kirby. Could he have been the Uncle Kirby of the journal? It rapidly emerged that he was no run-of-the-mill country clergyman, but was well known as an entomologist of distinction, and, as such, after his death in 1850, he had been the subject of a biography published in 1852. This work understandably focused on William Kirby's clerical and biological work and contained little about his personal life. However, of this, it recorded some key events, and these included his second marriage in June 1816 to Miss Charlotte Rodwell and, twenty eight years later, her death in 1844.

The combination of a Mrs Kirby, her death in 1844, and the village of Barham pointed strongly to the Rector's wife being the Aunt Kirby of the journal. Knowing that she had been born a Rodwell, one might gain full confirmation by discovering whether Aunt Fanny and Aunt Kedington were also Rodwells. A Suffolk directory of the period immediately revealed a Miss Frances Rodwell living at Baylham and the register of former students at the University of Cambridge included a Robert Kedington who had graduated in 1807 and, six years later, had married Catherine Rodwell of Baylham. His place of residence was recorded as Babergh Hall. All that was now needed to bring this line of investigation to a conclusion was to find a Wilkinson-Rodwell marriage. Here an internet search provided a pointer to a marriage in Suffolk in 1798, and a visit to the County Record Office in Bury St Edmunds confirmed that, on 13 November of that year, Robert Wilkinson of Kingston upon Hull had married Mary Ann Rodwell, resident in the parish of Little Livermere. It was now possible to reach the firm conclusion that this couple were to become the parents of Marianne, the writer of the journal.

After this breakthrough, the most pressing problems were finding out more about Robert Wilkinson and, if possible, locating the Wilkinson family residence prior to their daughter's departure for the Continent in 1844. Mentioned quite often in the journal, and strongly suggested as their place of residence in the entry for 10 September 1844, London seemed the best starting point. Everything pointed to Robert Wilkinson being a man of education and standing - not only his marriage into the Rodwell family, but also his literate daughter and some of the comments she makes about him in the journal. *The Post Office London Directory for 1834* listed two Robert Wilkinsons, one of whom was entered as an 'Accountant & Referee', a employment compatible with some social standing. It certainly seemed likely that it was this Robert Wilkinson who in the 1820s had been involved in investigating one of the most sensational bankruptcy cases of its day: that of the Banking House of Marsh, Stracey, Fauntleroy and Gresham. However, the address given in the *P.O. Directory* was clearly a business address and not a personal one - and thus provided no information through the census returns of Mr Wilkinson or his family. A search through later directories produced a number of Robert Wilkinsons living in London, and these were searched in turn, first in the 1851 census and then, after this produced a blank, in the 1841 census. Here, finally, at 8 Bedford Row in Islington, the right combination of names was revealed: Robert Wilkinson, accountant, aged 65, his wife Marianne, his daughter Marianne aged 35, and his son Josiah, solicitor, aged 25.

The discovery of the Wilkinson family living at Bedford Row in 1841 confirmed the profession of the journal writer's father and that the Josiah of the journal was indeed her brother and a solicitor. It also raised the question of why it had not been possible to find them in 1851. Could it be that Robert Wilkinson had died at some point between 1845 and 1851? At the end of the journal, the writer heard of her father being ill, and although she subsequently received reassurance that he was recovering, it was conceivable that this was premature. Certainly, if he had become seriously ill, the consequence might well have been the termination of the tour and an immediate return home. A search through the register of deaths for 1845 did indeed reveal a Robert Wilkinson who died in Islington in the second quarter of 1845. The certificate was sent for and when it arrived, it proved even more illuminating than expected - for the Robert Wilkinson who had died was not only Robert Wilkinson of Bedford Row, but the date of death was 3 June 1845, the precise date at which the journal had ended, mid-sentence, with the words 'the stillness'. How poignant that ending had now become!

The list of those living in Bedford Row in 1841 suggested that, at that point, Minnie had not yet come to be living with the Wilkinson family. Where was she then? Was it conceivable she was living with Joseph Hegan, and, if so, where was he in 1841? The time had clearly come to focus on Joseph Hegan of Dawpool. An examination of local directories showed that at some point between the mid-1860s and the early 1870s, Joseph Hegan had either moved from Dawpool or had died. A check at the Probate registrary confirmed that Joseph John Hegan of Dawpool had, in fact, died in 1865 and that he had left a will. This was sent for, and very interesting it proved to be. It showed him to have been a wealthy man and that he had two daughters, Agnes and Grace, the latter of whom was married. Amongst numerous bequests, there was no mention whatsoever of Minnie. However, the details revealed that the Hegan wealth had derived from South America and the will included one intriguing bequest: an annuity of £120 to a Dona Ana Nacarino, widow, of Lima, Peru.

Although both Minnie and Joseph Hegan had links with Peru, the nature of the connection between them was still far from clear - indeed the lack of any mention of Minnie in the will suggested that perhaps there was no close relationship. This unpromising conclusion began to be reversed when the will of Joseph's brother, John, was sent for. John Hegan had been Joseph's partner in some of his South American enterprises and one of the beneficiaries of his will. He had died some ten years later. His will not only mentions his 'good friend' James Pollock, physician, of 52 Upper Brook Street, and puts him forward as a possible executor, but also specifically leaves a bequest of the considerable sum of £5000 to James's wife, i.e. Minnie.

With this further evidence of a connection between the Hegans and Minnie, it became increasingly important to discover where Joseph Hegan was based in the years prior to Minnie going to live with the Wilkinsons. It had initially been assumed that Minnie's wedding to James Pollock had taken place in West Derby principally because James's brother, William, was a local clergyman there and would conduct the wedding ceremony. James himself, of course, was resident in Rome and would not necessarily have had a base in Britain. However, a chance find in the Probate Registrary revealed a request, in 1872, for Letters of Administration for the estate of Mrs Anne Elizabeth Hegan, late of Bankfield, West Derby, the wife of Joseph Hegan. It now seemed plausible that Minnie had been staying with the Hegans in the period prior to her marriage with James Pollock, but it would be of greater significance if it could be shown that she had been living with them prior to her moving in with the Wilkinsons. When a check against the census returns in 1841 showed that the Hegans were not then living in West Derby, another line of approach was called for. This was provided by an examination of the census information on the inhabitants of Dawpool in 1861, for here were contained details of the birthplaces of Joseph Hegan's two daughters: the older, Grace, had been born in 1840 in Arrow Hall, Cheshire, the younger, Agnes, in 1843 in Westerley, Lancashire. Checking these two places in the 1841 census returns located the Hegan family at the Cheshire address. Within the list of house residents was Mary Malves, aged 13 - undoubtedly our Minnie!

Having reached this point in the investigations, it was possible to gain a notion of the whole context of the tour. Joseph Hegan, South American merchant, brings back to England with him a young girl, possibly the daughter of some compatriot who has died, possibly even his own daughter born out of wedlock in Peru. He takes the girl into his family, but then decides it would be beneficial for her if the right person could be found to take her education in hand. For this purpose he finds, either by chance or through some mutual acquaintance, Miss Wilkinson, a cultured and well-read spinster living in London. An extended tour of the Continent had long been seen as one means of acquiring one or more foreign languages and of assessing and absorbing some of the culture of a few important European nations. In this connection, Miss Wilkinson agreed to take her charge on a tour of the Continent over a number of months. The journal itself suggests that it was Mr Hegan who was directly funding the journey and that it was the budget proposed by him which established what the two ladies were able to spend. It was the intention that the tour should last several months longer, but the news of Robert Wilkinson's death must have brought it to an abrupt conclusion. However, while the ladies were still in Rome, Minnie had met her husband-to-be. Understandably, no mention whatsoever is made of a budding relationship. However, James Pollock and his cousin were present in Venice when the sad news came through and so it is possible that he volunteered to accompany the ladies home.

Various leads in the search for a descendant of the Pollock-Malvars marriage were followed up and one finally proved successful. Thereby it was possible to confirm the unfolding of events and relationships as so far described. In correspondence, Joseph Hegan referred to Minnie as his daughter. When he married a widow in the early 1840s with whom he was to have two further daughters, it seems quite likely that he decided that it would be for the best if his illegitimate, Peru-born daughter was brought up outside his new household. Minnie probably went to live with the Wilkinsons at some point in 1842 - certainly her descendants still possess a letter written by Joseph Hegan to Minnie on the occasion of her 15th birthday in February 1843. The letter is addressed to Bedford Row and indicates that Minnie had been living there for some time.

While research into the background of the journal has revealed much about the background of the two ladies, many mysteries remain. In particular, I have failed to discover much about the journal writer after her return to England in June 1845. Marianne's father, Robert Wilkinson, left an estate valued under £500, suggesting that his accountancy firm had not been financially successful. Indeed, references to the firm in the 1830s indicated that it went bankrupt. Such financial misfortune would suggest why Marianne, a highly educated lady from a previously prosperous family, would have been ready to undertake the role of governess to the young Minnie, and why, after her father's death, she should have continued as a governess. In the 1851 census returns, she is recorded in Hastings with three pupils and two servants. Subsequently, the law business of her brother Josiah seems to have prospered, and, in 1881, Marianne is to be found, aged 80, living with him and his wife in Highgate.

Hitherto, I have failed to identify William, the young man who joined the two ladies in Geneva, remained with them in Rome, and was still with them in Venice when the journal entries terminated. I am also uncertain of the identity of Fanny, whose name occurs frequently throughout the journal in contexts which suggest that she could provide the link between the Wilkinsons and the Hegans. It is she who writes about the departure of William from England and she also corresponds with Miss Douglasse in Rome. She may, in fact be the Frances Douglasse who attended Minnie's wedding in 1846, but I have no evidence for such an assumption. How intriguing too are the circumstances of Minnie's birth and early childhood. Could it be that Dona Ana Nacarino of Lima, the recipient of an annuity from Joseph Hegan, was Minnie's mother? Perhaps a trip to Peru may be called for after all!

Index.

Academia Arcadi 126
Academia Sta. Lucia 143
Acland, Sir J. 130
Acquapendente 108
Adams, Mr 147, 155
Adams, Rev. & Mrs 83
Adelsberg caves 189 & n.
Agnano, lake 169,174
Agnew, Rev. & Misses 75
Ahorn 61& n.
Albano Lake 163,164
Alberghini, Joseph 113 & n., 116, 119,121,
129,158,162,165
Albert, Prince 113
Allen, Capt. 109, 124,139
Amalfi 175,177,178
Amsteg 61
Ancona 180,181,185,187
Andermatt 60
Antonelli, Monsig-re 140
Ara coelis 123,128
Ariosto 142,153
Arona 90
Avernus, Lake 174
Babergh 11
Babington, G. & Mrs 83,125
Baia 174
Balme, Col de 73
Barberini Library 142
Barham, Suffolk 34,135
Barras, Father Pierre Joseph 88
Barrett, Hester 164 & n.
Bartholomew, Miss & brother 103
Basel 24-6
Baylham 11,34,
Beckenried 56
Belcher, Lady 111 & n.,139
Berisal 87-8
Bernouilli, Mons. 57, 58
Bertin, Mons. 5,6,9,10,13,15,16,18
Bessarion 191 & n.
Blanc, Mons. (of Metz) 38
Boccatella 180
Bolsena 108
Bonneville 74
Borghese Palace 125,128,130,145
Borromean Islands 89
Bourgagnet, Mme 18,65
Bouss 65 & n.,68
Bremgarten 30-1,36

Brera 93 & n.
Brienz 43-7,50
Brochet, M. & Mme 75,77
Broglie, Mme de 78
Brooks, Misses 70
Brunig pass 55
Brunner (maid of Henzis) 48
Bulle 63
Bulwer-Lytton, Edward 8 & n.
Bunsen, Frances 6-7 & n.,29,122,130
Buonconvento 107
Burgess, Rev.Richard 82 & n.,115,129,141
Burns, Robert 155n.
Burton, Capt. & Mrs 103
Byron, Lord 64n,65,81-2,131 & n.,185 & n.
Caille, Pont de 78 & n.
Calame, Alexandre 81 & n.
Calandrin, Mme 82
Calcutta, Bishop of 129
Camaldoli monastery 181
Campana(ri) 156
Campana, Signor 124,144,163,165
Campo Santo 170,181
Canaletto 190
Canova, Antonio 140
Capitol 128,131,134,135,136
Capo di monte 171,181
Capri 169,174,175
Capua 167,181
Caracalla, Baths of 141,172
Caradini, Contessa 170
Carrara 97-8
Cashel, Bishop of (Robert Daly) 71 & n.
Castellamare 175,177
Casuti, Marchesa 136
Caucci, Marchesa 141, 143
Cepeano 183
Certosa 93
Chaillot 3, 6 & n., 9,13,21
Chamonix 71,72-4
Champ de Mars 15
Champs Elysées 9,10,15
Chantrey, Sir Francis 98 & n.
Charles X 7
Chawner, Miss 120
Cheever, George B. 69 & n., 70, 75
Chiesa Nova 148
Chigi Palace 155
Chillon, Castle of 64 & n.
Christem, R., 47 & n.
Cicero 162-3 & n.,167
Circus of Romulus 115

Civita Castellana 185
Clarens 64,66
Clarisse, Mme 111,113,154
Clarkson, Mrs 145, 147,157,158,160
Close, Mr & Mrs 181
Coddington, Rev. Henry 152 & n.
Coliseum 115,128,143,184
Collins, William 53n
Collyer, Mrs 112,115
Colonna Palace and Gardens 149,155
Como 90-1
Connor, Rev. James & Mrs 140 et seq.
Coppet 77-8
Cordès Mr, 83
Corinne 119 & n.
Correggio 102
Corso 137,138,139,140,141
Coulon family 126,128
Couvreu, Mme Emma & fam. 62 et seq.
Cracroft, Misses 69,170
Craigie, Mrs & daurs. 141,142
Croft, Rev. T. 70 & n.
Cullimore, Miss 79,81
Cumaean Sybil 175
Cupido, Amico 162,181-3,186
D'Arcamballe Mme 51, 67
D'Aubigné, Merle 83 & n.
D'Enghien, duc 7 & n.
Dentice, Principe D. 170
Deschwanden, M.P.v. 56 & n.
Devil's Bridge 60-1
Dickens, Charles 1,154 & n.
Dietler, J.F. 35 & n.
Diocletian, Baths of 141
Diodati 81
Diorama 30 & n.
Divoto, Jean-Baptiste 77,82,95 et seq.,162
Doge's Palace 191
Dolce, Carlo 102
Domenichino 112,145,148,153,163,164
Domo d'Ossola 86,89
Doria, Prince 89
Dornach, battle of 27 & n.
Douglasse, Miss 110 et seq.
Dufour, Mlles 62 et seq.
Durante, Vittorio 140
Edgeworth, Maria 8 & n.
Empoli 99
Engelberg 56-7
Entlibuch 62
Erskine, Thomas 144 & n.
Etruscan Museum 136,156-7

Evian 85
Exquisite 162
Farneran, (Zeerleder farm) 36-7
Farnese Palace 148
Feast of St. Agnes 134-5 & n.
Feder, Mons. 82
Fellenberg, Emanuel v. & Miss 48n.,50,62
Ferney 77
Fielding, Miss 115,124,145,162
Fingal, Lord & family 107 & n.,108,160
Fletcher family 166,168,169,170,174,180,181
Flue, Nicholas v. der 55 & n.
Foligno 186
Forbes, James D. & Mrs 73 & n.
Fox, Miss 149 & n.
Fox, Mr & Mrs 170
Fra Angelico 102,103
Frascati 148,162
Freudenreich family 29 & n.,31,34,51,67
Fribourg 62-3
Frith, Rev. & Mrs 119,123,128,137,150,162, 184
Fry, Elizabeth 29n.,53 & n.
Fuetter, Mons. 60
Gajotti 119 & n.
Galignani 4n.,17 & n.
Galileo, Gallilei 142
Galliano 91
Garofalini, Signor 112,116,118,139,165
Gaussen, L. & Miss 62 & n., 65,69, 70,82,84
Gelpke, Ernst Fr. 30 & n., 31, 32, 50
Genoa 94-6
Gessler 59 & n.
Gesú, Church of 125,143
Gibson, John 113 & n.,125
Giotto 101,140
Girardet, E. 46 & n.
Girardet, Jean 23 & n.
Goethe 130n., 153
Goldau 59 & n.
Grant, Dr 111,112,115,118,121,126,129,145, 146,148,152,155,162,164,184
Grimaldi, Cardinal 131
Grimsel pass 54
Grindelwald 42,54
Grotto del Cane 169
Guercino 100,146,148,155
Guido (Reni) 102,135,146,149,152,164,169
Gurney, Joseph 29n., 53 & n.
Gurten (hill near Bern) 30 & n.,38
Hallé, Charles 8 & n.,11,18
Hare, Rev. William 28 & n.
Harley, Mr 126